Imagined Liberation

Imagined Liberation

Xenophobia, Citizenship, and Identity in
South Africa, Germany, and Canada

HERIBERT ADAM and KOGILA MOODLEY

TEMPLE UNIVERSITY PRESS
Philadelphia · Rome · Tokyo

TEMPLE UNIVERSITY PRESS
Philadelphia, Pennsylvania 19122
www.temple.edu/tempress

Library of Congress Cataloging-in-Publication Data

Adam, Heribert.
    Imagined liberation : xenophobia, citizenship, and identity in South Africa, Germany,
and Canada / Heribert Adam and Kogila Moodley.
        pages cm. — (Politics, history, and social change)
    Includes bibliographical references and index.
    ISBN 978-1-4399-1189-1 (cloth : alk. paper) — ISBN 978-1-4399-1190-7
(pbk. : alk. paper) — ISBN 978-1-4399-1191-4 (e-book)   1. Xenophobia—South Africa.
2. Xenophobia—Germany.   3. Xenophobia—Canada.   4. South Africa—Ethnic relations.
5. Germany—Ethnic relations.   6. Canada—Ethnic relations.   7. South Africa—
Emigration and immigration—Social aspects.   8. Germany—Emigration and
immigration—Social aspects.   9. Canada—Emigration and immigration—Social
aspects.   I. Moodley, Kogila.   II. Title.
    DT1756.A33 2015
    305.8—dc23

                                                                                    2014045158

♾ The paper used in this publication meets the requirements of the American National
Standard for Information Sciences—Permanence of Paper for Printed Library Materials,
ANSI Z39.48-1992

Printed in the United States of America

9 8 7 6 5 4 3 2 1

For the next generation,

KIRAN, TALIA, MISHA, MILA, *and* MILAN,

to encourage future engaged citizenship

Contents

Part II   Variations of Migration Policies:
Africa, Germany, and Canada

Part III   Political Literacy

Appendices

Foreword

*Speech at STIAS (The Stellenbosch
Institute for Advanced Study)
at the launch of the South African
edition of the book*

BREYTEN BREYTENBACH

The Topos and the Topography of Utopia

I'm not sure whether I should be thanking STIAS for this opportunity to be associated with the launch of *Imagined Liberation*, the study on Xenophobia, Citizenship and Identity in South Africa, Germany, and Canada, written by Heribert Adam and Kogila Moodley—mainly because their eloquent and thorough study speaks for itself (and I dread not giving it its scope by speaking inadequately to a complicated subject, or intertwined themes, that they have been pouring over for so many years and with so much sympathetic understanding)—but also, because I am not at all clear in my own mind how to approach the phenomenon of *vreemdelingehaat* (the hatred of the other), or the further concepts they allude to.

Allow me nevertheless, first of all and before moving on to murkier matters, to pay my respects to this book and to the authors.

The title, *Imagined Liberation*, intrigues me. It seems to imply that our much vaunted post 1990 "liberation" is more imaginary than real; that our Rainbow is a mirage. But it also underlines, to my mind, the organic link between "imagination" and "liberation." If I may say so, the first attribute of "imagination" is generosity, or sharing, and the "liberation" of a people can only mean a freeing from bondage, iniquity, and oppression, also the fallacies that made it acceptable to oppress others, and thereby promote an environment where hospitality and tolerance and understanding may flourish. For both of these—the "imagination" and the "liberation"—a *dépassement*, a surpassing, a going beyond the confines of the personal, a striving for a decisive break with the norm and often the orthodoxy, will be needed. "Liberation," ideally, brings with it the enactment of altruism. To broaden our minds and deepen our hearts, liberation, in order to take root will have to be informed by the ethics of imagination. (This may be an oxymoron . . .).

In its subtitle, the book links Xenophobia, Citizenship, and Identity. It can be argued that these are quite discrete concepts emerging from different processes. Identity is not necessarily posited on Citizenship (the Touaregs and the Kurds may have a clear sense of cultural and historical identity but not consider themselves citizens of either Mali or Niger in the one case, Iraq or Turkey in the other). Furthermore, it would be nice to think (I nearly said "imagine"!) that Identity subsumed by Citizenship, when people are at ease with who they are, should diminish the grounds that breed xenophobia—but often, as this book points out, it is not the case. Indeed, one could reason that the more confirmed the identity, individual and collective, expressed in citizenship, the more easily people feel threatened by the presence of the diverse and thus the more easily xenophobia will be given a free rein.

It is said that the ethical fibre of a society is measured by the way it treats its prisoners—still true, and by this yardstick the United States fails miserably—or women (think Saudia Arabia) or child labour—with countries like India and Afghanistan in flagrant dereliction of decency. The merit of the book under discussion is that it reminds us of the imperative of hospitality and of encompassing differences in background and in origin, and that a society can also be measured by the way it reacts to the *amakwere* in their midst—indeed, that there is interaction between the quality of its liberation and the policies applicable to those who came from elsewhere.

The book then analyses at length comparable situations and processes in South Africa, Germany, and Canada. The authors, we know, have an intimate working knowledge of the three countries. In passing it ought to be noted that we are fortunate that Kogila Moodley and Heribert Adam should have consecrated so much of their learning and their energy to the understanding and interpretation of this construct-in-becoming, this work in progress (or is it decay?), which is South Africa. They may agree, though, that the three entities cannot really be compared except to the extent that the presence of xenophobia in one country, or the way tensions are defused and integration brought about, may clarify processes in other parts of the world.

As many other people in the world, I can only look at Canada and marvel about its essential qualities. For a moment in our South African history as well, there seems to have been the flicker of common purpose, maybe even a skyline where—to borrow a phrase from Kogila out of context—"difference was incorporated as a common good and not simply evoked for "cultural maintenance purposes."

It did not last long. Maybe it was never intended to be the veritable motivation for transformation into one multihued nation? Can it be argued that the falling apart of this ostensible purpose and the absence of a Center accounts for the extreme pathological expressions and acts of xenophobia? What does it say about the state of self-denigration that seems to underlie and inform so many of our violent reactions against the "foreigner"?

Andile Mngxitama, who states that the presence of even one white person in the same room as he and any number of black comrades will change the equation, will signify the death of the blacks, will deprive him of oxygen—said in a May 2008 interview with Ferial Haffajee in the Mail & Guardian: "Fourteen years of our democratic neo-apartheid existence has produced negrophobic bestiality, misnamed xenophobia. The barbarism of super profits for the few and the exclusion of the black majority has given us cannibalism. After the *makwerekwere* it's the Sotho, Venda, Xhosa and so on . . ."

What we are experiencing at present—the enormous increase in people fleeing their homelands to look for asylum, the clumsy ways in which the developed world deals with the phenomenon, the horrors of a Lampedusa or of desperate "people without papers," as the euphemism goes, literally using their own bodies and those of their companions as stepping flesh to try and climb the barbed fences around Ceuta, the European enclave in Morocco—has been building for many years. The tide of people trying to save their skins or to access a better life—how "better" it will be is an open question—cannot be stemmed.

I want to quote at some length from a text entitled "The Long March" that I presented at the New School for Social Research in New York, October 1990. Already then, it was clear that one of the defining characteristics of the world we were getting to know ("the end of history," some wag called it) was going to be the massive flow of people—refugees, clandestine migrants, guests workers, asylum seekers, wetbacks and other wall jumpers—from the poor and hungry and corrupt and over-populated south to the fortressed colonial north. It was as if a vast demographic redistribution was under way. And there may have been humanitarian concern for the destitute "foreigners" and sporadic attempts to regulate the flow in terms of the interests of the north, but no longer any internationalist solidarity—as experienced at the time of anti-imperialist wars—to significantly inflect the "problem" being solved by exclusion or deportation or arbitrary administrative measures, and of course by xenophobia and exploitation. This was to become an ever more important symptom of a disintegrating global community—together with the destruction of the planetary environment, the systematic disconnect between the filthy rich and the growing poor, and the tyranny of consumerism. What has changed since then is perhaps that huge numbers of desperate people now also try to get into whatever country they think they may survive in—Dubai, Australia, South Africa, even Israel—and that the world (if ever there was something we could define as "the world") has become even more indifferent if not inured to genocides and the large-scale extermination of people—those of another faction or belief or colour or origin— by their own rampaging armies.

"I want to enter a plea for the exiles," I wrote optimistically, "who are often enough admirable people. The courage and perseverance, the futile quest for survival of these stowaways, wetbacks, throwbacks, and other illegal humans, always astonish me. Tamils sneaking with false passports across the border, Ango-lans surfacing in Berlin from some 'underground railway,' Ghanaians passing themselves off as citizens from Zaire or the Ivory Coast, whole families making it to the 'capital' to be crammed into one room, boat people working like bea-vers to build dams for a future generation. And nearly always they are starving themselves to help provide for more unfortunate relatives back home.

"How resilient they are! See them come to terms with the writ of the rat. See how quickly they pick up the art of negotiating the labyrinths and warrens of Administration and Order, how rapidly they snick their tongues around the for-eign language, how keen they are to learn! Along the beaches of Europe, on the squares of its cities, you come across the young men of Mali—distant descendants of Ahmad Baba—tirelessly unrolling their bundles of African kitsch made in Hong Kong, the bangles and the beads and the imitation effigies. They peddle the instantly discardable. They squint at the grey skies and wind up plastic doves which they throw in the air to flutter and fall. Somehow they survive. Have you noticed the pride and the joy when these people manage to afford that first dress or leather jacket?

"Still, the personal compensation of survival and existential enrichment can never justify the willful destruction of hearth and habit, the forced removal of population groups or the expulsion of individuals. Will Romania ever recover from the mindless razing of the peasant villages? Can South Africa knit into a serviceable national cloth the torn fibres of Apartheid? How will the Touaregs, driven to give up their nomadic existence and herded into the shallows of West-ern civilization, survive as fly-swatters in shanty towns? And how can one ever explain—let alone understand or condone—the crimes perpetrated by Israel when they wall up and dynamite the homes of 'suspect' Palestinians?

"My personal declaration of human rights could be resumed in four brief points: 1. Every human being has the birth right to struggle for justice and equal-ity. 2. Every human being has the right to a home. 3. Every human being has the survivor's right to the preservation of our planet with all its life. 4. Every human being has the right to die with his or her dignity intact."

Thus far the quote from that distant document. We all know the story of what happened since. Maybe the most important slide has been the distension of public and international morals, the extent to which we have become used to "under-standing" and tacitly accepting the unacceptable, the ease with which we live beyond the shattered vestiges of our outrage of the time and our betrayed aspi-rations. How did we get to make do with the reality of nearly two million Zim-babweans surviving in South Africa, often illegally, while their country, the neighbouring country, is being sacked by so-called freedom fighters and now ever more appropriated by China?

Is it truly that easy? Can one look away—at the mountain, say, or at the Freedom Charter? How confident can they really be: the whites squeezing out the last juices of the good life, of the quality of lifestyle in a country that cannot absorb them and must side-line and in due time expunge them once they have coughed up enough for past sins, or the newly empowered blacks arrogantly trashing the poverty of the people who cannot forever be bought off with food parcels? Are these not the repressed fears that sometimes spill over in random acts of barbarism?

A few nights ago in Cape Town we had a gathering, already then discussing some aspects of the book of tonight. I'd wanted to shape my own contribution in *The Topos and the Topography of Utopia*—as I similarly entitled tonight's remarks. The "topography" part consisted only of a series of rhetorical questions.

For example: faced with the globalization of financial finagling and economic systems controlling us ("free" enterprise, capitalism, "the market"), as also the placebo of "communication"—can the movements (the incursions) of outsiders/incomers/clandestinos/undocumented ones/car guards and poachers . . . announce a new manifestation of the "solidarity" we seem to have forfeited or forgotten? Can the "world order" still be comprehensively undermined? Or are even these marginal ones just potential consumer junkies.

How do discourses/perceptions come about? What can the average citizen really know about how the *farenj* is treated, and the assumptions "justifying" the dehumanisation? Is it not true that we "liberals" are for once silenced by the impression that, for once, this is not our fight, that it is black-on-black violence, the poor putting fire to the foreign poor?

Structuralists hold that language ("understanding"/"communication") has its own innate structure. We sense its power, we know when we deviate from it and we know how it can convey (the illusion of?) order. Is language not the original delineation of inclusion and thus of exclusion? To exist consciously is to be aware of the texture, the associations, the emotions of words, sounds, metaphors; can we say that language is not only the territory and the history (the collectiveness of memory) but also the template through which the single consciousness negotiates its environment and thus its interaction with what is perceived as "different"? Are we not hoisted on the petard of our exquisite self-questioning?

In any case, what could the influence of arduous public thinking possibly be on a population where dumbing down is purported to be the way to democracy and security?

Do "morals" figure? Is it not angelic to expect that they who have internalized humiliation, who may have experienced the degrees of the abject, will not enact the same subjection or even worse scenarios to the "others" when they feel threatened? After all, they would know about the workings of *power*. (The Afrikaner and the Jew, for example, having been there, know this.)

What of *agency, time, texture*? Does "liberation," however much of a fool's game it might have been, of necessity not always bring its corollary of destruction? One is, after all, destroying the structures of the arbitrary, even if it is to replace them with another set.

Is there a time of forgetting? Is there not the near impossibility of time being kept alive and present in its implications? How much do we remember of our own idealism? One forgets in order to continue, to get back to "normal." Time does not secrete morals. How do we learn, then?

In the context of our failed revolution—how do we go about the premises of *belonging* and the precepts of *hospitality*? There is an apparent contradiction between the rights of citizenship and human rights. Is there a right *to* citizenship with its concomitant responsibilities, and how is this to be enacted in the absence of a shared moral centre?

Utopian thinking does not have a good press. It is assumed that one is being unrealistic—a cardinal sin in empirical practical politics!—escapist to boot, and, perish the thought, maybe revolutionary!

Yet, within the South African context it can be a useful tool. Surely, we can agree that it denotes in most places the nostalgia for what we imagine existed— in our case the magical moment of together becoming other, of a reckoning with ourselves and our conflicting histories and a desire to transform in depth, of a willingness to listen to each others' stories and actively tolerate, even encourage the dialectic between the specific and the general, also in our cultures and our mother tongues.

Maybe a start would be to admit that this dream had no legs. We were never a nation. Maybe a further necessary step would be to agree that without a utopia to strive for we are condemned to killing one another, that if we were to stop dreaming this shared "space" we call South Africa we shall revert to fighting factions, that we are obliged to provide for movement or else stagnate and destroy or self-destruct. Is it not true that the harmony or balance we strive for must be a radical agent for change?

I then thought of asking Kogila and Heribert: with all of their experience, insight and empathy—what would be the two or three measures they'd consider as capable of bringing about the forward movement towards utopia, maybe even realistically so?

Perhaps it is unfair to ask this of anybody. And if one were to be unfair, why not begin with one's own uncertainties? So, if you were to ask me, I'd say, again sticking to four points:

1. Bring about truly elective politics, constituency based so that Parliament can become vitalized and represent the interests and the aspirations of the people, and establish a true devolution of power that will reflect local concerns and responsibilities and conditions.
2. Bring about a "social contract" between the state and its citizens so that priorities can be agreed upon, explained, accepted, and the state be held responsible.
3. Allow for the vigorous and constitutionally guaranteed autonomy of institutions, free from party political interference.
4. Actively understand and enshrine that our essential richness is the diversity of our make-up, the depth of our languages, the force of our dreaming . . .

All of the above beg the question of how to get there. Nowhere on our continent
has a national liberation movement given up power—neither in Algeria nor
Angola nor Zimbabwe, not in Eritrea or Guinea-Bissau or Mozambique—and the
ANC in South Africa is no different, even now when the once generous struggle
is reduced to the banding of robbers. They can no longer drape themselves in
moral probity or even political sense (at least not to the benefit of the population,
and most definitely not to that of the "stranger within our gates")—these ideals,
together with "democracy" and "accountability" and "nation-building" were in
any event only lures to finesse their opponents out of power and lull the gullible
international community. Their lust for power, patronage, and entitlement—not
yet assuaged—is now petrified in historical legitimacy. "We won, therefore all of
it is ours." One might as well paraphrase: "We broke it, therefore we own it." And
our comrade capitalists have only one dream: how to morph from ostensible
communism as erstwhile servants to the people into party power monopoly
along the lines of the Chinese example where the state is the captured cow and
the people now the capital.

Yet, we all know liberation was a long time coming and that the ANC,
although the dominant factor, was not the only agent. In fact, the historical con
game was to have enough people believe the ANC, with the Stalinist worm in the
apple all along, is the agent for change, which in the South African context could
then only be equated with "liberation." Perhaps it's unfair to judge as harshly in
retrospect just because one has been fooled.

To mind comes a double-edged dictum of Marx that is still apposite:

"Men make their own history, but only in the circumstances given
to them."

One is going to have to resist in every possible way—by exposure ("sham-
ing" will make no dent), by keeping the Constitution alive and if possible
protected from raids by marauding power mongers, by promoting alliances
among parties and citizen organisations and in the process validating civics
and civil society, by working on a clear and comprehensive and complex
vision that will take account of our diversity, by really listening to the poor,
by trying to contain the unholy collusion between big capital and cadre corruption, by building firewalls between the state and the party in power, by
identifying and renouncing the rotten tongue Newspeak of political correctness . . .

The list is long and confused. It has always been a long walk. The way out, let
alone the way forward, is not to disqualify or to grade and degrade some people
found along the road. In fact, as always our capacity for imagining liberation—
and liberating our imagination—will at least in part be measured by the extent
to which we functionally recognize and receive the dignified human in the other.
South Africa has no other lasting and founding richness except the patchwork
of its people.

Justice is a function of social memory. Not to speak up, not to validate the living archaeology and magic of our languages, not to be aware of the *roots* and the *reach* of our experiences as expressed in our cultures and the extent to which these cohere into a sense of belonging (or not belonging), not to test the boundaries of the forces defining our identities (or destroying them), not to go to the limits of what is within reach of transformation and of creative citizenship, would be to acquiesce to the cynicism of what passes for politics and the thieving incompetence of what presents itself as leadership. It will be like saying: all of this is too big and abstract and ugly and dangerous for me to engage with. Not to speak up would be a maiming of our own dignity and potential, and a failure to the dream of liberation.

We would then be the silent and angry and disillusioned accomplices to our own failure of imagination, and thus of liberation.

To conclude: We have only this passage, this window of opportunity on the eternity of dust and the oblivion of what came before. I believe we are doomed (programmed, you might say) to strive for a certain human dignity, to extol a given tenderness of life—and these can be measured by our capacity for recognizing in the other what we share, and by our willingness to become other. I believe this is how; in all creole honesty, we may still fabricate the commons.

Acknowledgments

M ost of the research and writing for this book was carried out while we were fellows at the Stellenbosch Institute for Advanced Study (STIAS) for three short stints during 2011–2013. The cosmopolitan company of a changing cast of local and international colleagues in this splendid environment provided tranquility for reflection as well as stimulation. We thank its director Hendrik Geyer and its founder Bernard Lategan for this opportunity. We benefited particularly from many valued discussions with our friend and co-fellow Njabulo Ndebele. At different times issues were clarified by co-fellows Raymond Suttner, Bob Hepple, Ivan Vladisovic, John Dugard, and George Pavlich. Reiner Klingholz and Ulrike Davy suggested additions to Chapter 6 on Germany.

Renowned Stellenbosch historian and seasoned analyst of Afrikaner politics Hermann Giliomee critically commented on several draft chapters. Longtime friend Pierre van den Berghe in Seattle generously agreed to read the entire manuscript, and Solly Benatar provided feedback on a portion of the text. While we have not always been persuaded by their different perspectives, they nonetheless strengthened our arguments. Carla Spinola made cogent editorial suggestions that improved the readability of the book.

As in the past, we were sensitized to South African politics by many Cape Town friends across the political spectrum: Alex and Jenny Boraine, Michael Savage and Lucia Thesen, Wilmot James, Crain Soudien, Milton Shain, Ken and Kate Owen, and that gentle but feisty veteran activist and treason trialist Norman Levy. The Saturday afternoon tennis matches with their sacred ritual of tea and cake, comprising Geoff Budlender, Andre du Toit, Johann Maree, and Richard Honikman at the Burton's garden court, inevitably veered into political discussions when Mary Burton joined. Another player, UCT law professor Jonathan

Burchell, drew our attention to the four constitutional court cases discussed in Chapter 2.

In Germany, Bodo von Greiff and Hanne Herkomer, Fritz Sack, and Walter Heinz served as invaluable sources of information to sharpen our understanding of German politics. In Vancouver, Gary Teeple and on Pender Island, Harvey and Rhona Weinstein from Berkeley, Maria Tippett, and Peter Clarke, as well as the genius artist Karl Stittgen, always raised thoughtful questions. Another islander, lawyer Jane Morley, one of three members of the ill-fated first Canadian Truth and Reconciliation Commission, clarified many questions about Canadian First Nations. We are grateful to renowned poet and global public intellectual, Breyten Breytenbach for his thoughtful address at the South African launch of the book. The speech is included here as the Preface.

Finally our cosmopolitan daughters and sons-in-law, Kanya and Simon Pimstone and Maya and Lawrence Seeff, patiently subjected themselves to discussions about South Africa and probably wondered how we could sustain preoccupation with one topic for decades. Five exuberant grandchildren no doubt assume that all grandparents are born with books and newspapers attached to their hands and are sentenced to imprisonment for long periods in their studies. They provided the background of laughter and relief from stress.

Chapters 8 and 9 on political literacy synthesize arguments from our previous publications. We thank the respective publishers for permission to use short excerpts. Chapter 5 on Settler Colonialism has been expanded and translated from German in Daniela Klimke and Aldo Legnaro, eds, 2013, *Politische Ökonomie und Sicherheit*, (Weinheim und Basel: Beltz Juventa). A shorter version of Chapter 7 on Canada has also been published in *Intercultural Education Journal*, vol. 23, no. 5. We gratefully acknowledge the support of the Social Science and Humanities Council (SSHRC) in Ottawa. None of the persons and institutions that assisted us, however, are responsible for the opinions expressed, biases inherent, and inevitable errors in our writing. We alone take responsibility for the latter.

Abbreviations and Acronyms

AA	Affirmative Action
AB	Afro Barometer
ADL	Anti-Defamation League
ANC	African National Congress
ANCYL	African National Congress Youth League
AU	African Union
AWB	Afrikaner Weerstandsbeweging ("Afrikaner Resistance Movement")
BCM	Black Consciousness Movement
BD	*Business Day* (South African national daily newspaper)
BEE	Black Economic Empowerment
BRIC	Brazil, Russia, India, China, South Africa
BUM	Botshabelo Unemployed Movement
CC	Constitutional Court
CDU	Christian Democratic Union
CEE	Commission for Employment Equity
COPE	Congress of the People
COSATU	Congress of South African Trade Unions
CP	*City Press* (South African Sunday newspaper)
CSU	Christian Social Union
CT	*Cape Times* (Cape Town-based daily morning newspaper)
CV	Curricula Vitae
DA	Democratic Alliance
DAAD	Deutsche Akademischer Austauschdienst
DG	Director General

DHA   Department of Home Affairs
DLF   Democratic Left Front
DRC   Democratic Republic of Congo
EE   Employment Equity
EFF   Economic Freedom Fighters
FDI   Foreign Direct Investment
FFP   Freedom Front Party
FLN   National Liberation Front
G&M   *Globe and Mail* (nationally distributed Canadian newspaper)
GDR   Germany Democratic Republic (GDR)
HSRC   Human Sciences Research Council
ICD   Independent Complaints Directorate
ID   Identity Document
IDASA   Institute for Democracy in Africa
IDP   Internally Displaced Persons
IEC   Independent Electoral Commission
IFP   Inkatha Federal Party
IJR   Institute for Justice and Reconciliation
IPTC   Israeli and Palestinian Truth Commission (or IPTRC)
JSC   Judicial Services Commission
KZN   KwaZulu Natal
LRB   *London Review of Books*
LRC   *Literary Review of Canada*
LSE   London School of Economics
M&G   *Mail and Guardian* (South African weekly newspaper)
MP   Member of Parliament
MPLA   People's Movement for the Liberation of Angola
NA   National Assembly
NEDLAC   National Economic Development and Labour Council
NP   National Party
NP   *National Post* (Canadian newspaper)
NPC   National Planning Commission
NDP   National Development Plan, South Africa
NDP   National Democratic Party, Canada
NGOs   Nongovernmental Organizations
NUM   National Union of Mineworkers
NYT   *New York Times*
OECD   Organisation for Economic Co-operation and Development
PAC   Pan Africanist Congress
PAGAD   People Against Gangsterism and Drugs
PAIA   Protection of Access to Information Act
PASSOP   People Against Suffering Oppression and Poverty
POIB   Protection of Information Bill
PP   Public Protector

PR	Proportional representation
PSA	Political Science, Sociology, and Anthrogology
RCMP	Royal Canadian Mounted Police
RDP	Reconstruction and Development Program
RSA	Republic of South Africa
RSD	Refugee Status Determination
SA	South Africa or South African
SABC	South African Broadcasting Corporation
SACP	South African Communist Party
SADC	Southern African Development Community
SADTU	South African Democratic Teachers' Union
SAIRR	SA Institute of Race Relations
SAMP	South African Migration Project
SAPS	South African Police Service
SARB	South African Reconciliation Barometer
SARS	South African Revenue Service
SFU	Simon Fraser University
SI	Sunday Independent
ST	*Sunday Times* (South African newspaper)
STIAS	Stellenbosch Institute for Advanced Study
SWAPO	South West African People's Organization
TAC	Treatment Action Committee
TRC	Truth and Reconciliation Commission
TRT	Tactical Response Team
UBC	University of British Columbia
UCT	University of Cape Town
UDF	United Democratic Front
UNHCR	UN High Commissioner for Refugees
UNHRC	United Nations Human Rights Council
UNISA	University of South Africa
UNITA	The National Union for the Total Independence of Angola
ZANU	Zimbabwe African National Union
ZAPU	Zimbabwe African People's Union

Imagined Liberation

Introduction

Our book explores xenophobia empirically, comparatively, and theoretically. We portray xenophobia in postapartheid South Africa, postfascist Germany, and multicultural Canada. Have these societies learned humanistic lessons from their racist past? With the main research in South Africa and focus on the current situation, we probe what went right and wrong with the vision of liberation.

Imagined Liberation traces how the dream of an inclusive nonracial democracy faded in South Africa. For many former anti-apartheid activists the vision has turned into a delusion, while others are still imagining liberation through outdated policies. To support our analysis we use xenophobia as a prism for South African society at large. Our empirical evidence probes perceptions about foreigners in selected all-black township schools, because xenophobic violence signifies how the imagined postapartheid solidarity is being jettisoned. A marginalized underclass displays extreme hostility toward fellow Africans. Through the lens of xenophobia, we aim at capturing revealing aspects of the current collective mindset, twenty years after legalized apartheid has been abolished.

What puzzled us is a society that freed itself at the very least from institutionalized racism but that nevertheless practices new forms of black-on-black racialization. Strangely, whites are not considered *amakwerekwere*, hated foreigners. Whites, whether locals or visitors, are welcome tourists, investors, and job creators. Hardly any white ever enters the sprawling slums. On the whole, racial groups still live apart and hardly socialize but interact respectfully, even amiably, at work and in the marketplace.

Our ethnographic research in townships in the Western Cape aimed at discovering empirically what motivates a strongly anti-apartheid township population to turn violently against fellow Africans. We explore the reasoning and rationalizations behind the hostility. For successful intervention, it is not sufficient to merely register and document xenophobia through preformulated statements found in attitude surveys. Instead we let the respondents themselves give the reasons for their hostility in open-ended replies. Furthermore, how political figures, police personnel, teachers, and community leaders react to xenophobia—whether they tolerate, deny, condemn, or even incite it—seems an important factor. We portray this reality as we experienced it through focus groups, surveys, and interviews in impoverished township schools and through participant observation in the racialized affluence of Cape Town and Stellenbosch during our annual research visits.

The research literature on xenophobia highlights foremost competition for scarce employment, demands for entitlement, scapegoating for poor living conditions, and entrenched habits carried over from the apartheid era. Yet how do they relate to one another, and what about the new human rights culture of a progressive constitution? A society that liberated itself in the name of universal human rights nevertheless demonstrates extreme hostility toward persons who moved to South Africa because they lacked human rights at home. This includes restricted life-chances with no jobs, civil wars, or environmental disasters. The liberal democracy that the end of apartheid had ushered in guaranteed rights for all South African residents, regardless of citizenship. Yet these inclusive human rights jar with the exclusive entitlements of citizens that underlie the legitimacy of a liberal democracy. Of all countries in the world, South Africa has admitted the most refugees. Is there a limit, dictated by a state's resources and the hospitality of citizens? This so-called liberal paradox characterizes all Western democracies that have enshrined rights of refugees and asylum seekers.

Modern xenophobia harks at entitlements for citizens from which foreigners are excluded. How can universal human rights be reconciled with closed rights of citizens? Can hostility toward strangers be considered a universal phenomenon, perhaps an evolutionary conditioning for maximizing survival, as sociobiologists assert? Is the antagonism toward perceived foreigners an issue of an insecure identity? Can xenophobia be unlearned and be corrected through appropriate political education? How can empathy with refugees be nurtured? The strangers in this case are not visibly different but share the same phenotype, sisters and brothers who assisted South African liberation, as the story goes. Therefore, are the "dangerous strangers" invented or constructed, just as European anti-Semitism once attributed all kinds of imaginary features to Jews? In a similar vein, Islamophobia now ostracizes Muslims and predicts an Islamic "tide swamping" of a childless Europe, turning it into "Eurabia" after emptying its welfare budgets.

Is xenophobia a collective paranoid delusion? Mental health textbooks define delusions as "beliefs held with great convictions in spite of having little empirical evidence." Foreigners' swamping, flooding, drowning, polluting a nation, introducing diseases, peddling drugs, defrauding the locals, and seducing women conjure up threats. The stranger lurking to invade and undermine a virtuous people is an age-old tactic to construct an enemy. Anti-Semitism under Nazi rule had perfected the mobilization against a worldwide Jewish conspiracy. Xenophobia resembles this fictitious logic but differs from the paranoid delusions of anti-Semitism.

In economic terms, newcomers compete with locals for scarce resources, especially jobs. Migrants are a real threat under conditions of scarcity. This gives xenophobia a rationality that anti-Semitism lacks. Therefore xenophobia should not be pathologized. A similar caution applies to the conflation of xenophobia with racism. The "figment of the pigment" lacks a scientific basis. It was invented to rationalize colonial domination with the "civilizing mission" of the "white man's burden." In contrast, the "othering" of strangers rests on the nepotism of the locals. Citizenship legitimizes excluding noncitizens from the rights of natives.

Xenophobia cannot be reduced to problems of a labor market alone. We soon had to question whether an impoverished township life suffices to explain scapegoating. The neglect of the shantytowns was embedded in the overall political development of the country, where an urban elite pays only lip service to the fate of the poor. This led us to revisit a once-glorified liberation movement that is still politically strong but morally weak. Chapter 4, "Falling from Grace," sketches in broad strokes the collective state of mind of the "rainbow nation." We identify various moral turning points: the HIV/AIDS denial, the continuing high crime rate, the crisis of corruption with the waste of public funds in the arms deal, the reracialization through black economic empowerment, and passivity by the African National Congress (ANC) toward the Mugabe regime. We argue that South Africa is not threatened by an unlikely descent into a Zimbabwe-type dictatorship, but by the opposite: a disintegration into anarchy once liberation ideals lose their appeal. The disillusionment with an imagined liberation can trigger all kinds of irrational reactions, given the widening inequality that no longer is based mainly on race but now is based also on class.

As is well known, South African decolonization was achieved not by military means and departure of the colonizers, as happened in other African settler societies (Algeria, Rhodesia, Kenya, Mozambique, and Angola), but with the cooperation of power holders who could have delayed their ultimate demise for some time. This unprecedented "negotiated revolution" has forced compromises on both antagonists that constrained implementing the initial visions of the new regime. Transforming a colonial economy, capturing its "commanding heights," redistributing wealth and land or nationalizing the mines, proved impossible when the compromise essentially rested on the replacement of the political class in return for maintenance of the old property relations and neoliberal market order.

What needs clarification is how much of the current malaise should be attributed to the apartheid past and how much should be ascribed to the short-sightedness of the new leadership. The legacy of racial oppression obviously is not wiped out by new nonracial legislation. Internalized habits of domination and submission last, often even unrecognized by well-intentioned progressive forces. However, blaming the apartheid legacy for most of the current political deficiencies too easily exempts inept, self-indulgent new rulers. Failing to deliver textbooks in Limpopo or paralyzing Eastern Cape education by a "selfish teachers' union" cannot be explained by referring simply to Verwoerd's Bantu education six decades earlier.

In Chapter 6 on Germany, we portray the dilemmas of a modern welfare state that needs to attract migrants with the right skills but ends up with non-integrating asylum seekers—criminalized Roma and Sinti—who are seen as defrauding the system. We discuss the European Islamophobia and the myth that an incompatible religion prevents integration. We also seek answers to why xenophobia is much higher in former East Germany (GDR) than in the Western part, although few foreigners lived in the German Democratic Republic (GDR).

In Chapter 7, we portray an official immigration society as an alternative to the South African model: an immigrant integrating, multicultural Canada. Why did South Africa not follow the Canadian or Australian example of a vision that not only regulates immigration through a sophisticated point system but also celebrates cultural diversity as well as cherished multiculturalism? Why do South Africans reject the benefits of regulated immigration of scarce skills? While in some ways South Africans are ahead of Canada by intuitively living comfortably with diversity in daily reality, Canada leads in the teaching of mutual respect and integrating difference consciously, by encouraging tolerance of dissent and equality through citizenship.

In the Conclusion, we scan the social science literature for theoretical conceptualizations of xenophobia, ranging from the notion of "moral panic" to Fanon's postcolonial condition and Freud's "narcissism of small difference," to psychosocial concepts of "identity assertion" and "reversal of honor." Merely invoking and preaching noble constitutional principles overlooks that the progressive ideals, enshrined by an urban elite, barely resonate with substantial sections of a depoliticized population. Therefore, we argue, only increased political literacy can create a cosmopolitan identity that immunizes against a violent citizenship of exclusion. However, has a complacent ruling group a real interest in such nuanced, critical political education when it is better served by uncritical conformity?

Given the vast literature on the "Mandelaland," "What is new and different about your book?" friends frequently asked. Our answer is fivefold. First, we unashamedly try to explore neglected dimensions of the landscape—what orthodox Marxists dismiss as mere "superstructure" or "false consciousness"— such as identity, perceptions, and attitudes as well as moral commitments. Second, we write from a comparative perspective as inside-outsiders, who have lived and taught intermittently in Germany, South Africa, Egypt, and the United States and for the longest time in Canada. We bring these experiences to bear on the interpretation of South Africa. Third, we minimize the popular journalistic focus on political leaders and emphasize more the sociological conditions in which they succeed or fail and what makes a following susceptible to the calls of government. Fourth, our own modest empirical research tends to be more ethnographic than representative. Therefore we complement it extensively with representative countrywide opinion surveys and reflect on immigration policies worldwide. Fifth, we focus on perpetrators rather than the experience of victims or the vast refugee assistance programs in civil society organizations. We believe that foremost a deeper understanding of collective hate is a precondition for minimizing it beyond the well-intended charity. Finally, we apply social-psychological and psychoanalytical concepts in theorizing South African ethnic relations, superimposing these over common economistic explanations. We are interested in the fantasies that sustain xenophobia and other collective outbursts of hate. We also try to write for a politically interested general audience, South Africans and non–South Africans, seeking to communicate in a more journalistic style. We did not confine ourselves to academic treatise but deliberately utilized media pundits extensively in order to enliven the portrait of South African society with everyday descriptions.

Regrettably, we continue to use apartheid racial labels, because South Africa is not yet a race-free, color-blind society and probably will not be one for a long while to come. Even in the postapartheid state, the old race categorizations are officially retained, but now to measure progress toward transformation (greater representivity) through affirmative action policies. In addition, the legacies of varied identities, associated with the phony ethnoracial categories, persist. The common label of African for the black majority does not preclude that the members of the other groups are also African in the political sense of citizens belonging to the African continent as their only home and origin. This is clarified in Chapter 5, "Settler Colonialism," which also compares SA liberation with Israel/Palestine. In contrast to the Middle East, all parties in South Africa, including the Pan-African Congress (PAC), have accepted this status of original "settlers." Therefore, not all Africans are black, and not all blacks are Africans. It should also be noted that since the rise of Stephen Biko's Black Consciousness Movement (BCM) in the late 1960s, "black" had become a proud political term, comprising politically conscious members of all three disenfranchised groups, including "Indians" and "Coloureds," the 10 percent 'mixed-race' people in the apartheid hierarchy.

So that there may be greater author transparency, two mini-autobiographies have been added in the appendixes. As the viewpoints we adopt and the research topics we chose emanate from personal histories, autoethnographies allow the reader to judge biases and vantage points of the authors. Kogila, as a Durban-born South African, sketches how her family managed to overcome systemic discrimination in a period when Indians were considered unassimilable aliens. Heribert, of German background, outlines other obstacles he had to overcome to liberate himself as well as many academic controversies in which he has been involved since graduating and working as an assistant at the Frankfurt

Institute of Social Research under Theodor Adorno and Max Horkheimer in the 1960s. This book synthesizes our fifty years of academic involvement with South Africa. It can also be read as a series of essays on the rich South Africa trajectory, a country that embodies the problems of both the first and third worlds in a microcosm.

I

Integrating Difference

1

Comparative Xenophobia

South Africa in Global Context

Xenophobia generates much violence and psychological harm. Hardly any country, whether classified as a Western democracy, a former communist state, or a developing nation, seems to be immune to hostility toward economic migrants, asylum-seeking refugees, and even legal immigrant residents. Xenophobia, racism, and nationalism (like misogyny or homophobia) are closely related but are not identical. Although all these antagonisms are frequently displayed as a common syndrome in a prejudiced person, these resentments are directed against different collectivities, and different rationalizations are used for unequal treatment. Xenophobia is not necessarily racist, and racism is not always xenophobic. Traditional racism, based on relationships of power, ascribes innate superiority and inferiority to physical characteristics or ancestry, while xenophobia uses putative markers of foreignness, cultural incompatibility, or religion as a basis for exclusion. That would make an intense nationalism a prime suspect in fostering xenophobia. However, not all nationalisms single out immigrants as polluters of cultural identity. Knowledge about the conditions under which xenophobia waxes and wanes, how violent or dormant hostility toward outsiders expresses itself, and which groups are "othered" with which rationalizations are all questions that need to be understood for successful intervention.

Such a project benefits from a comparative perspective. While focusing primarily on South Africa, we compare it with Canada and Germany. We refer to Israel and the United States occasionally, because both ethnically divided societies faced seemingly intractable problems but chose different solutions to confront their predicaments. These societies on three continents are sufficiently different in political culture to allow for meaningful comparisons. On a spectrum of current xenophobic attitudes, South Africa is located at the worst extreme, Germany in the middle, and Canada at the other end. These are also societies with which we are reasonably familiar, because we have lived and taught in the three contexts for much of our academic careers. Canada is the only Western democracy where a slight majority of citizens considers immigrants as an asset. In contrast to most European countries, a right-wing, anti-immigrant national party, does not exist in Canada, although Canada annually admits twice as many immigrants per capita (0.8 percent—260,000 in 2013) as the United States and Australia. Even the ruling Canadian Conservative Party has embraced multiculturalism. Most West European governments (particularly Germany, Holland, France, Britain, and Denmark) now advocate more compulsory assimilation and antidiscrimination laws in place of multiculturalism, which is blamed by political elites for ethnic ghettoes and an alienated, terrorist-prone youth. Canada so far has escaped the backlash against multiculturalism in Europe, where it had hardly been implemented in the first place. In South Africa, Canadian-type multiculturalism is stigmatized, because it is associated with the divide-and-rule policy of the previous apartheid regime. Instead, a utopian "nonracialism" in a glorified "rainbow nation" is propagated as the formula for "nation building" in a still deeply divided society. Yet black migrants from other African countries, not whites, are regularly singled out for attacks. A marginalized underclass of unemployed young males in shantytowns finds meaning by constructing scapegoats below themselves. It is ironic that South Africa, which once mobilized against one of the worst systems of institutionalized racism, has experienced widespread waves of xenophobia.

South African townships provide a particular vantage point not only because of the relevance of xenophobia here but also because of their non-Western character. Perspectives from the South are relatively absent in a field where the moral panic of the North about migrant invasion from the South dominates. In the emerging literature on citizenship, the comprehensive analysis by Christian Joppke (2010) stands out as a sophisticated review of the debate on immigration policies in different periods and geographical contexts. Yet even Joppke admits that his is still a book with "a view from the comfort zone" and no doubt there is a dire need to understand better the "upside-down" world of non-Western, developing countries' citizenship (viii). South Africa, with its fragile national identity, its non-Western political majority, and its Western economy, presents itself as a rich laboratory for moving the focus from the West to the Rest.

In May 2008, sixty-two migrants from other African countries, including some people who were mistaken for South African citizens, were killed by agitated mobs in various parts of the country; scores were injured physically and scarred emotionally; hundreds of shops and homes were looted; and tens of thousands of displaced persons sought shelter in churches and police stations or returned to their home countries. Since then hardly a week goes by without smaller but similar incidents of harassment being reported. While most SA municipalities and police agencies now have "disaster plans" in place to respond to attacks, the simmering hostility has only disappeared from the newspaper's front pages and is buried as "service delivery protest" in the back. A typical newspaper notice (*Business Day* [BD], February 15, 2012) four years later under the heading "Crime" reads, "Mpumalanga police arrested 51 service-delivery protesters in Masoyi, south of Hazyview, yesterday. They were charged with public violence, theft and malicious damage to property, Capt Leonard Hlathi said. 'They broke into shops belonging to foreign nationals and looted them," he said. In January 2013, dozens of shops of foreigners were looted in Zandela township near Sasolburg in mass protests against the proposed merger of two municipalities, totally unrelated to the presence of foreigners. As reasons for the attacks residents mentioned that foreign shop owners did not join the protests, did not contribute to community initiatives, such as sponsoring local sports teams and schools, don't assist with funerals in the neighborhood and instead send their profits to relatives in their own countries.

In the province of Mpumalanga, poor water had become a major grievance, and the agency entrusted with facilitating water supply in the provinces municipalities could not account for R20 million allocated. According to media reports (BD, March 6, 2014, p. 3), "protests in KaNyamazane village were fuelled by rumors that water in the area had been poisoned by Somali shop owners, who had allegedly shot dead a child recently." Why would Somali shop owners want to poison water? Who spreads such rumors, amounting to typical urban legends, that mobilize a community against foreigners? According to credible allegations, in many protests the instigators were allegedly ANC functionaries who had been sidelined for council elections for whatever reasons and now wanted to be reinstated on election slates for lucrative positions. These allegations seemed to be confirmed by many demonstrators in ANC garb and the increase of demonstrations before elections. It is therefore problematic to assume that the many protests express disillusionment with the ANC government and voters turn against the ruling party.

There are other worse examples where newly liberated people turned on each other despite their common struggle against a colonial oppressor. In the most prominent case of the India-Pakistan separation in 1948, an estimated one million people died in internecine atrocities. The conflict over the disputed territory of Kashmir still lingers between the two nuclear armed rivals. The failed Biafran war, following a few years after Nigeria's independence in 1960, produced a staggering toll of victims, as did the ongoing Kikuyo-Luo rivalries in Kenya or the prosecution of the Algerian Harkis by the victorious National Liberation Front (FLN) after independence in 1962 or the massacres of an estimated twenty thousand Ndebele Zimbabweans by Mugabe forces in the 1980s (H. Adam 2011).

One has to applaud the ANC for a long-standing "anti-tribalist" vision that embraced a "land for all the people who live in it," as the "Freedom Charter" states. So far the ANC held the fragile line on interethnic strife, although rivalries simmer under the surface. Mutual resentment between Africans and

Coloureds or envy of more successful Indians is seldom expressed publicly. These taboos may be viewed as mere political correctness, but they also prevent incitement. Compared with the rest of Africa, with its artificial borders, one of the great achievements of the ANC lies in establishing an expanded, broader "ideological border" (Etienne Balibar). These borders of the mind are ill defined; they can become deadly when stirred as communal rivalry but also stay inclusive when based on a common identity. The imagination of a borderless world contrasts with real geographical borders.

None of the 200 sovereign states of the world allow open borders. The developed global North—particularly Western Europe, North America, Japan, and Australia—have ever more fortified themselves against the influx of economic migrants from the global South. In sub-Saharan Africa, relatively developed South Africa represents the global North, as does Australia for some Asian countries. South Africa, with relatively porous borders, attracts large numbers of African migrants from as far afield as Somalia, Ethiopia, Sudan, and Nigeria. With the disparity and inequality between the two worlds of development growing, more young migrants are driven by desperation or ambition to seek their fortune abroad. This is particularly the case in disintegrating failed states and countries engaged in civil wars.

Despite ever more sophisticated border security in Southern Europe, electric fences along the U.S.-Mexican border, militarized sea patrols in the Caribbean and the Mediterranean, or extended and restricted visa requirements elsewhere, no country in the world has succeeded in stopping clandestine entry. People smuggling has become a lucrative business. Frontline states, such as Muammar Gadhafi's Libya, have been paid by the European Union (EU) to establish holding pens for African migrants as well as deportation costs, but to little avail (Harding 2012). Before the uprisings and civil wars in the Arab world, Britain and some other European states reported a decline in migrant numbers but often merely drove "illegals" and visa overstays underground.

In South Africa widely varying numbers of foreigners indicate that no reliable figures are available and all statistics are guesstimates. South African estimates of foreigners in the country vary between 1.5 million and 10 million, or about 3 percent to 20 percent of the total SA population of 52 million. In the Western Cape, Provincial Police Commissioner Arno Lamoer (BD, February 9, 2012) reported, 8,000 foreign nationals arrive every month in his southernmost province of the continent. One academic study (Landau 2011: 232) mentions "approximately 3% of the total population," which would amount to 1.5 million foreigners, which is an extremely low estimate. However, according to a widely quoted conference speech by deputy Home Affairs Minister Fatima Chohan, "427,000 new asylum seekers arrive in South Africa each year," with only 123 officials to process them (Netherland aid, June 22, 2011). She reported that her department "receives 1,200 applications per day" and that South Africa already houses ten million refugees. This high number would amount to 20 percent of the total population being foreigners and would surpass the number of migrants in the twenty-seven EU countries combined. In South Africa it is widely believed that the country indeed admits the most refugees of all states in the world.

The source country from which most claimants originate is Zimbabwe. In 2010 South Africa launched a "regularization scheme" for Zimbabwean passport holders only, during which 275,000 Zimbabweans applied for work, study, or business permits. The scheme was terminated in July 2010 with many decisions still outstanding, but was reinstated in 2014. The country profile of 2012 by the United Nations Human Rights Council (UNHRC) reports a backlog of more than 300,000 applications for refugee status awaiting a decision and projects for January 2013 a total of 480,520 persons, of whom 94,360 are assisted by UNHRC. Refugee Status Determination (RSD) is neither efficient nor fair in a country plagued by a notoriously understaffed and disorganized Department of Home Affairs.

According to the political scientist Jean-Emanuel Pondi, "only 5% of African migrants go to North America or Europe: 92% migrate to another African country" (*Le Monde Diplomatique*, November 2012). The European media image of an invasion of the continent by Africans is contradicted by these figures. While most African migrants move to a neighboring country, the dreamland remains distant South Africa. Most who have made the strenuous journey had paid heavy bribes to smugglers and border officials in half a dozen countries to reach South African soil. The glamorous SA 2010 soccer world cup had further reinforced the image of the country as a peaceful, reconciled Mandela nation.

The unexpected South African violence is important, not only because xenophobia runs counter to all the ideals of pan-African solidarity, unity, and cosmopolitan identities that African leaders usually espouse. The violent rage could also spread to other targets. The respected vice-chancellor of the Free State University, Jonathan Jansen, already warned, "Make no mistake, the people who are now pursuing foreigners will sooner or later turn on the rest of us" (*The Times*, July 14, 2010). The popular rage against foreigners disproves the Mandela-Tutu vision of an inclusive "rainbow" nation or a glorious "African Renaissance." It makes a mockery of the much-heralded African Ubuntu philosophy that self-development depends on the well-being and care for all other community members. Instead the ongoing hostility could well be seen as a forerunner to an impending civil war between a growing underclass and an indifferent, self-enriching state elite.

In Europe and the United States, anti-immigration sentiment is instigated from above by right-wing political leaders, while in SA xenophobia originates from below and is unanimously condemned by the political elite as "shameful." Theoretically, it would also seem problematic to view xenophobia as an "irrational" fear of strangers, as the dictionary definition reads, when "insiders" clearly benefit from excluding "outsiders" from scarce employment.

Giving preference of kin over nonkin—however imagined and constructed such fluid boundaries of communities are—is explained by sociobiologists (Van den Berghe 1990) as bestowing an evolutionary advantage. If this explanation of mobilized ethnicity as nepotism is correct, then one solution would be broadening in-group membership. In the case of xenophobia, this means redefining citizenship to a more cosmopolitan notion, embracing diverse members in a nation in place of an imagined homogeneity. Authors who view the nation-state as outdated in light of global migration propose extending citizenship rights to foreigners and blurring the lines between citizens and noncitizens. In this vein Yasmin Soysal (1994) in her book *Limits of Citizenship* suggests "a model of post-national membership that derives its legitimacy from universal personhood, rather than national belonging." Migrants are characterized by multiple belongings and multiple identities that need to be recognized and accommodated, rather than erased by an enforced new nationality. Multiculturalism in a multiethnic state fits this need. Still, legal citizenship cannot include all of humanity and in reality is tied to the restrictions of existing states. When is such discrimination on the basis of citizenship legitimate? Yet once "indigeneity" has been exalted, even those "foreigners" who have acquired citizenship but do not fit the image of "natives" become targets. Twenty-one of the sixty-two killed in 2008 were in fact South African citizens, guilty of being Venda or Shangani speakers from Limpopo, linguistically resembling and associating with the tainted foreigners.

States that do not assist the integration of outsiders and instead leave them to fend for themselves risk lasting tensions. Citizens or not, newcomers compete with established residents for limited state resources in employment, education, or health services. Since the insecure newcomers usually work harder at lower pay and are therefore preferred by employers, they are perceived as a direct threat by the locals. Can one expect the locals to adapt to the competition, utilizing the skills of immigrants, instead of discriminating against the outsiders?

It is necessary to return to the question, is xenophobia racism? Should "autochthony" be used instead? The concept, as defined by Peter Geschiere (2009), denotes a nativist obsession with land and belonging, to which genuine locals only are entitled, who must expose 'fake' claimants. There are many writers who maintain that the label "racism" should not be confined to the construction of phenotypes or ancestry and, as Nira Yuval-Davis (2011) argues, should include all signifiers of boundaries between "us" and "them." Thus discrimination on the basis of differences in inherited skin color should include language, religion, origin, sexual orientation, and accent and can be subsumed under the racism label. Any discourse with the logic of exclusion and exploitation amounts to racialization, in Yuval-Davis's definition. It is questionable which new insights are gained by this extension of racism to all kinds of "othering" or exclusionary practices. One only loses sight of the specificity of discrimination by lumping everything together under the label "racialization."

There are exclusionary rules and "othering" that can be justified. Most democratic settler societies, such as the United States, Australia, and Canada, have recognized "aboriginal rights" of "First Nations" from which later newcomers are legitimately excluded. It would be absurd, for example, to label the differential rights of citizens and noncitizens "racialization." If everything is

racism or fascism, then nothing is racism or fascism. The amplification of analytical concepts occurs at the expense of specificity. This applies in particular to
the institutionalized racism of the apartheid state. Surely the exploitative
racism of a white minority toward a subordinate black majority during apartheid must be distinguished from the hostility of a disempowered black underclass toward black newcomers, who are perceived as competitors for jobs and
retail business. Their demand for exclusion aims at improving the survival and
life chances of the poor. In contrast, apartheid's exclusionary policies reinforced the privileges of the already privileged. Therefore some analysts doubt
that one can talk about black racism altogether. They argue that such a reversal
ignores the power relationship that is embedded in all racialization. Powerless
people, in this view, cannot be racist.

Yet racism and xenophobia are universal in different guises. Without asserting an essentialist definition, predominant supremacist attitudes of Japanese
toward Koreans, Chinese Han toward minorities such as Tibetans, or Arabs
toward black Africans resemble the racialization of colonized people by Europeans. However, only Europeans developed an elaborate ideology of genetic and
cultural differences to justify their conquest with a "civilizing mission." Xenophobia lacks this systematic ideological rationalization that characterizes European old biological and new cultural racism. Xenophobia assumes national
entitlement on the basis of indigeneity as a "natural" defense against "intruders"
who want to partake in the entitlements of the insiders without their consent.
The insiders resent sharing their space with outsiders, not because they feel
superior as in settler colonial racialization, but because newcomers are perceived
as threatening their accustomed sense of belonging and entitlements. In short,
colonial racism was aggressive and therefore needed rationalization; xenophobia
is construed as self-defense and hardly needs justification in the view of the
perpetrators. What justification does exist takes the form of a moral panic about
intruders who cut into the native's rightful space, bring disease, introduce drugs,
seduce women, rape children, and engage in fraudulent business practices.

In addition to being portrayed as an "economic threat," migrants are also
labeled as a security risk. There seems a widespread consensus among most
South Africans that foreigners are overrepresented among criminals. The
political analyst Moeletsi Mbeki (the brother of former president Thabo Mbeki)
simplifies the problem when he criticizes the government for not "controlling
the borders, leading to a flood of poor people into SA" in order "to help fellow
Africans" by allowing them a refuge in South Africa. "Not thinking that illegals
cannot legally get jobs, but they need to eat to live. I believe that most of our
crime is by non–South Africans from north of the borders. They need to do
something to survive! Remove the illegal problem and you solve most of the
crime problem" (M&G, July 15, 2011). However, these popular "solutions" over-
look that most "illegals" work and survive without resorting to crime.

The ANC too adopted the security anxiety. *Business Day* (BD, December 27,
2012) on its front page reported after the December 2012 Manguang conference

that the "ANC mulls tough plans to curb tides of refugees." These followed a report by the ANC general-secretary that "during the last five years there were developments that pointed to the need for a more comprehensive approach to the question of management of foreign nationals entering SA." The developments of concern mentioned first "the high number of cases of crime involving foreign nationals." Behind the bureaucratic language of imbalances and "reducing the ambiguity on immigration policy" lies also for the first time the fear that "competition from nationals from Asian countries was having a negative effect on small business" (BD, December 27, 2012). While most hawkers and small shops trade with Chinese imports, the Chinese-owned corner shop, like in North America a century ago, slowly constitutes a "yellow peril." In Africa generally, Chinese projects are not popular, because Chinese investors frequently import their own labor. Howard W. French's book, *China's Second Continent: How a Million Migrants Building a New Empire in Africa* (Knopf, 2014) was listed by the *New York Times* among the 100 best books of the year. With this protectionist worldview, the South African government taps into a national consensus. Inveighing against "too many foreigners" is not confined to the urban poor. Blacks and whites, regardless of class position, share this skepticism. One can already hear informally that Zimbabweans dominate the management of too many South African companies and Nigerians hold too many professional jobs. Soon indigenization of corporate executives could become the next demand of South African nationalists.

Comparative research on xenophobia poses the classic liberal dilemma between universalist human rights and the individualist rights of citizens. The French revolutionaries of the Enlightenment tradition in their Declaration of Rights of Man and Citizens introduced the two distinct concepts. Both aim to achieve equality, eliminate unmerited discrimination, and ensure justice. Global human rights have advanced with economic globalization. Even birthright citizenship is now considered, like inherited property, an unmerited advantage.

Human rights strive for equality among all human beings as well as between richer and poorer states. Human rights universalize the rights of "man" and women, regardless of national origin. Quota of immigrants according to national origin or religion had been abolished in most democratic states during the 1960s, although tightened admission, even of visitors, according to selected national origin has been reintroduced in North America and Europe since 9/11.

Citizenship rights, on the other hand, are bounded by nation-states in which they apply. Advocates of citizenship rights argue that human rights can be realized only within and through nation-states. In his compelling book, *A Man of Good Hope*, Jonny Steinberg (2014: 270) states: "Perversely, xenophobia is a product of citizenship, the claiming of a new birthright [in South Africa]. Finally, we belong here, and that means that you do not." In this view redistribution and solidarity cannot be extended to everyone without limits but are grounded in identity, trust, and loyalty to fellow citizens. But does that mean that belonging together and communal identity require closure? Is connectedness, or what Max Weber calls "Zusammengehörigkeitsgefühl," a precondition for social rights? People from all over the world can harmoniously live together in the same democratic welfare state with subnational identities, as the elaboration of the Canadian model shows in Chapter 7. Similarly, South Africa's parallel ethnic enclaves may not be the "imagined community" of solidarity and rather "less a nation than an agglomeration of disparate tribes, riven by collective envies and rivalries," as Ken Owen (2012: 49) argues, but they do coexist relatively peacefully and freely with equal citizenship rights. Some even embrace the Habermasian "constitutional patriotism."

The problem with a high number of immigrants arises from a labor market from which locals feel shut out by too many newcomers. Does the South African state have the resources to accommodate refugees from the rest of the continent and the high number of unemployed indigenes? Does South Africa have a special obligation toward a less developed continent? Many convincingly argue that if the South African substantial resources of human and material capital were more effectively deployed and not wasted by foolish policies, the state would soar. In an expanding economy with less inequality and a more just distribution of scarce resources, the "immigration problem" would be minimized.

In light of increasing numbers of desperate refugees and migrants in search of a better life in more developed and democratic countries, receiving states basically face seven options of dealing with migrants. These options and their drawbacks are listed as follows and will be elaborated subsequently:

1. **Fortify borders**—which is costly and at least partially unsuccessful, no matter how well fences, surveillance, special police forces, or visa restrictions are implemented.
2. **Turn a blind eye**—ignoring the death of migrants, which has been advocated by right-wing parties in Europe; tolerating increasing casualties of unwanted migrants on the high sea (European Union, Australia), in the deserts (U.S.-Mexico, Sinai), and under the control of smugglers. It is inhuman to deny aid to refugees and also violates international law and national constitutions.
3. **Implement the "Arizona Option"**—strengthen internal policing of undocumented immigrants by increasing penalties of employers of "illegals" and extending arrest warrants. Increased deportation leads to racial profiling and local strife and is also opposed by influential business sectors.
4. **Focus on socioeconomic development**—pacify strife-torn states, so that incentives for emigration decrease. This ideal can be achieved only in the long run. It also does not address the question of refugees from large-scale environmental disasters (such as climate change, drought, earthquakes, tsunamis, or contamination) or persistent harm from homophobia or gender atrocities.

5. **Relax immigration control**—favor open or porous borders despite rejection by the national populace. This laissez-faire policy could overwhelm existing welfare systems and social services. It also risks xenophobic backlashes when locals feel shortchanged.

6. **Increase regularized immigration**—which would meet stern voter resistance and increase support for far-right parties, particularly in Western European societies that do not consider themselves immigration countries. Yet the shortage of specialized skills and aging populations could make this "Canadian Option" increasingly more attractive.

7. **Educate a skeptical population**—with the aim of integrating newcomers, foster understanding to empathize with the plight of refugees and migrants, who will be part of social life, regardless of all the attempted responses outlined above. How a prejudiced society can not only be infused with more tolerance but also be made hospitable to difference remains the challenge.

Whether the migrants are a net benefit or liability to the economy of the receiving country is hotly debated. In most settings, illegals provide an exploitable, low-wage labor force, particularly for unskilled jobs that locals reject. Immigrants mostly supplement but do not replace indigenes. Newcomers frequently fill economic niches, such as child and elder care, food processing, low-skilled construction jobs, farm labor, waitressing, and gardening in South Africa and California. They also remit earnings to kin in their country of origin, which amounts to small-scale global redistribution. If big capital had an exclusive say, immigration restrictions would be relaxed, particularly for skilled migrants, such as IT professionals. Migrants add to the industrial reserve army of labor. As unorganized cheap labor, migrants drive wages down. Therefore unions everywhere are generally opposed to unregulated free immigration, unless a "split labour market" (Bonacich 1972) can be prevented through state regulations, as was the case with the state contracts for "Turkish guestworkers" in West Germany of the 1970s.

Yet even without the influx of migrants, the downward trend on wages would not be stopped, because globalized capital is mobile and can relocate. Outsourcing of production into cheaper labor areas achieves the disciplining of unions. On a global scale, the South African labor market itself is part of this reality, and the influx of migrants reinforces this working-class dependency. However, even if the economic benefits are clearly demonstrated, the Indian computer geeks are still rejected and the foreign medical doctors in South Africa are still considered *kwerekwere*. When the former social-democratic German government tried to introduce temporary green cards for high-tech specialists along the American model, the battle cry from the conservatives too was "Kinder statt Inder" (babies in place of Indians).

David Abraham (2010: 977) has correctly stated, "Immigration discourse generally ignores the welfare state." A welfare state is based on a social contract among contributing citizens. If any of the developed welfare states would allow noncitizens from underdeveloped parts unearned equal access to the social rights of citizens, the benefits of a modern state would be severely strained under the pressure of sheer numbers of newcomers. Already, the influx of Eastern Europeans with legitimate claims for social assistance as EU citizens is strongly resented in the original EU states, particularly Britain. Cosmopolitan citizenship appeals as an ideal but flounders on the reality of competition for scarce resources. Indigenes would feel massively shortchanged. Border abolitionists ignore the fascist potential among insiders. Spreading violent xenophobia is an indication of a potential that could worsen conditions for both locals and migrants. Once populist agitators hark on a repertoire of national pollution, such as making people foreigners in their own land of birth and the undermining cherished traditions, particularly replacing sacred religious symbols with competing religious markers, the scene is set for worse violations of human rights for insiders and outsiders alike. In a Swiss referendum, adding more mosques to the existing six minarets in the country was rejected. Holland and Denmark exemplify how quickly two relatively tolerant societies abandoned multiculturalism for xenophobic cohesion after a few incidents. In his 2012 reelection campaign, Nicolas Sarkozy courted right-wing voters with absurd chauvinistic slogans, like legislating processed meat labels so that true French people would not have to eat halal food unwillingly.

In Germany, the dictionary definition of xenophobia as "fear of strangers" misleads insofar as xenophobia does not so much express fear as disdain and resentment of undeserved welfare recipients. Constructing a self-image of shortchanged indigenes establishes for the xenophobic mind a superior identity and for its instigators an opportunistic role as self-styled, farsighted leaders, preventing "cultural pollution" and draining of scarce resources. Thilo Sarrazin's best seller *Deutschland schafft sich ab* (Germany abolishes Itself; 2010) is an indicator of a popular lingering xenophobic sentiment, articulated by a leading social democrat who embarrassed his political allies by espousing a dormant anxiety. Yet Germany differs from other European countries, like France or Britain, in having a relatively small and fractured right-wing movement that, however, can hark back to a nostalgic Nazi past which at the same time has discredited its ideology. It has also more stringent legal provisions for criminalizing hate speech together with extensive memorialization and education programs, and comprises a relatively secular Turkish minority since the 1970s that has dampened the Islamophobia of other European countries. Yet attacks on foreign residents occur regularly, particularly in former East Germany.

In South Africa, most reports (Everatt 2011: 22) emphasize the sentiment that patience with better-educated and "hard-working entrepreneurial foreigners had expired" and "the post-apartheid dividend needed to be claimed by South

Africans, violently if necessary." Sarrazin's central thesis asserts the opposite: lazy, nonassimilating foreigners with many children bring the hardworking, increasingly childless German nation down and undermine traditional virtues. While the SA discourse concerns mainly economic entitlement and material implications of migrancy, the German debate in addition is overladen with ideological concerns about *Leitkultur* (dominant or guiding culture) and *Überfremdung* (cultural alienation), in short, the contamination by permissive multiculturalism.

The harsh European immigration restrictions and expulsions of undocumented migrants contradict the professed humanitarian values that Europe adopted as its self-image after World War II. The deportation of Jews still lingers as guilt in the collective memory of Germany and France. Therefore the pretense of the universality of human rights is not easily shed. Similar considerations shape the contradictory responses in the former apartheid state, which cannot openly violate its liberal constitution and evict asylum seekers in the same way as the white minority expelled undesirable blacks to the rural hinterland. All nominal liberal states, including the United States, face this conundrum between universal justice and communitarian injustice toward nonnationals. The compromise with which the contradiction is marketed to a xenophobic constituency adopts a hard line on illegal would-be migrants in exchange for a more liberal immigration policy and temporary entry for asylum seekers. This American consensus asserts that without detention centers, expulsions, and imagined border security, an even more right-wing sentiment among insiders against threatening outsiders could emerge.

Should stronger law against xenophobia be enacted? The criminalization of xenophobia and hate crimes in general, as necessary as this may be, hardly functions as a deterrent. The delusional Norwegian mass murderer Anders Behring Breivik, who systematically killed 77 and seriously injured more than 150 Norwegians in July 2011 in order to draw attention to the alleged "pollution" of the nation by foreigners, actually sought the publicity of his punishment to spread his message. For such pathologies enhanced retribution of a criminal code would nevertheless seem useful, if only to deter copycat actions. The perpetrators of hate crimes usually act collectively as conformists to the group they feel is significant to them. Therefore, the law and respected political leaders speaking out may put brakes on latent predispositions.

However, hoping to eradicate xenophobia by criminalizing it fails to be successful for a variety of reasons. Attitudes cannot be legislated; only behavior can be influenced by laws. If strong attitudes of hostility toward out-groups persist, those attitudes find expression regardless of official prohibitions. Moreover, belief in the power of the law falls into the trap of a conservative law-and-order mentality that holds the individual, rather than the social conditions that predispose people to hateful behavior, accountable for outbreaks of violence. Ethnic riots do not so much result from individual choices as avert attention from the social, cultural, and economic conditions that underlie collective hostility.

2

South African Perspectives
on Xenophobia

R eviewing the South African empirical evidence on xenophobia against the backdrop of the vast general literature on ethnic hostility could expose shortcomings of accepted theories and hopefully advance our understanding of a significant social problem that counteracts peaceful development in many parts of the world. Hardly any of the existing studies on SA xenophobia reviews the incidents with a comparative and interventionist focus. Most accounts are rich in descriptions of the local dynamics, but "surprisingly little attention has been paid to underlying political causes" (Klotz 2012: 189), nor has there emerged any sustained or coordinated national effort for intervention. One of the informative papers of the South African Migration Project (SAMP) states, "South Africa urgently needs an antidote to a decade of political inaction on xenophobia" (Crush 2008: 8).

Many social scientists in South Africa have written about or commented at numerous conferences about the 2008 countrywide riots against foreigners. The edited volume by Loren Landau (2011) that is advertised as "the first academic text to fully theorize the events" contains twenty-five pages of bibliography. We found, among the many analyses of xenophobia, Landau's book together with a special issue of the South African journal *Politikon* (vol. 38, no. 1, April 2011), edited by David Everatt, particularly useful. Landau's contributors mainly focus empirically on local causes with much detailed quantitative analysis.

Landau, the director of the African Centre for Migration and Society at Wits University, deplores that "a universal humanistic recognition" for foreigners and fellow citizens alike is prevented by the exclusive government focus on correcting the material inequities of the past. Since this requires using racial categories with whites as a reference group, it implicitly depoliticizes and ignores other social divisions. Foreign blacks in this logic are not a historically disadvantaged group. Landau and his contributors controversially also accuse migrant organization, clamoring for inclusion and protection to "become active participants in entrenching and naturalizing differences based on history and citizenship." Instead of inclusion as equals, he argues, migrants allow themselves to be turned into charity cases: "By demanding participation as strangers, they grant citizens a power and authority by entrenching a relationship of subjugation and outsiderness" (234). But everywhere do citizens, not newcomers themselves, determine the status of immigrants in a new land. It is utopian to expect the abolition of citizenship rights, because such rights by definition, Landau asserts, "retard rather than enhance the possibility of professional, personal or even political solidarity" with foreigners (234). In contrast, we argue that hospitality and recognition of all migrants cannot be demanded and granted automatically but depends on a mutual relationship. In the real world, newcomers more than locals have to foster this relationship, even if it means demonstrating utility as a precondition for recognition. Landau also underestimates the struggle for scarce urban resources by downplaying the number of migrants having entered South Africa. He maintains that given the approximately 3 percent of foreigners in the total population and the level of unemployment in postapartheid South Africa (between 25 and 45 percent) "the logic of a foreign demon undermining the wealth of South Africans does not stand up to careful scrutiny" (232). While immigrants generally enhance the wealth of a country as a whole, particularly when they can offer superior skills, it is inevitable that they are preferred by employers and thereby disadvantage locals competing for the same jobs.

The articles in Everatt's collection offer interpretive summaries of responses by civil society (media, business, unions, and churches). Shireen Hassim, Twana Kupe, and Eric Worby's (2008) collection *South Africa: Go Home or Die Here*, with superb photographs by Alon Skuy, is an equally compelling indictment of the "rainbow nation." The pre-2008 fifty SAMP Migration Policy reports by the Queens University–based Jonathan Crush, revealing South Africa as one of the most hostile societies to immigrants, laid the foundation for the growing awareness of problems of migrancy. We found, among all the academic journal articles, the piece by David Mario Matsinhe (2011), "Africa's Fear of Itself," most insightful and closest to our perspective, while the essay by Andreas Wimmer (1997), "Explaining Xenophobia and Racism," provides a theoretical overview of the general literature on xenophobia which unfortunately stops at 1993.

Two guiding threads inform most SA analyses: the apartheid past as one root cause of xenophobia and, more controversially, the many deficits of the postapartheid state that are held responsible as key causes. The shortcomings of the new order cannot all be blamed on apartheid but are clearly linked to and derived from the past. Habits formed during the apartheid era, when "surplus" people were moved around, "endorsed out" (meaning forcefully relocated to rural areas in the jargon of apartheid planners), contained, and denationalized in the country of their birth, are reenacted in the new South Africa. As Everatt has written, perhaps with some exaggeration, "The echoes with the language of apartheid are uncanny. The language and practices of the past were internalized by participants as solutions to the present. The former victims of apartheid's influx control and attempt to animalize black South Africans and restrict them to orderly movement from one prescribed area to another, conducting their business in urban areas and then returning to rural Bantustans while treating them as potential criminals who were guilty until proven innocent through producing a 'dompas' (permit) had by 2008 become the language of those enfranchised by apartheid democracy" (2011: 12).

In the postapartheid era, up to three hundred thousand persons declared illegal annually were deported, many only to return as quickly as possible to escape poverty and war. Anchoring the new xenophobia in the history of the country is of merit, but it hardly explains the specifics of violence: why some communities were heavily affected and others, like Soweto, which had a similar percentage of foreigners, not at all. In addition one has to ask, if apartheid conditioning is the main explanation, how must similar or worse policies against migrants in Alabama, Arizona, many African states without apartheid, and other parts of the world be understood?

To what extent the apartheid legacy of socioeconomic inequality accounts for xenophobia, as most argue, is highly contentious. Michael Neocosmos (2010) denies that "the problems of xenophobia are fundamentally economic" and does not think "xenophobia is a problem of the poor at all," because a majority of South Africans are xenophobic, regardless of class, gender, or racial differences. Indeed, 84 percent feel that South Africa is allowing too many foreign nationals into the country, and 74 percent want anyone not contributing economically deported (*ibid*: 19; see also www.afrobarometer.org). However, while xenophobic attitudes are among the highest in the world in South Africa, the residents of predominantly white and affluent suburbs, such as Sandton or Bishopscourt do not go on a rampage against foreign shop owners. Only the very poor in informal settlements loot and kill in their areas. Why?

New-left academics and organizations like Abahlali sneer at the charitable interventions of liberals and educational efforts about xenophobia by civil societies' do-gooders: "The solution is not to educate the poor about xenophobia. The solution is to give the poor what they need to survive so that it becomes easier to be welcoming and generous" (Gibson 2011: 179). While everybody agrees about the need to improve the lives of the poor, it is naive to expect that wealth alone will change xenophobic attitudes, as the survey cited in the preceding paragraph indicates. Ignoring the immediate exigencies and belittling educational efforts means waiting for Godot. On the other hand, left organizations or religious nongovernmental organizations (NGOs) are often the only voices that take notice and promise mobilization and education. They issue high-minded press statements of condemnation and exhortations to desist from scapegoating foreigners and instead blame the governing culprits for not doing enough to alleviate poverty. A typical example is a press release from local activists: "The Botshabelo Unemployed Movement (BUM) and the Democratic Left Front (DLF) call on informal traders in Botshabelo not to use foreign traders in the township as a scapegoat for their anger at the attacks they have faced from the Mangaung Metropolitan Municipality last week and their dire economic circumstances. The BUM and the DLF regret last week's outbreak of xenophobic violence in Botshabelo. The BUM and the DLF call on informal traders and all unemployed people to desist from continued attacks against foreign traders in Botshabelo. Rather, Botshabelo informal traders and other unemployed people must direct their anger at the Mangaung municipality. We call for sustained mass action to expose failed service delivery, corruption and how the municipality's policies maintain apartheid geographies and continue the systemic marginalisation of the unemployed. The BUM is now undertaking local mobilisation and public education against xenophobia in Botshabelo" (BUM press release, July 2, 2012). Whether such promised redirection of pent-up frustrations from the foreign competition to the political power holders will succeed remains to be seen. The envisaged socialist international solidarity of the working class failed during two world wars in Europe when pitted against nationalist mobilization. One may rightly doubt a different outcome of similar efforts in South Africa, particularly when the target of the independent left is an uncaring liberation bureaucracy.

In addition, in the public debate the causal relationship between poverty and xenophobia is flatly denied by some analysts. The influential columnist Aubrey Matshiqi (2010) holds the strong view "that socio-economic conditions" were not "the cause of the xenophobic attacks." Matshiqui blames "the many layers of prejudice that afflict South Africa . . . as the root cause." Yet this explanation merely renames the phenomenon that it purports to understand. A related journalistic view holds "that countries that treat foreigners well will tend to experience high economic growth," while one also hears the reverse, that countries with economic growth do not experience xenophobia. A comparative examination of Western Europe and Canada can shed light on this overgeneralized proposition.

While no consensus exists about the causes of xenophobia among SA analysts, even the label "xenophobia" is questioned or the phenomenon is ignored altogether. In the first diagnostic report of Trevor Manuel's National Planning Commission (NPC), "nine key challenges" facing South Africa are identified, but xenophobia is not among them. Former President Thabo Mbeki has wondered what those who accuse "my people" of xenophobia know about "my people." In his view, they are trying "to explain naked criminal activity by cloaking it in the garb of xenophobia" (quoted in Hassim 2008: 4). By criminalizing the popular sentiment, the illusion of the virtuous national citizen is resurrected and the government's responsibility for neglecting the marginalized underclass obscured. Similarly, R. W. Johnson (2009: 630–631) writes, "When the fact of popular xenophobia became clear, ANC leaders behaved as if they were priests attempting an exorcism, by preaching and prayers to cast out the devil (xenophobia), as if the real problem was inside the heads of the rioters, when, quite clearly, the root causes lay in high unemployment and the government's failure to control the country's borders."

Andile Mngxitama (2008: 204) has added, "The fact that ours is a neo-apartheid state managed now by yesterday's anti-apartheid revolutionaries is also concealed." Similarly, Nico Trimikliniotis and colleagues (2008: 133) call the stance of the postapartheid state simply "racist" and "a continuation of the apartheid regime." They conclude that "there is no reason why one should refer to the exclusionary ideology merely as 'xenophobic.'" Other writers (in Hassim 2008: 198) diagnose "Afrophobia" or "negrophobia" as "a more accurate term" and call the self-hate of blacks a "psychological disease of the mind" that has "killed more blacks in the last five hundred years than epidemics and plagues of all sorts."

Most SA scholars also highlight the liberal, inclusive South African constitution with its emphasis on rights for all residents, not just citizens, and lament the violation of its spirit. It has only gradually dawned on this privileged class that the nonracial "rainbow nation" did not resonate with "throw-away citizens" in "permanent refugee camps," as the shantytowns have been called. After all, the rainbow notion dissolves difference, while the urban poor rely on and invoke the difference between entitled insiders and dangerous outsiders. Francis Nyamnjoh (2006: 40) argues that the outsiders pose a threat to the insiders, who are "eager to prove their modernity and harvest the benefits of full citizenship for long mystified by whiteness." He views xenophobia as deriving from "a narrowly nation-state-based citizenship" and advocates a model of "unbound, flexible citizenship." However, such a notion of a "cosmopolitan African identity," briefly envisaged by a 1995 Southern African Development Corporation (SADC) protocol of greater regional integration and open borders for the Southern African region, was vetoed by South Africa. The liberal opposition Democratic Alliance (DA) supported this stance. Its current leader, Helen Zille (cited in Hassim, 2008: 248), is quoted as, "The recent wave of xenophobic attacks is a direct result of the government's failure to properly control immigration into South Africa." Apart from the incapacity of controlling South Africa's borders, Zille's statement implies that xenophobia would disappear or at least be reduced with regulated immigration, an implication that can also be doubted.

Others go further and question the whole process of SA nation building. Ivor Chipkin (2007) doubts that South Africans exist as a nation and speaks of "foreign natives" and "native foreigners" as a legacy of the "Bantustan mentality." Sabelo J.Ndlovu-Gasheni (2010: 293) blames the uncertainties of the globalization process for worsening "the degeneration of African nationalism into nativism and xenophobia." Others refer to Mahmoud Mamdani's (2001a)

insistence on colonialism as responsible for artificial African borders and reinforcing or even creating divisive ethnic identities. But what is true for Rwanda,
from which Mamdani draws his evidence, does not necessarily apply to the
internal settler colonialism of South Africa. Once "indigeneity as the central
imperative of citizenship" is introduced, as Michael Neocosmos (2006) asserts,
the slide into xenophobia away from an inclusive civic nationalism to a narrow
ethnic nationalism is almost inevitable.

Since 9/11, the Western discourse on foreigners is preoccupied with Islamophobia. Islamist terrorists have been elevated to the principal representative of
the foreign threat, including those Muslim adolescents born and educated in the
new country but alienated from Western values. Although about 2 percent of the
South African population identify as Sunni Muslims, Islamophobia does not
feature in the debate about SA foreignness. There were some terrorist bombings
by a Muslim group, PAGAD (People Against Gangsterism and Drugs) in the
Western Cape during the 1990s, but these were locally motivated turf wars. It
never escalated into jihad rhetoric. PAGAD was quickly infiltrated and marginalized by the community itself. Although South Africa is soaked with religi-
osity in a variety of faiths, ecumenical tolerance has prevailed. Even the
ongoing media warfare on the Israeli-Palestinian conflict between an avowedly
Zionist Jewish community and an equally ardent Muslim Council has become
stale, boring, and predictable. Physical attacks on each other have not taken
place, partly because of the joint struggle against apartheid in which both Jews
and Muslims were active.

Another crucial difference between migrants in South Africa and migrants
in the West relates to their vision of the future. Migrants in Europe or America,
regardless of whether they are legal or undocumented, prefer to stay permanently,
integrate, and hope for a better life as new citizens. According to our interviews,
most migrants in South Africa, particularly Zimbabweans, would return to their
country of origin if conditions improved. Most view themselves as sojourners or
reluctant immigrants, not voluntary emigrants. Writing about Somalis, Jonny
Steinberg (2014: 271) asserts: "They do not want to make friends. They do not
want to make South Africa their home. They want to make money." Had the
South African ANC government put pressure on Mugabe in a similar way
as J. B. Vorster forced Ian Smith to sign the Lancaster House agreement in 1980,
the country would not have been emptied of half of its productive youth.

Foreign corporations and African governments added to the refugee stream
from the Congo by supporting local warlords in order to gain access to rare
minerals, particularly columbite-tantelite ("coltan"), used in cell phones and
turbines, and cassiterite, a mineral used for the production of tin, another essential component of computer circuit boards and mobile phones. The Cape Town
journalist Tony Weaver (CT, January 18, 2013) who often writes on the eastern
Congo civil war, has pointed out that 80 percent of the world's known reserves
of these rare minerals are located in the Democratic Republic of the Congo
(DRC) in areas controlled by rival militias. Rwanda, Burundi, Zimbabwe, and

Uganda back different warlords. "It is estimated that close to six million civilians have already died in the civil war in the DRC, and over half a million women and girls have been raped," writes Weaver. A large UN peacekeeping force in the area has not made much difference to the bloodletting of humans and animals for the commodities of "modernity."

While officially deploring the Zimbabwean strife and for a long time deporting Zimbabwean refugees until 2009, both the Zuma and particularly the Mbeki government ensured the continuous stream of refugees through their passive tolerance or even support for a tyrant at their doorstep. In January 2013 it was revealed that South Africa even supplied Zimbabwe with helicopters for an army that acts as an instrument of political repression at home and looting of assets abroad. Roughly two million Zimbabwean migrants are estimated to live in South Africa and just fewer than 700,000 have work permits, according to the SA Institute of Race Relations (SAIRR) Survey 2012. More than 160,000 Zimbabweans were deported annually before 2009 when a moratorium came into effect, following the xenophobic attacks. This was rescinded in 2011, and deportations resumed. According to the Department of Home Affairs (DHA) Annual Report 2010–11, currently between 200 and 300 Zimbabweans are deported back every day, or 7,500 per month. Most Zimbabweans are ready to return voluntarily, if conditions in the homeland improve. Simon van der Westhuizen (Letter to CT, March 1, 2012) expressed the situation well: "I have spoken to many Zimbabwean workers employed in this country—I am one myself—and most would really like to go home to a prosperous and free country without a president who regards it as his personal property. Surely if the SA government took a more active role in sorting Zimbabwe out politically and economically, at least 1 million jobs would become available to South Africans almost immediately—that's more jobs that any scheme or ministry could create in 10 years."

Our research in the Western Cape produced some overlooked facts. The assumption that rightless foreigners are preferred by employers mainly because they are cheaper may not be correct in South Africa. Various acquaintances pay the same R150–200 for a local or a Malawian gardener per day, the same for a cleaning lady from the Cape Flats or from Zimbabwe. Inquiries among restaurant waiters established low identical wages for everyone. However, virtually every employer, white or black, from a supermarket chain to a small business owner, from a commercial farmer or a bank administrator to a private household head, view the foreigners as "working harder," being more reliable, "going the extra mile," being flexible, "taking initiatives," and being eager to please as reasons for preferential recruitment. The attributes mentioned characterize powerless people. Yet this powerlessness also qualifies as a hard currency in a competitive labor market. In contrast, local labor is considered "generally lazy"; "they take jobs for granted"; they "work with an entitlement mentality"; "they are nonresponsive as waiters." Even one strong African nationalist told us "our people [had] better wake up" before they all get shortchanged. Confronted with such stereotypical perceptions in a national division of labor, the locals inevitably resent foreigners who expose them as lacking essential qualities for obtaining the most scarce and most desirable commodity: a regular income.

Such different opportunities for employment are exacerbated during a strike, when needy foreigners are perceived as "scabs" because they are willing to continue working for low wages they need for survival. This gives locals the justification to act out their xenophobia, as happened in the 2012–2013 Western Cape farm workers' strike. About four thousand Zimbabwean seasonal fruit pickers refused to join the strike. This was further complicated through inter-foreigner hostility. Undocumented Basuto fruit pickers were not hired, because they lacked work permits and some farmers had been fined for employing them. In most cases the vulnerable foreigners serve as an easy target for a frustrated unemployed youth. A similar situation exists within the ubiquitous private security industry. Most of its low-paid guards are foreigners who bear the brunt of angry locals. The literature on xenophobia sometimes emphasizes the difference between skilled and unskilled immigrant labor. It is argued that skilled labor functions as a complement to domestic labor, whereas unskilled labor acts as a substitute. While broadly true, the preceding examples show that unskilled labor also complements local supply when foreigners fill niches for which domestic employees are not available or are considered unsuitable.

As was previously mentioned, in Europe and the United States, anti-immigration sentiment is mobilized from above by right-wing leaders, while in South Africa xenophobia originates from below and is unanimously condemned by the political elite. The South African violence did not aim at control of the state, as the simultaneous interethnic violence after the 2008 Kenyan election did. There the strife and ethnic cleansing, as Loren Landau and Jean Pierre Misago (2009: 105) have observed, were both national and state centric, while "South Africa's xenophobic violence was decentralized and rooted in the micro-politics of township life." All our research did not discover a central agency or "third force" that had planned or coordinated the hostility, as was originally hinted by some ANC leaders. "Third Force" is usually a code word for Inkatha, the Zulu party of Chief Buthelezi. However, there is no Inkatha presence in the Western Cape. The attacks stemmed from the weakness of the state and disorganization of ANC local branches, which gave gangsters and freelance politicians space to appropriate state authority for their own benefits. Some analysts (Horwitz, in Helen Suzman Foundation Roundtable, 2010: 25) assert that "the ANC has disempowered its ward councilors. They are treated like dirt and they don't do their work." Self-appointed xenophobic entrepreneurs exploit a political vacuum when they establish themselves as a substitute leadership. As Landau and Misago (2009: 105) perceptively diagnose, "the stake of wealth may not be as high as in the African civil wars for control of the capital, but community leadership is an attractive alternative for the largely unemployed residents of the informal settlements. It is a form of paid employment or an income-generating activity whereby supposedly voluntary leaders often charge for services, levy protection fees, sell or let land and buildings, and take bribes in exchange for solving problems or influencing tender processes." The more the official local councilors are perceived as corrupt and on the take, the more parallel, informal leaders gain legitimacy. Nor is petty corruption—or other illegal activities—restricted to local political leaders, particularly when it comes to dealing with foreigners. Border Crossings in many countries are particularly amenable locations for bribery. In the weekly SA blog GroundUP (October 13, 2014) a reporter, Tariro Washinyira, describes how she crossed illegally into South Africa, pretending not to have a Zimbabwean passport: "The truck driver shows his passport then the officers ask for the passengers' passports. The driver replies, reaches for his wallet and takes out R100. The officer refuses. 'These people paid you more than this,' he says. He is offered R200 and lets us through. A few meters away we reach a place where lots of cars were parked and immigration officers are patrolling. The truck driver tells us to get out of the truck and sit outside pretending we are waiting for something while he checks if it is safe to drive off. When he thinks it is safe, he asks us to hop into the truck. Before he drives away two officers appear and demand to see our passports. The driver gives them R200 each and is allowed to drive away." Without documents the rightless migrants are victimized by locals and officials alike: "Sitting in a taxi at the filling station in Musina is a woman with a three-year-old baby. She has paid R250 to the taxi driver for transport to Johannesburg but the taxi has not filled up in two days and the driver has refused to refund her. She cannot report the driver to the police because she is also a border jumper—she and the child do not have passports' (GroundUp, October 13, 2014).

In an interview with the authors, one senior policeman with almost thirty years of service defined xenophobia as "pure looting," including by the police. When asked how many of the police in the Cape he considers corrupt and taking a bribe when offered, he replied, "Up to 60 percent." He told the story of an acquaintance who was consigned to a border post where "everyone is involved": "When he [his acquaintance] tried to check the papers of a full mini taxi, the driver became agitated and said, 'But I have already paid R20,000.'" The Sotho speaking supervisor arrived and said, "My new colleague here is a Xhosa speaker who does not fully understand our rules. I'll sort this out" and waved the taxi through. The policeman vowed rather to quit next time than face this again. We probed further what to do about police corruption and heard the common refrain, "Look, two successive national police chiefs have been dismissed and are in prison. The mess starts at the top," followed by the classic sentence, "In South Africa everyone makes his own gravy train." The R500 that the Home Affairs official receives to have the papers ready when the "refugee" from the DRC arrives in Cape Town is "peanuts" compared with the losses in other areas.

On the basis of many informal talks with police personnel, we obtained the distinct impression that this arm of the state is even more contemptuous of foreigners than the students surveyed. Although cagey not to express hostility openly, many hinted that the government is too lax in enforcing immigration control. Therefore the country becomes "ungovernable." The reemergence of vigilante activity and necklacing, although directed against local thieves, is largely ignored by law enforcement. Indifferent enforcement of laws encourages abandoned populations to take the law into their own hands. One should also not forget that even under apartheid the majority of policemen were blacks and the distrust of police has carried over to the new era. Hundreds of "service delivery protests" nationwide are put down with the same force and with the same armored cars as during the hated minority rule. Sometimes the police also collude with the community whose sentiment they echo.

One policeman told the story of the eviction of Nigerians. Two houses, rented by Nigerians, were identified by the community as "drug dens." Whenever the police raided the houses and broke down the front doors—without a warrant, as the narrator proudly stressed—the tenants had apparently flushed the drugs down the toilet and the police had no evidence on which to arrest the suspects. Frustrated community members therefore gave the tenants two ultimatums to move out, but the deadlines were ignored. A final deadline was set with the knowledge of the local police, who turned up to watch the events. "Fortunately," the narrator explained to us, "this time a truck turned up, the tenants loaded their belongings, and the foreigners left." The policeman was relieved that the problem was solved peacefully, but he also hinted that he would not have intervened had the locals chased out the foreign criminals violently.

High unemployment in the formal economy makes it difficult for an undocumented foreigner to integrate into a regular occupation. Setting up a small business, mostly operating from home, is an obvious alternative for survival. "Spaza shops" (informal convenience stores usually run from home) have developed as the preferred route for Somali immigrants. Other foreign nationals sell handicraft at street corners; set themselves up as hairdressers with a plastic chair, a mirror, and scissors; work long hours as waiters; fill gas at petrol stations; or guard parked cars or fancy houses at night. As in most immigrant societies, new arrivals drift to areas and occupations where fellow ethnics are already established and usually assist each other. Somali newcomers, we were told, help out without wages in the shop of a relative but are provided with food, accommodation, and a bit of pocket money. After a while they are "set up" with their own shop and pay back with a cut from their profits. An ethnic division of labor has developed with certain nationalities specializing in certain occupations. Some compete more; others less or not at all with locals. The higher the competition, the greater the risk of xenophobic violence. High on the list as targets of choice for criminals and envious locals alike are Somali-run small businesses. The Somali traders operate in direct competition with local spaza shops but offer their commodities at lower prices. More than half of the informal stores on the Cape flats are owned by foreigners, and about three-quarters of those are owned by Somalis. Locals prefer the Somali shops because of their lower prices, which are a result of bulk buying. Somalis can fall back on a clan and extended family network, which researchers have called "collective entrepreneurship" (Laurence Piper, *Weekend Argus*, February 18, 2012). Local spaza owners, mostly women in contrast to the all-men Somali shops, lack this "social capital." Our interviewees frequently described Somalis as "natural-born traders" but could not explain why South Africans did not employ the same methods of bargaining collectively for the lowest price from wholesalers. Several teachers replied that "South Africans don't trust each other." This lack of communitarian solidarity may hark back to a "history of being cheated" as well as the atomized survival in a dangerous environment.

According to Western Cape provincial police commissioner Arno Lamoer, giving evidence at Parliament's police committee (BD, February 9, 2012), almost 70 percent of business robberies in the province were of foreign nationals who were running spaza and tuck shops (small food retailers). While foreigners are generally considered the main culprits in crime, they are in reality its main victims. Since many of the victims are in the country illegally, they have no recourse to the law. Obstructed from opening bank accounts, migrants keep their cash at home. Despite many owners' sleeping at their business premises, criminals break in and force the traders to hand over their money. Members of Parliament (MPs) described the situation as "bordering on xenophobia." The commissioner Lamoer blamed the victims when he explained since most were trading without the required permits, they were reluctant to report the robberies to the police. He failed to mention that many traders do not expect protection from a corrupt police service and even suspect the police to collude with criminals. In addition, local gangs often demand protection money from these foreigners, with the police not interested or unable to intervene. In some cases, the traders pay the gangsters as well as the police to avoid being harassed.

While Somali spazas are liked and frequented, paradoxically, Somali traders also bear the brunt of hostility. Tara Polzer (in: Helen Suzman Foundation Roundtable, 2010) points out that "over a 100 people from the Somali community alone have died each year over the last few years." All Somali-owned spazas in Khayelitsha we visited were recognizable by their heavy iron shutters and meshed grills, with a small hole through which the owner hands out the goods and receives money. The barricaded shacks are still not an effective defense against petrol bombs that force the occupants into the street. Literally living like a frightened animal in a cage, the visibly poor migrants eke out a living nonetheless. They have even formed a Somali shop owners' association. It is therefore problematic, as Caroline Wanjiko Kihato (2007) correctly points out with the example of women migrants in Johannesburg, to portray migrants exclusively as victims. They also exert agency by adapting to a hostile environment. Ascribing sole victim status to foreigners disempowers and disenables migrants anew by lumping them into an abstract category. It hinders recognizing migrants as individuals, each with a unique life history. Jonny Steinberg (personal interview, March 17, 2011) has further illuminated the successful business techniques of the Somali traders despite the surrounding threats. Locals frequent them because their shops are always open and they pay close attention to having available every stock in demand. However, an even more important reason lies in the psychological satisfaction that powerless customers experience when they can bully the foreigner without reprimand.

Yet in Khayelitsha the 2,477 foreign nationals (0.6 percent of the population, according to the 2011 census), most of them Somalis with an average of five years residency, are the prime victims in many respects. Not only are the foreigners at risk from local criminals, but neglect, indifference, and sometimes extortion by the police deprive them of any protection. The social anthropologist Vicki Igglesden and other witnesses reported high levels of dissatisfaction and discrimination by the police to a thorough official commission of inquiry, established by the Western Cape government in the face of ANC opposition. The "Khayelitsha Commission on Policing" (released August 2014) by former Constitutional Court (CC) judge Kate O'Regan and advocate Vusi Pikoli heard testimony from crime intelligence officers that 96 percent of all business robberies reported involved Somali shops and only 4 percent Xhosa spaza owners. About 50 percent of the shops in the township are owned by Somalis and the other half by locals. The commission found it necessary to remind the South African Police Service (SAPS) to "take urgent steps" to change biased police attitudes toward "respect and concern" for foreigners and gay people. In the compelling documentary novel *The Man of Good Hope*, Jonny Steinberg (2014) vividly portrays the brutality and insecurity the refugees suffer. In a case before the Western Cape High Court in March 2014, a group of Somali community leaders and businessmen argued that Somali people feel threatened because they are robbed and killed in township attacks on a "daily basis" (CT, March 5, 2014, p. 3). A police captain, Johannes Theron, testified that foreign businesses were seen as "soft targets," people with money who appeared scared to testify or identify suspects. According to Theron's official police statistics of the sixty incidents of robbery with aggravated circumstances reported in Thembalethu (George) in 2013, forty-eight involved shops owned by foreigners. The judge, Vincent Saldanha, remarked that "there was a perception that the State and police did not take these kinds of cases seriously." He praised the exceptional police efforts in this case for which the Somalis also expressed their gratefulness.

South African courts have been much more sympathetic to refugees and asylum seekers than the government. In several cases they have struck down government restrictions in light of the Human Rights Charter. "Everyone" entitled to dignity was interpreted as applying to noncitizens as well. The following four cases are most relevant. In *Minister of Home Affairs v. Watchenuka* 2004 (4) SA 326 (SCA), the Supreme Court of Appeal held that a decision by the Standing Committee for Refugee Affairs that a permit issued pending application for asylum must contain a prohibition against work infringed the applicant's right to dignity by prohibiting him or her from working and, in fact, forced the applicant to turn to crime since there was no state support for asylum seekers. Similarly, a general prohibition against study was also an infringement of dignity.

The prohibitions in question were regarded as unconstitutional and therefore unlawful.

In *Dawood v. Minister of Home Affairs, Shalabi v. Minister of Home Affairs,* and *Thomas v. Minister of Home Affairs* 2000 (3) SA 936 (CC), the Constitutional Court (CC), interpreting the right to dignity to include the right to family life, held that a provision in the Aliens Control Act 96 of 1991 that empowered immigration officers and the DG (Director General) to refuse to grant a temporary residence permit to spouses of SA citizens infringed the right to cohabit by forcing SA citizens to choose between going abroad to be with their partner or remaining in SA alone. Of course, this decision protects the SA citizens' rights, but it also extends protection of family life to the non-SA citizen.

The CC in *Lawyers for Human Rights v. Minister of Home Affairs* 2004 (4) SA 125 (CC) held that s 26(2)(a) of the Aliens Act 96 of 1991 (i.e., application for work permit may be made only while the applicant is out of the Republic of South Africa [RSA] and the applicant shall not be entitled to enter RSA until a valid permit has been issued) seriously disrupted family life and impeded the possibility of persons' living together and giving each other marital support. Furthermore, the CC held that even aliens are entitled to administrative justice and that the applicant was entitled to a hearing.

In *Khosa v. Minister of Social Development; Mahlaule v. Minister of Social Development* 2004 (6) SA 505 (CC), where the right to social security was extended to permanent residents, the word "everyone" in s 27(1) of the Constitution is not restricted to citizens.

"Dignity" is, of course, the basis of all social rights, which in turn can be implemented only within the limits of government resources. These are strained when, for example, as Wilmot James has pointed out, every fifth person who comes to a state hospital in the Western Cape is a non–South African. The debate about migration management and xenophobia has overlooked that the court decisions cited in the preceding paragraphs together with the liberation euphoria under Mandela's presidency have led to what researchers Tara Polzer and Aurelia Segatti (in Landau 2011: 206) have called "the adoption of an exceptionally progressive asylum regime in 1998." It is now reported, though without any evidence provided, that "South Africa has the highest number of asylum seekers in the world and an unknown number of illegal immigrants" (Carol Paton, BD, December 27, 2012).

South Africa has a long history of employing foreign migrants since the gold mines were established. The migrant labor system of single men in compounds at the same time undermined the African family system, where the social costs of children's education and eldercare were borne by the women left behind in the rural areas. The SA union movement has been ambiguous toward migrants, who were seen as too compliant to employers. With the exception of the National Union of Mineworkers (NUM), the Congress of South African Trade Unions (COSATU) failed to organize and incorporate the outsiders as members.

Neither did it educate its constituency about xenophobia or participate in the civil society marches and protests after the 2008 violence. While condemning the hostility and providing some humanitarian aid to the victims, unions did not achieve the elusive left working-class solidarity. As Mondli Hlatshwayo (2011: 176) has written, "COSATU's response to the xenophobic attacks of May 2008 indicates that the federation needs a lot of debate and engagement on the political significance of xenophobia in order to see migrants in working-class areas as part of their class brothers and sisters." The average black worker views the foreign migrants as competitors, not as "class brothers." No left-wing movement anywhere has been able to overcome the nationalist identification of its members in favor of international solidarity. Inasmuch as the Marxist internationalization of class solidarity has failed, the noble intent of world citizens to establish cosmopolitan nations without borders seems destined to a similar fate for the time being. In South Africa's vision for 2030, the "National Development Plan" (2011: 87) states in vain, "Policy-makers are asking why people should be confined to nation states, when barriers to the movement of capital and goods have progressively fallen."

The immigration policy of a country is always intertwined with its national identity. How a state constructs its national vision and imagines its nation-building project is expressed in its shifting definitions of who belongs and who does not. The ANC's Freedom Charter, for example, allocated equal rights to all who live in the land, not just citizens. By excluding noncitizens from most social rights and benefits, the rainbow nation violates and ignores its own Human Rights Charter. Sally Peberdy's (2009) book, which analyzes South Africa's changing immigration policies historically until 2008 but not the problem of illegal migration and the new fear of outsiders, concludes, "By clearly defining what defines South Africans and who they are, the state has clearly defined who South Africans are not, and so who does not belong to the nation. But until the principles that underpin the Constitution are realized for South Africans and immigrants, migrants and refugees, the nation will lay itself open to the rupturing of the very principles on which it stands and on which its binational identity is built." Citizenship represents a form of "social closure" (Brubaker, 1992) that affirms the citizens as symbolic owners of the state, exclusively entitled to the solidarity of the imagined national community. Brubaker's compelling insight points to citizenship as inclusive internally but exclusive externally.

One may hypothesize that the very uncertainty and confusion about the "South African Nation" and its maladies—crime, HIV infections, who belongs and who does not, who is entitled to preferential treatment for historical disadvantage and who is excluded—contribute to the general suspicion about foreigners as criminals, linked to chaos, disorder, and contamination. Some analysts (Amisi et al. 2011: 61) simply diagnose "the root causes of xenophobia in structural oppressions" and list unemployment, "a tight housing market, extreme retail competition, world leading crime rates, Home Affairs Department corruption and patriarchal processes and cultural conflicts" as the leading stress factors without weighing them.

On rare occasions the migrants themselves protest against their home governments, which they hold responsible for their fate. In early 2012 several hundred Congolese demonstrated at Parliament, calling on South Africa to withhold recognition of President Joseph Kabila. The expatriates were admonished by Zulu King Goodwill Zwelithini: "We respect our leaders and we discourage people who protest and criticize our government and president."

There are remarkable incidents of solidarity among foreign nationals as well as violent conflict when this solidarity breaks down. For example, in December 2012 in Durban's Albert Park, jobless Tanzanians went on the rampage, stabbed five people, hacked to death others with pangas, damaged cars, and set spaza shops alight. Those with jobs had, until recently, been donating some of their wages to their unemployed countrymen "in a gesture of brotherhood." Stopping this support ignited the violence, which could be called reverse intraclass hostility. The thousands of jobless Tanzanians had moved from rented locations on the South Coast closer to the city and were "living rough" along the railway line near the Berea station. The employed Tanzanians felt "they had enough" and accused their "brothers" of giving the community a bad name. Utilizing the very same labeling to which they themselves were subjected not so long ago, they described their compatriots as follows: "These people are here in South Africa not willing to work, but are surviving by committing crime and selling drugs to young South Africans. We don't want anything more to do with them" (*Natal Mercury*, December 22, 2012).

Such incidents demonstrate how desperate conditions turn conflict inward and give rise to intra-out-group violence, when migrants turn on each other. Of course this reinforces the South African image of "foreigners as nuisance." These perceptions obscure the fundamental questions to be asked: Should the city not provide emergency shelters, so that people do not have "to live rough"? Can the newcomers be expected to share their meager resources and negotiate the distribution peacefully? Given the uneven wealth of South Africa and the abundance of luxury goods stashed away and wasted by the elite, should this upper crust not accommodate starving neighbors? Is it justified to remove the refugees forcibly as "illegals," as happened to the arrested Tanzanians in this case?

While those aspects of the "moral economy" are foregrounded, xenophobia also needs to be seen as an affective emotional issue. Without dismissing the economic explanations, what needs to be added is a more psychological and psychoanalytic explanation in line with Freud's "narcissism of small difference" and colonial conditioning for self-hate. The projection of undesirable traits onto outsiders by insecure insiders illuminates why abandoned victims perpetuate the discrimination against fellow Africans.

3

Youth Voices

Views from a Township

There is no better way to strip difference of its mystique than to deal directly with practices of everyday life on their own terms while also linking them to the wider world.
—JACOB DLAMINI, *NATIVE NOSTALGIA*

Aim and Methodology

We researched the face of xenophobia in South Africa with the aim to gauge empirically whether the massive attacks on foreigners in May 2008 could reoccur, whether the efforts of public education impacted attitudes, and how the relationship of township dwellers with foreign migrants manifests itself. When schoolchildren in their neat uniforms look on laughing while a Mozambican man slowly burns to death, as the most iconic image of the 2008 riots shows, investigating their mindsets seemed a pressing task. At the same time, the research also touched on the general political consciousness of township youth and probed race relations, governance, and development in the postapartheid state. All our empirical data were collected in the Western Cape, because it is a high influx area for new foreign migrants. The mining industry in Gauteng (Johannesburg) historically employed large numbers of workers from neighboring countries; locals are accustomed to migrants from Mozambique, Malawi, or Lesotho on the streets. In the Western Cape with its majority of so-called 'Coloureds' in still highly segregated residential areas and the only provincial government not controlled by the ANC, the rapid change of the ethnic composition of whole areas on the Cape flats makes for an explosive mix.

When the premier Helen Zille complained about internal "refugees" from a dysfunctional school system in the Eastern Cape moving to Cape Town, she was accused of racism for questioning the right of internal mobility of South African citizens by labeling them refugees, because the term is normally applied to external migrants, that is, hated "foreigners." The controversy was triggered by pitched battles between Coloured and black African residents, who had destroyed school buildings in protest against overcrowding in Grabouw. What this linguistic controversy unleashes is the stigma associated with the term as well as the lack of consensus around the meaning of the label "refugee" at the symbolic level. Whereas in other countries there is empathy for the refugee as one whose life chances have been threatened, here it is likened to "foreigner" and *amakwerekwere.*

No claim is made that our sample is representative of other South African areas, or even of all the township schools in the Cape. Our study is more of a vignette in the ethnographic tradition—a more qualitative than quantitative analysis, although we also employed survey techniques. However, judging from media reports and an extensive literature, our findings are likely to apply equally to Johannesburg or Natal, though this remains to be confirmed in future research. Our survey covered only Xhosa speakers, the almost sole African presence in the Western Cape. While there are some significant differences between Xhosa and Zulu speakers' cultural traditions, the countrywide riots in 2008 and the earlier 1949 attacks on Indians in Durban testify to similar "us and them" perceptions across the land.

Our study excluded so-called Model C independent schools, now integrated semiprivate schools in former white areas, because no xenophobia has ever been reported in these areas. We also did not focus on the simmering Coloured-African antagonisms, although those frictions were sometimes referred to in the group discussions. The SA public discourse avoids these cleavages as "politically incorrect" distinctions in the apartheid tradition. Yet the mutual social distance and animosity between Coloured and African in the Western Cape is of long standing, reinforced by the previous official labor preference for Coloureds in the province and the majority electoral support of the Coloured group for non-ANC parties.

Apart from a content analysis of various local newspapers and radio discussions, the study is based on a variety of data: personal face-to-face interviews with (a) teachers and school principals in four township schools in the Cape; (b) police personnel in Stellenbosch and Cape Town; (c) dozens of foreign migrants in various settings; and (d) academics, journalists, judges, and a few politicians with expertise and interest in the topic. Despite considerable efforts, we were unable to elicit any cooperation from Home Affairs officials, as two senior Cape Town managers would not even agree to a short telephone interview about departmental policies.

The most important source for our findings is a written survey with five open-ended questions, conducted in four secondary schools with grade 11 and grade 12 students, followed by focus group discussions with the same "learners" after they had filled out the questionnaire. Open-ended questions and free-flowing, semistructured discussions yield richer and more nuanced insights than the usual tick beside preformulated answers. Such closed questions merely describe, measure, and categorize xenophobia. They often contain replies that would not have emerged spontaneously. In contrast to the preformulated items to be tested, open-ended questions allow the reasons for an opinion to be spelled out. To combat hostility, its rationalization and specific logic must be known. Our contribution to the literature on SA xenophobia aims at this detailed exploration of xenophobic predispositions which has been neglected. In addition we encouraged expressions of opinions on a range of politically broader controversial issues in the group discussions, not necessarily related to the xenophobic focus.

Altogether 150 respondents participated in the survey and focus groups at the beginning of 2012. The 150 grade 11 and grade 12 learners in the four township schools ranged in age between 17 and 21. Pilot studies on the same topic had been conducted a year earlier while based at the Stellenbosch Institute for Advanced Studies (STIAS). It was assumed that if there was any potential recurrence of xenophobic violence, it would show in the attitudes toward foreigners among adolescents in all-black poor township schools. Our theoretical aim was to gain deeper insights into the specific rationalizations and characters of xenophobic perpetrators. If any educational interventions for empathy and tolerance were to be attempted, a detailed understanding of perceptions would be a prerequisite. For this purpose our study prioritizes potential perpetrators and prevailing everyday understandings rather than victims who have been amply documented in the literature.

Interviews with teachers, in-depth group discussions, and questionnaires were administered in different sections of a sprawling township on the outskirts of Cape Town. The names of the schools must remain confidential as well as the identity of the students, who filled out the questionnaires anonymously. They were only asked to indicate their age, gender, and home language. The average age of the pupils was 18, with an even gender ratio among the groups. With two exceptions in one group, all 150 students were Xhosa speakers. We did not tape the focus groups, as this might have inhibited the students, but recorded the highlights from memory immediately afterward. In the following summary of findings, the verbatim quotes from the written survey are intertwined with the records from the group discussions. The two numbers in the brackets behind each answer refer to the subsequently numbered blank questionnaire and the four schools in which it was administered. The school visits included discussions with principals and teachers. We also explored the school surroundings and engaged in conversations with some nearby residents and shopkeepers.

In our survey we avoided using the term "xenophobia" altogether. The danger that the students in an authoritarian system regurgitate the politically correct version had to be countered. As was also indicated at the top of the questionnaire, when we entered the classroom, we introduced ourselves by name as two Canadian university professors from Vancouver who study the attitudes toward foreigners and immigrants in different countries, including South Africa. We talked briefly about our own history in South Africa and our work in Canada, to humanize the exercise and make it appear less bureaucratic, stressing our curiosity as foreign visitors about student thinking. We stressed emphatically that we would like to know what the students "really feel and think, honestly and frankly," not what the government or the teachers tell us about foreigners. We also mentioned that participation was voluntary and if the students did not like the questionnaire, they could simply ignore it and wait for the discussion after the others had responded. We experienced no refusals or return of blank questionnaires. In two cases the teachers left us alone with the class, which we preferred; in the other two cases the teachers chose to stay with us in the classroom. However, the teachers did not interfere in our discussion, and it is impossible to gauge whether their very presence influenced the subsequent oral expressions, but it certainly did not impact the anonymous written survey.

An Ethnography of Township Schools

Before we report and interpret our research findings in four secondary schools, it is important to understand the environment in which learning and teaching take place in the majority of South African schools. We first sketch in general terms the background of the students we surveyed, what we learned from the teachers with whom we interacted, views about their union, and opinions of more knowledgeable insiders about the state of education in the country. Without an ethnographic picture of the life and circumstances of our respondents, their answers will only be partially appreciated. We are also conscious of presenting township life as the opposite of "normal," uniformly a world of deficits and suffering. As Jacob Dlamini (2009: 118) in his rich memoir of Katlehong has written, "To define townships in terms of their problems is to reduce township residents themselves to problems—instead of seeing them as people with problems, some of which are personal and others collective: just like every human being on earth, in fact." This does not mean normalizing poverty, but interpreting complexity and uniqueness as accurately as an outside observer can muster.

The adolescent African learners we interviewed showed limited historical consciousness. Apartheid constitutes an abstract term for the postapartheid, so-called born free generation. When asked about a school in the neighborhood, named after a struggle activist, the students could hardly associate anything with the name. History, geography, and social studies are no longer taught as separate subjects, but at best subsumed under the amorphous label "life skills." Students who were once a highly politicized group of anti-apartheid activists now resemble a depoliticized, consumer-driven generation of aspirant money makers. While similar trends have been observed and lamented the world over, it is particularly striking in a country with an opposite tradition. In short, political education is nonexistent or has utterly failed. Historical amnesia hides under a superficial "good versus bad" familiarity with media and political celebrities exposed by TV or radio. SAfm, the state broadcaster, which describes itself as "information leader," broadcasts the same three-minute banal snippets about weather, accidents, crime, sports, and political leaders' announcements every half hour. The saving grace of the country is the fiercely independent and outspoken print media and some informative phone-in radio shows. However, local daily newspapers (*Cape Times* and *Argus*), let alone books, are not readily available in the townships, and the few libraries that do exist are located some distance away, making safe access difficult, especially for the female students. Reading is a middle-class activity for people with leisure, not township dwellers struggling to survive. In addition, unlike Natal with several isiZulu newspapers, no vernacular newspapers or books exist and reading in a second language is an effort. Countrywide, 93 percent of public schools have no libraries, 95 percent have no science laboratories, and 45 percent still use latrine toilets, although the Basic Education Ministry has been forced by the civic activism and court action of the "Equal Education" NGO to rectify this inequality in educational facilities.

Indications of political illiteracy and the appeal of populists should not be dismissed as harmless, to be corrected in later life. In classroom discussions, even digressions from the main theme were informative. For instance, when the issue of leadership came up, a student questioned us about our preference for Jacob Zuma or Thabo Mbeki as president. When we in turn posed the same question to the students, there was a short silence, until one student seemed to articulate the dominant feeling: "Neither." Then whom? The whole class collectively shouted, "Malema!" Why? "He talks straight; he is honest." But "he has just been disciplined and suspended from the ANC? If you support Malema, you turn against the ANC." The obvious sympathy for the rabble-rousing youth leader had not been reconciled with their traditional ANC loyalty. Julius Malema, himself an uneducated yet skilled agitator, appeals to a politically illiterate constituency, because he presents himself as an evangelical populist, a savior from township poverty through confiscating white wealth without compensation in the name of "economic freedom." Most students appeared unaware that Malema had himself already amassed considerable wealth through corrupt tender procedures. Others even admired his high lifestyle, as is expected from African strongmen. When asked "Would a President Malema not scare away foreign investors and impoverish the country like Mugabe did in Zimbabwe," the students were hesitant and surprised and obviously had not thought about these implications. Yet in all the focus groups, we did not detect any antiwhite hostility per se. On the contrary, whites were frequently associated with skills and knowledge "from which we can learn." The ANC, we concluded in light of the predominant sentiment, may come to regret the expulsion of the ANC Youth League leader, who could have been better controlled inside the organization than outside as a free agent. Despite his mere seven percent support in the 2014 national election, his party's disruption of stale parliamentary proceedings, the working class dress of its *Economic Freedom Fighters* (EFF) and blunt, aggressive rhetoric, have elevated the EFF to the real opposition in township perceptions, rather than the much stronger but more measured official opposition Democratic Alliance (DA). As one teacher explained, "Blacks in the DA are just token bait to hook us!" Since instruction occurs exclusively in a second language,

English, which is not spoken at home, the students were initially insecure when they expressed themselves in discussions. We explicitly encouraged them not to worry about grammatical mistakes and to just express their opinion as they felt.

In South Africa as a whole, an estimated nine million children (43 percent of the total) are growing up in single-parent households (Denise Robinson, Politicsweb, November 20, 2014), often without maintenance benefits despite court orders. In the Cape Flats the overwhelming majority of black students live without supporting stable family structures. Most are born to single mothers or have fathers who live elsewhere and do not partake in family life. This trend was initiated by the migrant labor system of the past, which split families. Many migrants from rural South Africa established a second family or informal relationship at their urban workplace and in the process neglected and alienated both. If there ever was a "fatherless society" in Christopher Lasch's apt description of similar American trends, it is found in South African townships where the micro-family no longer exists and fathers take little responsibility for their offspring. An extended family of women, grandparents, siblings, and neighbors raise children under the most trying conditions. Other pupils have been sent from a dysfunctional school system in the Eastern Cape to stay with relatives in the townships. In essence, the learners have to fend for themselves in a materially and spiritually impoverished environment, sometimes in child-managed homes. Crain Soudien (2012: 238), among many SA educators, has drawn attention to "the absence of emotional intimacy" in addition to the sheer scale of physical deprivation: "Hungry children cannot learn. Emotionally alone children have difficulty in seeing in the school a source of hope. The physical realities that surround children hound them. . . . They do not have access to the kind of intimacy in their lives which makes experimentation with their potentialities reasonably safe." At their most vulnerable age, they are at risk of exploitation from drug dealers and criminal elements. Another local observer (Gavin Silver, Politicsweb, August 17, 2012) familiar with township life, remarks, "Children sent to schools with the hope of securing a better future find not a place of learning and security, but rather a gang warzone where young 'gangsters' fight with screwdrivers, pangas, knives and guns. During the past month thousands of children have stayed home from school for fear of being caught in the crossfire, while others had to flee to the Eastern Cape. When children are not at school, they must play in overcrowded and under-served slums amongst heaps of uncollected rotting waste in pools of excrement and wastewater." Despite these hardships, it is moving to see how women launder clothing by hand and children emerge in neat school uniforms. Little credit is usually given to the networks of women's cooperation and the ingenuity of the most disadvantaged who are more pathologized than recognized for their skills in surviving.

The principals and teachers we encountered without exception impressed us with their openness, dedication, and professionalism. Relying on their hospitality, we obviously could not raise with them delicate issues of the failings of the South African Democratic Teachers' Union (SADTU) and frequent accusation against individual members. Incidents of male teachers exploiting female students sexually are commonly reported. Teenage pregnancy is high, resulting in high dropout rates. It has long been known that the sexual abuse at schools has reached the stage of a "pandemic," reports Victoria John (*Mail and Guardian*, November 15, 2012). At civil society conferences the sexualization of pupils and the sexual violence by minors and teachers is regularly bemoaned, without provincial education authorities having found the means to reverse the trend, despite court cases and teacher training sessions. In one Gauteng conference (M&G, November 15, 2012) an attorney, Nikki Stein, of the rights organization "Section 27" reported about disciplinary hearings against teachers but also cases of "teachers and principals who knew about the violence, but did not report it, as they were legally required to." The same conference heard about pupils trading video clips of child and adult porn among themselves as well as "taxi queen" pupils who offer sex for taxi rides. The absence of school buses or other safe transport from township schools puts young girls directly at risk of abuse. "Sometimes if we are two girls it's easy to get money," a learner who identified herself only as Siya told GroundUp (October 7, 2014). "When we get a lift, a driver would want to kiss one or both of us and we don't mind. We first see what he offers, then we decide what happens. At times he just kisses, or he would want to touch your chest, but it's nothing hectic and it's the most easy way to get at least R20," says Siya. The 13-year-old girls go to a friend's shack to change from their school uniforms into a "sexy" outfit to attract attention.

When the two vital educational institutions of home and school disintegrate in a society, the repercussions go much deeper than currently visible. International medical research has proven that childhood trauma affects adult brains; that memory is impaired by poverty; and that in adults who had suffered abuse as children, blood pressure disproportionately increased in response to stress (*Guardian Weekly*, October 26, 2012, p. 32). While disturbing incidents of videoed gang rape have also taken place at Canadian schools or mass shootings in American educational institutions occur several times per year, the frequency and casual acceptance of violence in South African townships stands out.

The bleak, inhospitable schools, with graffiti on the walls and without libraries or sports facilities, offer no substitute for a nurturing home environment. Frequently underqualified but militant unionized teachers look after their own interests first and seldom serve as role models. On the whole, they work far fewer hours than their counterparts in independent schools. Like nurses, the unionized teachers join frequent walkouts, protests, and strikes, regardless of the effects on their custodians. In one notorious incident, nurses abandoned a maternity ward and mercilessly let a dozen infants die, because the union insisted on a total walkout without maintaining essential services. During our survey, a nationwide one-day COSATU strike against tollbooths on Gauteng highways and labor brokers, which had nothing to do with Cape schools, closed most Western Cape township schools, left students unsupervised, and wasted another day of instruction.

Njabulo Ndebele, whom the editor of the *Business Day*, Peter Bruce (BD, March 26, 2012), describes as one of the "brightest African brains of our time," writes that SADTU "has almost single-handedly destroyed the schooling system across much of South Africa, particularly in townships. 'Almost' allows for the fact that the trade union has had the ruling party's political support, making the party complicit in the destruction. This happens at the same time that the ruling party yearly allocates billions of rands to improve a system that can never be improved under the prevailing circumstances. The quantum of wasted money is the stuff that causes revolutions" (*City Press* [CP], March 25, 2012, p. 26). The suggestion by some ANC leaders to declare teaching an essential service was vehemently opposed by the union, because it would make teachers' strikes illegal. The union rejects performance contracts for teachers and principals that the education minister wanted to introduce. The department itself regards 60 to 80 percent of schools as "dysfunctional." Yet nobody in the fractious tripartite alliance dares to hold the second-largest COSATU union accountable. As Anthony Butler (BD, September 23, 2012) has written, "The South African Democratic Teachers' Union (SADTU) has enjoyed patronage under Zuma in the form of unsustainable pay rises, immunity for poorly performing public servants, and high office distributed to union barons."

The opposition DA constantly specifies and hammers the destructive power of the teachers' union, but even the most absurd examples of selfishness cannot motivate the weak Zuma government to impose some rational changes for fear of losing union support. The DA has assailed relentlessly the overspending on salaries and the underspending on learning resources and school infrastructure in the Eastern Cape without triggering action. "Some schools are grossly overstaffed (in one case 22 teachers serve just 55 pupils) while other schools are seriously under-staffed and are forced to hire 'contract teachers,' resulting in a ballooning provincial salary bill. SADTU is defending teachers who refuse to be 're-assigned'—and no-one in the ANC dares to take on SADTU in the year of Mangaung" (DA Weekly Statement, August 3, 2012).

Comparing the schools in the townships with the dozen former Model C schools ten kilometers away in Rondebosch is literally facing day and night. Dedicated, punctual teachers, scrutinized by watchful parents, work an average of seven hours a day in whitewashed buildings, set in sprawling lawns with expansive rugby and cricket fields. A motivated, multiracial student population is already conditioned by class status to "naturally" continue in this role. The relatively high fees of these semiprivate schools ensure a class selection that perpetuates itself by outpacing the all-black schools at every level. The leading Cape ANC activists always had their children enrolled in these private institutions of privilege, even during the apartheid era, when the slogan "Liberation before education" was propagated. In contrast, teachers in the no-fee township schools work alone with little parental support, since most mothers can barely afford to feed their families or purchase the school requirements and have a limited capacity to assist with homework or become involved in time-consuming school affairs.

Nationally, South Africa has achieved an almost 100 percent enrollment in 24,451 public schools in 2010, a slight decrease from 26,789 public schools in 2000 and an increase of independent (partly state-subsidized) schools from 971 in 2000 to 1,399 in 2010. However, after grade 10, half of the youngsters drop out of the system. In 2008 there were more than a million pupils in grade 10, yet two years later there were only 537,543 in grade 12, of whom only two thirds pass matric (matriculation) with much lowered standards. Universal schooling with annual higher pass rates camouflages the quality of education offered. World Economic Forum data for 2012 ranked South Africa 143 out of 144 countries surveyed for mathematics and science education, yet every year an increasing matric pass rate with lower standards is celebrated with great hype. While South Africa led the African continent in literacy and education for a long time, it is now assumed that general education in many African countries has surpassed South African standards. As a leading SA educationist, Jonathan Jansen, has written,

> If I had to make the choice with my own children today, I would seriously consider not sending my child to school in South Africa, for one simple reason: I do not trust a system that makes it possible for a child to pass Grade 12 with 30% in some subjects and 40% in other subjects. I would be filled with fear when I discover that you can get 32% in mathematics and 27% in physical science and still get an official document that says you can continue to study towards a Bachelors degree at university. I would worry myself senseless when I enroll my child in Grade 1 knowing that she could be among the more than half-a-million children who would not make it through to Grade 12. I would be horrified at the possibility that the principal might force her to do mathematical literacy because someone decided she could not do pure mathematics, because it would make the school's pass averages look bad. And I would be angry when I find that she is guaranteed to be among the 96% pass rate for Life Orientation when all the other subjects in the national Senior Certificate have pass rates way below this number. It is extremely difficult to fail Grade 12 in South Africa today. You have to put in a special effort, miss your classes, deliberately provide wrong answers to questions, and hand in your paper early during an exam session and maybe, just maybe, you will fail.

> (ST, January 9, 2012).

Our survey and observations in four township schools confirm and reflect this assessment. No foreign nationals were in any of the classes we interviewed. Teachers explained this absence of foreign learners because they attend independent schools that their richer parents can afford. This assessment seems doubtful. A more likely cause appeared to us that most foreign nationals in South Africa are young male and female singles without schoolgoing children, who often were left in the care of relatives at home. In addition, many foreigners in South Africa are unregistered and therefore ineligible for schooling and other benefits, while the legal migrants are hesitant to enroll their children in a potentially hostile township environment.

How Students View Foreigners

In gauging attitudes toward "foreigners" and focusing minds on the subsequent group discussions, we asked five open-ended questions in simple English, trying to avoid any bias in the questions and making it easier to respond to controversial issues by attributing sensitive sentiments to other, unnamed people rather than the respondent. We pondered whether we should use the term "foreigner" at all, since it may have negative connotations and logically includes non-Africans as well. However, since there are no whites living in African townships, it was generally understood that "foreigner" in the township lingo exclusively refers to black Africans from other African countries. So does the derisory term "amakwerekwere," whose origin is unclear. The derogatory name seems to have been given by Tswana and/or Sotho-speaking people to speakers of other languages, ridiculing the foreign sounds to Tswana speakers.

The first question aimed at capturing the general attitude towards foreigners was, **"Should foreigners be allowed to settle in South Africa? If 'yes,' under which conditions? If 'no,' why not?"** The term "settle" left open the where and how and how long, to be specified under "conditions."

The surprising positive feature of responses was that only a minority in our sample objected to foreigners settling in South Africa. A clear majority of 69 percent affirmed the right of foreigners to settle here and listed a variety of reasons for welcoming or tolerating foreigners, though most insisted that they should have papers and not be "here illegally." In this category of "conditional presence," some mention employment: "They should be here only for work; if somebody is not working should hit the road; the working ones should have a contract of 5 years" (1-02). Similarly, "qualifications" are cited by a few as conditions for entry. Others point to conditions that are common for immigration permits anywhere: "Before they enter they should be checked for any criminal offences that they might have made in their country" (1-03). "Yes, as long as they will not contribute to the increasing crime rate of the country" (1-15). "Yes, but they should be told to pay tax" (3-37). The underlying suspicion of migrants as potential deviants is clearly evident, even among the majority, who would not oppose their admission.

Only a small minority of our respondents favor unconditional acceptance of foreigners. Moral, religious, and humanitarian considerations are cited together with historical gratitude for exiles' acceptance and utilitarian aspects of benefits from foreigners. In view of this predominant humanitarian predisposition, a common humanity overrides everything else: "Yes they should be treated as citizens of South Africa; by doing that we would be building humanity in our country. This will help us when visiting other countries also" (3-36). "Yes, because they are also human beings like us who have needs and responsibilities" (3-01). "Yes, they should settle in SA without any conditions, because we are all people of God" (3-05). Frequently the impoverished conditions in the countries of origin are quoted for immigration as a right of all Africans: "Everyone has a right to stay wherever she/he wants to stay and most of all we are all Africans" (3-02).

A minority of respondents invoke the African assistance to SA exiles as reasons for solidarity: "Yes, these people are our brothers and sisters. If they are running from poverty and war in their country we should help them, because they also did the same during the time of apartheid" (4-44). "During apartheid people from here went to different countries; they were welcomed there, treated with love and care" (4-12). "Our forefathers used to escape to those countries of foreigners and they were not discriminated against" (2-23). One person in this category reveals his historical ignorance: "Yes, because when Dr. Mandela was in exile and he was a foreigner and they did not say he must go away" (1-05).

Those with this general outlook of compassion, inclusiveness, and care for people in need may be characterized, using a Weberian ideal type of construct, as representing a *humanitarian character*. Taking answers to all five questions together, 51 percent of our sample fall into this category. Humanitarians are able to differentiate between people in a category and generally have a realistic understanding of the plight that motivates migration. This leads to empathy. An opposite attitude of overt hostility, hate, and prejudice toward foreigners may be dubbed a *xenophobic character*. This type generally stresses the negative features of foreigners and refuses to assist and displays various degrees of paranoia about outsiders who "intrude, swamp, overcrowd." The written comments identify 24 percent in this class. A middle group may be termed *ambivalent characters*. Students with this syndrome are not consistent in their attitudes and consider foreigners as brothers in need of assistance but are hesitant to help or make it contingent on circumstances. They show understanding as well as hostility: "I like them, but not their behavior" (1-02). People in this category constitute 25 percent in our sample. They could be expected to behave in a number of different ways: participate in a xenophobic riot or act as bystander but also come to the rescue of victims.

The 28 percent who categorically answered "No" to the question of admission mainly emphasize job losses, overcrowding, and crime: "Because they will cause more unemployment. The foreigners will settle for any amount of payment, even R200 per week, but South Africans know their rights and how much they should be getting" (4-34). "They use young girls to be their sex partners by giving them money" (4-37). Others elaborate on specific negative behavior of migrants (drug trade, fraud, or sexual offenses) as reasons for rejection. It was beyond the scope of this survey to establish to which extent these alleged experiences and features attributed to immigrants were based on fact, fantasy, or projection. In short, they displayed classical prejudices of the in-group against members of a constructed out-group, described by a vast social science literature.

To our surprise, no major differences could be discerned between male and female respondents, who were evenly represented in our sample. Only an over-representation of female respondents among the ambivalent characters could be detected. From all the pictures of xenophobic rampages, it appears that the perpetrators were exclusively young males. No empirical data are available as to whether female locals exhorted or restrained their male counterparts, as confirmed by Loren Landau (email correspondence, November 8, 2012).

In contrast, there were some clear differences in the response patterns among the four schools surveyed. Given that all other variables in the sample were identical, clearly some prior teaching about xenophobia or political education in general seems to have impacted on the attitudes of students in some schools. If this assumption can be substantiated in further research, important lessons about best practice political education can be drawn.

While our research, as has been pointed out, cannot claim to be representative of the whole country, the 2011–2012 Afrobarometer, based on face-to-face interviews of 2,400 randomly selected respondents across the country, is representative. This survey of the general adult South African population did not probe reasons for attitudes expressed, but asked for agreement or disagreement with two similar statements, one formulated in the positive and one in the negative, about foreigners in the country. The first statement, formulated in the positive, read, "People who are persecuted for political reasons in their own countries deserve protection in South Africa." Only 38 percent countrywide expressed agreement; in the Western Cape, only 31 percent. The second statement, formulated in the negative, read, "Foreigners should not be able to live in South Africa, because they take jobs and benefits away from South Africans." This statement elicited 45 percent agreement countrywide and 51 percent in the Western Cape. Compared with our sample of black students, the intolerance toward foreigners is higher in the general population (which includes whites, Coloureds, and Indians proportionally) than among the impoverished township learners. One would have expected the opposite, so the results of this survey give hope that xenophobia among black youngsters is on the decline.

A second, open-ended question in our survey allowed respondents to amplify: **"What do foreigners contribute to South Africa (Good or bad)?"** Again, a surprisingly high number of 61 percent emphasized the good contributions, usually together with various negative features which dominated in 39 percent of answers. Given the image of black Africa in the media as a backward, "dark" continent, as opposed to the modern, civilized, industrialized South, reinforced by apartheid indoctrination, we expected the SA respondents to display a similar arrogant, supremacist view. However, many expressed the opposite sentiment that South Africans can learn and benefit from the skills foreigners bring with them. We could detect little of the South African exceptionalism of an older generation—that South Africa as an industrial powerhouse is not of Africa—in this younger group.

"As we all know they know technology more than us; they can help us a lot. They even do teaching mathematics for us in our schools, because rare South African people know mathematics" (2-07); "They fix our phones and television with a good price" (2-19); "they have knowledge of everything" (2-25); "they are good in technology and they are highly educated and responsible" (1-14). Opening of shops is viewed by many as "good," "because they are cheap and we can afford what they sell" (3-11). "Foreigners are also showing us their skills of doing business" (2-22). "Most foreigners are educated, so it boosts our economy" (2-24).

More self-hate shines through when students loathe their own consistently: "It's not that they came here to take the jobs away. Black people can't do a thing for themselves; they just don't want to work. So they expect that other people from another country must not work too" (1-05). There is repeated evidence of low self-images and a fatalistic acceptance of self-defined inability. In contrast to us, "they are hard working. They open businesses and don't wait on government to give them something" (18-year-old female). Another 17-year-old female said "they are not liked because South Africans can't open spazas for themselves, because foreigners who come from poor countries open supermarkets and spazas competing with black people." "They can teach us how to manage business and create business and their prices are cheaper." Self-diminishing comments reiterate a similar self-perception: ". . . . most of them they . . . become employed while most South Africans can't, but what I can say is that there is nothing wrong with them and Xhosas are lazy; they don't wanna [sic] work and they expect to be paid big, while the foreigners accept what they are given"(18-year-old male). "They bring their skills and ideas into the country . . . can fix stolen phones . . . and know about technology." These utterances echo their own shortcomings in navigating the routes to survival in a competitive, changing world.

Among the hardcore xenophobes, who answered "No" to any admission of foreigners and emphasize insurmountable differences, clear disbelief in any advantage is stated: "I belief they can't benefit us with anything, especially economically" (4-22). Among the bad features of migrants, a clear ranking emerged in terms of frequency mentioned: Selling drugs ranks number one, followed by robbery; rape and prostitution; faking goods, money, and ID books; practicing witchcraft; and, not the least, "taking jobs." One respondent quotes "the propaganda belief of that they are witches, human traffickers, drug dealers, alcoholics and people with no manners" (2-23). Cheating with witchcraft ranks prominently among the bad characteristics: "They come here with no houses. Then you offer a house to rent, maybe for about two years. When you come back, the house is in their name; they are dangerous, they use *muti* and they are crooks" (2-24). "Some pretend as if they are doctors whereas they do not have experience at all" (3-38).

We did not expect that the accusation of witchcraft would figure so prominently in many narratives. We were skeptical when we read about the emphasis on superstition in other similar studies, for example, in the analysis by Pierre du Toit and Hennie Kotzee (2011), based on the World Value Survey. Usually witchcraft is associated with rural unenlightenment, not a modern city such as Cape Town, where even many shacks have multiple-channel TV and most youngsters own a cell phone. Perhaps more recently arrived students from rural Transkei were particularly prone to blame the magic of witchcraft for what they could not explain rationally. Could it be that the dismal living conditions require the belief in magic that explains the unexplainable, just like religion gives meaning to a meaningless life? "They also kill their babies taking their private parts to make their medicine" (4-06). "Some kill for *muti* and also they rape" (1-05); "they do bad things like *amakwirikwiri*; they rape young children" (3-41). Like traditional anti-Semitism that attributed child killing to Jews, the violation of children which is widespread in South Africa is attributed to foreigners by several students: "They are dangerous to the children, because they take the body of a child to do their thing like *ukuthawala*" (1-27). Like anti-Semitism in the fake "Protocols of Zion," the dangerous and clever outsiders lurk to seduce, pollute, and pounce on the innocent, helpless insiders. People who refer to witchcraft have clearly grown up outside any Enlightenment tradition. Superstition still prevails in some sections, as is evident in the popularity of *muti* shops.

While the obsession with witchcraft may be a typical SA phenomenon—where even some ANC leaders participate in rituals to kill a bull in order to communicate with the ancestors—the paranoia about outsiders stealing, molesting, and raping local women features in xenophobia worldwide. It probably originates from the historical experience of conquering armies abducting the young women of the vanquished, from Alexander the Great in India to the Russians in Berlin in 1945. In the Bosnian war, Serbian men were officially encouraged to rape Muslim women in order to shame and ostracize them from their community and make Serbians out of their offspring. In both world wars, German armies were successfully mobilized with the imagery of protecting the virginity of the maidens from the dirty designs of the enemy. Similarly in South Africa, romantic contact between local sisters and foreign brothers is deeply resented, particularly given the African patriarchal tradition where the outsider ignores local customs, like paying *lobola* (bride price). "They do traffic and sell our sisters to other countries" (4-23). In the minds of several respondents, foreigners invade the space and exploit not only resources but also bodies, because they "know us and understand how we think and do things . . . ; they pollute our place, and when they come here they always come with their family invading our space. They don't see us as people like them. They got this advantage of that South Africans like money they see [us] as filthy and strippers, prostitutes" (4-24).

Among the sexual offences, a 17-year-old male asserts, "They have a tendency of dating 14, 15, 16 years old which is wrong" (4-02); "Some of them took their sisters, girlfriends and left them with nothing" (2-20). "They marry [our] daughters and make them pregnant. After they got the ID they dump them. So all in all they are opportunists" (1-02). A few hold foreigners responsible for all the maladies in the country: "The price of food in SA is too high; it increases every day, because we have the people who do not belong to South Africa" (2-18). In the misery, insecurity, and inequality of township life, the basic enabling conditions for xenophobia are found. The foreigner serves as the ready scapegoat, even though the causes lie elsewhere. Scapegoating absorbs frustrations and empowers disempowered people by providing explanations to their misery.

A third question directly targeted xenophobic attitudes in the guise of other people's hostility: **"Some people do not like foreigners ("amakwerekwere"). Why do you think they are not liked?"** Mentioning the derisory term "kwerekwere" signaled that respondents should be free to express their negative feelings.

There are a few respondents who critically reflect on the manipulation of negative images that they do not share: "I think it has something to do with myths that are being spread around our communities. Most of us we end up being brainwashed by all sorts of these gossips, e.g., that they brought HIV and drugs to our people" (2-29).

However, many more respondents list here obvious differences (language, color, hair) as well as stereotypes as reasons for dislike: "stinking under their arms" (3-07); "Somalis in SA own businesses, but they do not wash and sleep on the top of their groceries" (1-24). A few point to jealousy: "Amakwerekwere have skills and they work harder than the Xhosa people. It is all about jealousy" (2-08). "They don't like them, because they say that they take their jobs and wives" (2-31).

In the group discussions we asked specifically why whites are not singled out for hostility. The students had never thought about why whites *(mlungus)* were not considered "kwerekwere." Andile Mngximata answers this question succinctly in the title of his work "Whites Are Tourists, Blacks Are Kwerekwere." It was obvious, several respondents said, whites spoke English or Afrikaans and were part of the country. The discussants readily supplied more answers: whites ensured investments and thereby provided jobs; whites had knowledge and skills needed for development; as tourists they brought in money; whites did not live in the townships and crowd out the space.

South Africa successfully decolonized in 1994, but only politically and legally. Mental colonization continues. Historical conditioning of habits and worldviews do not readily change with the color of the government, although it democratically represents the majority for the first time in the country's history. Afrophobia is only one manifestation of an internalized value system that despises the local but subconsciously glorifies European ways. Biko's BCM attempted to change this and instill pride in the colonized, but succeeded only in a limited way. Biko primarily focused on "freeing minds" and strengthening self-esteem, in addition to abolishing structural oppression.

Mental colonization revealed itself among our subjects in a strange way that can be termed "consumer colonialism." Many are incensed that kwerekwere fake commodities, such as CDs, DVDs, and brand-name clothing. They long for the authentic, genuine clothes and watches, not the cheap imitations offered by the foreigners. In South Africa, equality is measured by how whites live, not how

African traditions would suggest. Gandhian austerity and a return to self-reliant simplicity are rejected by the colonial mindset. Consumer colonialism celebrates an Americanized lifestyle, represented by Hollywood celebrities and rock stars. English soccer clubs can count almost more fans among the black youth than local teams. In the fashion parade that marks the opening of Parliament, outsized English hats, Gucci bags and shoes, and Rolex watches dominate among the female MPs. Single-malt whisky is served at the receptions afterward, not indigenous Marula brews. The head of the Communist Party is not alone among government functionaries driving a most expensive German car. Given such consumer colonialism at the top of a liberation culture, it is little wonder that a deprived youth desire the same the poorer they are. Holding public office and being "deployed" as an ANC loyalist rather than a competent professional is now viewed as the surest way to realize the goal, as will be elaborated in Chapter 4.

A fourth question tried to gauge perceptions of difference among foreigners as well as between foreigners and locals: "**Based on your experience with foreigners in your area, are there any differences between the nationalities you have met or heard of? If yes, what are the differences?**" We wanted to know whether respondents tend to generalize and lump outsiders together or differentiate between the dozens of nationalities in the townships.

Most of those who answered with "No differences" did not do so in order to generalize and lump all foreigners together, but meant it in a positive sense, by emphasizing the unity of Africans: "No, because we are the same people and we look the same and I don't see any difference between nationalities" (3-08). "No, I do not think that there is any difference between nationalities, because we are of the same colour and race" (1-03). Those holding these views were, however, clearly a small minority. Others laud qualities of foreigners that South Africans are said to lack: "I haven't seen a foreigner starting a fight" (2-22). "South Africans are lazy, while refugees are self-reliant" (2-28) is frequently echoed in the narratives.

Among all the nationalities, Somalis are viewed most favorably and frequently described as kind and providing cheap goods. Some identify Somalis with their own poverty and even exempt them from being foreigners: "The Somalis are not selling us drugs; they came here because they are poor too, so they came here to make money and feed their family. That is the difference between foreigners and Somalians" (4-08). "In our area there is a difference between Somalia and amakwerekwere, who have more experience about any business than Somalia, especially electrical things" (3-42). "Somalians at my village if we asking for a donation they giving us anything" (5-01). One respondent states that Somalians are "destroying our townships, like Belville" but contradictorily also asserts that Somalis "are assisting in the rural areas that are poor" (2-02). Bellville, a predominantly "Coloured" industrial town, is frequently referred to as "looking like Mogadishu," probably because of a preponderance of small stores and some burqa-clad women seen on the streets. So far no discussion on how women should dress in public along the French example has emerged in South Africa. Quite the opposite took place when local African women at taxi ranks in Gauteng were molested for being "too provocatively" dressed. Among those who indicate differences between South Africans and foreigners, a range of markers—language, religion, dress, smell, hygiene, accent, and color—are all mentioned. These differences are generally not understood as value-neutral distinctions, but put-downs, with local habits being the superior and "normal" features.

"Yes, we are very different the way we preach god, the way we dress, the way we talk, also the way we handle things" (2-24). Obviously no comparative religion has ever been taught, as other comments about different gods reveal: "The god that we worship isn't the same" (4-41); "They don't believe in one god and their traditions are not the same" (2-07). "They don't believe in one religion" (3-39). One has to keep in mind that South Africans in general consider themselves a very religious people, with multiple denominations represented. In the representative Afrobarometer survey, 72 percent rate religion "very important" with an additional 13 percent stating religion to be "somewhat important." Mainstream Christian churches are underrepresented in the black townships; various self-styled ministries of religious services combined with communal living assistance prove far more popular.

Many respondents assert the usual stereotypes about the different outsider: "They speak too loud and like to shout and you think that they are fighting" (4-09). Foreigners are contradictorily portrayed as both poor and rich: "They make money that South Africans never do. They are living in hotels and fancy houses and South Africans are living in shacks, so that is what's make them dislike" (3-40). Hygiene always figures prominently in designating outsiders and supposedly protects insiders from infection. The depiction of the outsider as unhygienic derives from a universal repulsion and fear of dirt, disease, and contamination and is used to justify the social distance that goes with "othering." Education in multicultural understanding of different traditions of eating and cleaning is clearly lacking when one considers the following comments: "When they [Somalis] go to the toilet they don't use toilet paper, they are using water as a form of toilet paper" (1-06). "Yes, in their shops, they smell very bad. They are dirty" (3-31). "Some wash their children outside" (3-30). "Many of them have a bad smell or odour and their food is different. Some eat things that we South Africans see as a taboo to eat" (3-37).

Among the different nationalities, Nigerians have the worst image and are mostly associated with drug peddling and other crimes. While Zimbabweans, Ethiopians, or Somalis are perceived as poor, "Nigerians are not poor, they come here to make fraud and take over" (3-09). A teacher corroborated this image of Nigerians as able to reprogram cell phones so that they could use their account numbers to make long-distance calls back home, landing locals with huge bills. Typical is the contrasting picture by a 20-year-old female: "Yes, Somalis are very friendly and they even opened a shop near my house and they are not here to stay, they are here to work for their families in Somalia. Zimbabweans are also doing business going around risking their lives because they want their families to eat every night. Nigerians are here to be in love with our sisters and change their ways like not listening at home and they make them drink" (1-05). "The Nigerians and the Ghanas are the violent ones in my experience" (4-43).

So stigmatized are the 24,000 Nigerians living in South Africa (according to the 2011 census) that some of their South African wives formed a support group, United Nigerian Wives in South Africa (UNWISA), to combat their image of "gold diggers" and prostitutes (M&G, January 24, 2014). The organizers reported Home Affairs officials saying they should "deport 'the dog' and detain the South African women," who are stereotypically suspected of accepting cash for faked marriages in order to assist the Nigerian men to qualify for citizenship. Nigerians not only encounter the most suspicion by local residents but also are automatically viewed as fraudsters by state-linked institutions. This was demonstrated by an incident at the Oliver Tambo airport in early March 2012 when all 125 Nigerians, including a senator, were deported for allegedly presenting bogus yellow fever certificates. Although South Africa apologized when Nigeria retaliated by sending SA businessmen back, Nigerians were collectively accused of fraud without examining the individual papers. Nigerian Foreign Minister Gbenga Ashiru, a former ambassador to South Africa, correctly responded, "What you see playing out is xenophobia by South Africans against all Africans, not just Nigerians, even those from their neighbouring countries" (BD, March 9, 2012).

A final question asked about assuming responsibility and personal intervention in xenophobic incidents: "**Sometimes foreigners are attacked. If you saw such an incident what would you do?**" Again, a majority of students indicated that they would not passively stand by, let alone cheer, but that they would call the police and try to help the foreign victim.

"People that are attacked also have rights" (4-36). Even some of those who dislike foreigners would summon intervention, because of a common humanity or an aversion to violence: "I would call the police, because they are not animals, they are human beings just like us, but they must stop what they are doing, because it is not good to our people" (4-08). "I would report the matter, because nobody deserves to be attacked, no matter what conditions" (4-12).

Others sympathize but admit that they fear being attacked themselves: "So in my heart I would be willing to save them, but also scared of being attacked. It will all depend on how many people are attacking them" (4-43). Civic courage remains a rare virtue given the nature of the violence they encounter: "Personally speaking, I wouldn't do anything, not because I hate them; I just would be fearing for my own safety and it is very violent in the township" (4-34). "I'd do nothing in fear of me getting tortured for trying to stop the locals beating the foreigners" (1-15). Other bystanders state, "I will not do anything. I will just talk to my people and find out what the problem is then start judging" (1-16). "I don't do anything. I just stay in my home watching TV" (3-43). Others distinguish between "good" and "bad" foreigners: "I would stop them if they are attacking the good foreigners, because foreigners are not the same" (2-02). A total lack of principle and moral judgment is evident in comments like: "I believe everyone is entitled to his her opinion and if some people think that attacking is the way to go than they should go with what they believe in, but I wouldn't be part of it though" (4-22).

A substantial minority (18 percent) admits not only passive bystanding but active aggressive support: "Talking from my heart I think I would attack too because seriously I don't like those people" (4-05). "Honestly, I would just watch or attack them too, because people cannot tolerate what they do to our country and I think they have overpowered the government" (4-10). "I would just ignore and hope they beat him/her to death. I don't like them and they make me sick. They should just pack their bags and go to their countries; we could do much better without them" (4-23).

Again, two similar statements about active hostility were tested in the 2011–2012 Afrobarometer survey, which asked, how likely is it that you "take part in action to prevent people who have come here from other countries in Africa from moving into your neighborhood?" Thirty-two percent affirmed likely participation, and 36 percent expressed the same willingness to join action against foreigners "operating a business in your area." It has been pointed out that these xenophobic attitudes increased, compared with responses to the same question previously. This is likely a result of the general economic crisis and increased anxiety about poverty. Yet again, our sample of black students expressing active hostility is smaller than in the general population.

How to combat xenophobia effectively, how to create empathy and progressive civic engagements among black students, requires a separate study. The results of our research show that previous efforts of political education have not been particularly successful among a substantial section of learners. That invites reflections on the state's responsibility for better teacher education and curriculum design, which also cannot be sketched here save to conclude that such measures have not been implemented. In light of our findings, the 2008 xenophobic violence was not the first and most likely will not be the last event of this nature.

The very ambivalence of most respondents in our sample suggests space, opportunity, and a need for meaningful discussions. However, such a conversation about integrating difference is not taking place. Neither the classroom nor the public sphere has clarified the role of migrants, except creating moral panic about being "swamped," "flooded," and "crowded out" by "aliens." Repeated official association of foreigners with crime exacerbates distrust and aggression. For example, on March 20, 2012, SAfm radio reported the Mphumalanga police commissioner warning employers, with the threat of imprisonment, against hiring illegal foreigners; "otherwise this would make fighting crime more difficult." By implication, therefore, the foreigners, not the locals, are the criminals who need to be registered and controlled.

To such official incitement one has to add the collective delusion of South African exceptionalism and superiority of being *in* but not *of* Africa. The survey agency "futurefact" (Politicsweb, September 22, 2014) reports that "64% of South Africans believe that, in general, people from South Africa are superior to those from other parts of Africa." Half of the 3,050 adult sample also think "that most criminals in South Africa are foreigners." Local ethnocentrism trumps continental identity, as a majority do not view themselves as Africans but South Africans, akin to Europe or the United States. Selfishness by far outweighs solidarity, as almost three quarters state "that South Africa should look after itself and its own people and not worry about the rest of Africa."

The South African public discourse focuses far too much on rights and hardly discusses responsibility around integrating difference. This is understandable in light of the imposed difference in the past, to be overcome by a unified "rainbow nation." This ideology of colorblindness, propagated by the ANC and the liberal opposition alike for different reasons, is contradicted by the continuing racialization of everyday life, from racial segregation and schooling on the basis of poverty, to elite-privileging "Black Empowerment" and ill-conceived, noninclusive affirmative action quotas that neglect class background. These footprints of difference are written much larger into the minds of people than the noble dreams of a blended rainbow nation. "Where is the brown in the rainbow?" ask the colored people, who bitterly complain, "In the past we were not white enough and now we are not black enough." Racial identity may be the "figment of the pigment" for liberal academics, but as the famous Thomas theorem stated, "when people perceive something as real, it is real." When everybody's opportunities and life chances hinge on their place in a scale of "nativeness," the foreigners obviously occupy the lowest rung. To teach learners such constellations of reality rather than preach the official doctrine would be a crucial first step to understand and combat xenophobia.

However, the state not only passively stands by but indirectly encourages xenophobia. The state indeed bears major responsibility for nudging people into xenophobic action which state agencies themselves have legitimized. The SA Alien Controls Act of 1991 "allows officials to make random arrests on the basis of skin colour, vaccination marks, pronunciation of words, or understanding of local dialects" (Everatt 2011: 13). Equipped with such arbitrary discretion together with physical and verbal abuse of illegalized persons, it is no wonder that the township dwellers merely emulate illegally the hints they receive from the legal authority. What immigration controllers could not achieve, the locals undertook on their behalf. Given that the police was perceived as not only ineffective but also in cahoots with foreigners by accepting bribes from them, the local xenophobes in their minds merely rectified a rotten situation for the benefit of the community.

The official denial of the existence of xenophobia adds to this dilemma. Consider the odd logic of former President Mbeki (*Sunday Times* [ST], October 17, 2010, p. 2), known for his sharp intellect:

"When I walk down the streets of Johannesburg and this other black person approaches me, there is no way (of) my telling that they are Zimbabwean or

Mozambican. There is nothing there that says 'ah, this is the enemy I must hate.' But if a white person comes up, they are different. So I am saying if there was xenophobia, I would expect it to be expressed against people who might stand out as being different from me and also, given our history, these are the people that oppresses us. But you don't have any evidence of racism among our people."

Given the rarefied realm of security and luxury that distances an ANC president from his constituency, it is highly unlikely that he would ever experience life on the street like an ordinary person. If he did, he would hear from every taxi driver in Johannesburg that Zimbabweans, Congolese, or Nigerians can easily be distinguished from South African blacks. The same was told to us by policemen on the beat in Cape Town, who were absolutely certain about their "instincts" just as Protestants and Catholics in Belfast asserted the recognition of difference by merely looking at their enemy. In any case, to hinge the existence of xenophobia and racism on visibility displays a remarkable ignorance. The 2014 World Human Rights Report by the New York–based Human Rights Watch (HRW) also points out that the national government's "denial that the attacks were xenophobic had undermined the development of an effective long-term strategy by the police to prevent xenophobic crimes" (CT, January 22, 2014). Still, the question remains, why is it so obviously painful for an ANC leader to admit the prevalence of xenophobia among those who valiantly fought against colonial racism? The columnist Aubrey Matshiqi (in Helen Suzman Foundation Roundtable, 2010: 25) provides one answer: "If we were to concede that we are xenophobic, we run the risk of being dislodged from the moral position that apartheid bestowed on us as black people, and it's a risk that we are not willing to take." Rare among black analysts, who usually revictimize themselves in their writing, Matshiqi (ibid.) also points out that this black exceptionalism means "arguing that the black man is not fully human if we are arguing that the black man lacks the capacity for evil" that "pre-exists the coming of the white man to the continent."

The legacy of apartheid with similar practices in the postapartheid state cannot be denied. People are products of their upbringing and conditions of socialization, even if they fought against them. However, they can also overcome such legacies by understanding and reflecting on questionable roots. Such political literacy has not happened in South African townships, where the reasons for poverty and inequality are poorly understood. Almost all South African analysts of xenophobia vividly describe these connections with the past, but they fail to explain why such legacies were so readily internalized—in the case of our sample, by a generation that was not even born during apartheid.

In this study we posit, simply put, that a failed liberation can be held responsible for the high level of xenophobia in a society that was supposed to turn out differently. Why and how the dream of an alternative derailed has many dimensions. The elusive goal is explored in Chapter 4, beginning with the high hopes and gradual disappointment of outside observers and progressing through the moral turning points of the new regime.

4

Falling from Grace

Moral Turning Points

If Biko were alive today, his cry to Africa would be to put its house in order. He would be appalled at the civil wars, the failure to feed and educate the people, the greed of government officials, and the general failure to live up to the promise of the great struggles for liberation.
—BEN OKRI, THIRTEENTH ANNUAL STEVE BIKO LECTURE, UCT, 2012

Shifting Views on "Mandelaland"

The current South African political culture outlined in the following discussion of HIV denialism, sexual violence, corruption, and affirmative action appears to have little to do with xenophobia. Yet sociologically sensitive readers can easily detect parallels: the contempt and sense of entitlement over females by young male outcasts resemble the hate of foreigners; race-based affirmative action reinforces "us versus them" attitudes of divisions rather than common goals and national unity; widespread corruption introduces political cynicism that foregrounds selfishness rather than solidarity. When people hate themselves and their misery, they also resent others. This background offers a fertile substrate in which xenophobia flourishes.

Xenophobia is embedded in a country's history, its political culture, and the habits and relationships formed in this process. When a country's bureaucracy detests refugees, queuing for days at disorganized Home Affairs offices to renew their residence permits, and the police shoot rubber bullets at frustrated protesters followed by security guards spraying cold water on the huddled crowds in midwinter (as happened in Cape Town in May 2013), it is no wonder that the general population takes its cues from such callous abuse.

The following sections sketch this background for South Africa, which is hardly new to all area experts but worth revisiting for readers who are unfamiliar with the field. More romantic outsider perceptions are contrasted with the more gloomy assessments by insiders. Our portrayal of a failed liberation, despite its successes in some areas, does not paint a pretty picture as a whole. Yet it seems necessary to face a stark reality first as a precondition for improving it.

For the increasing number of tourists to South Africa, a paradise of natural beauty, exotic animals, and friendly people await the visitor, just as the glossy brochures of the travel agency present the holiday idyll. The magic of a smiling Mandela has reconciled the different races in what Desmond Tutu envisioned as the "rainbow nation," a "one-ness" in diversity. His famous Truth and Reconciliation Commission (TRC) has made some former supremacists confess, not necessarily repent, in return for forgiveness and amnesty. For the American public in particular, South Africa represents a microcosm of global harmony with far better race relations than at home.

Not so for the visitors from African countries, particularly the estimated millions of irregular migrants, legal or illegal, who eke out a living as street hawkers or car guards. Denounced as drug dealers, petty criminals, and competitors for scarce jobs, these invisibles bear the brunt of xenophobic exclusion. Yet surviving on South African streets is still preferable to starving in Zimbabwe, languishing in the slums of Luanda and Lagos, or being killed in the civil wars in the Congo. As such migrants are unable to reach a walled-in Europe, modern South Africa with a relatively booming first world economy remains a second-best choice. For an unemployed teenager from an impoverished African city, a grossly underpaid teacher in Zimbabwe, a medical doctor in Nigeria, or a harassed shopkeeper in Somalia, South Africa embodies "the West" with much greater opportunities for advancement and upward mobility.

So what is the current mood in a society that advertises itself as a reconciled "rainbow nation" but is portrayed by critics as a deeply divided, unequal, crime-ridden, and poverty-stricken pseudo-nation? Our analysis is based on dozens of personal interviews with persons across the political and ethnic spectrum as well as participant observation. We draw upon parliamentary debates, media reporting of controversies, radio talk shows, and dozens of blogs. Our aim is to give the reader a bit of the flavor of the South African public debate during the second and third decade of the postapartheid era.

After spending several millions of rands on consulting agencies, the SA cabinet in 2011 approved a new international advertising slogan: "More than you can imagine!" Indeed, for first-time visitors it is difficult to imagine the physical beauty of the Western Cape winelands, the magic of the Mpumalanga game reserves, the lush flora of subtropical KwaZulu-Natal, the ubiquitous energy of frank political discussions, the outspokenness of a free media and the quality of investigative journalism, and the total obsession with soccer, rugby, and cricket together with the gratuitous violence of increasing break-ins, 15,000 annual murders, and countless abuses of women and children.

Ordinary citizens of all hues demonstrate in their everyday behavior and interactions that they want to get along with each other amicably. Blacks and whites respond to small gestures of friendliness from each other, and even former diehard Afrikaner nationalists have changed their attitudes for whatever reasons. The occasional racial confrontation occurs, particularly in rural areas, but that such incidents are newsworthy is in itself an indication that overt racial frictions are rare. To be sure, the former rulers look at the ANC government as utterly incompetent or corrupt, just as they had predicted and often had been themselves, but that does not affect the bantering cooperation at the workplace or the respectful interchanges at government offices and public institutions.

On the whole, blacks and whites still live in separate worlds, following residential segregation. In an Institute of Justice and Reconciliation (IJR) survey, 60 percent said that they do not socialize across racial groups, but 53 percent now also would not oppose a close relative marrying someone of another race (IJR, SA Reconciliation Barometer, Cape Town: 2011). Yet when these two solitudes mingle on the street or in shopping malls, less so socially in homes or in restaurants, normal, polite relations prevail. The former social distance between the racial groups has waned. Even rates of sexual partnerships across racial lines have increased among the educated middle class. Close to 20 percent of youngsters are now educated in integrated multiracial Model C schools. Most English-language universities are attended by a majority of black students, although the old apartheid academic hierarchy of liberal English, Afrikaner-dominated institutions, and so-called bush-colleges, once set up exclusively for the different black ethnic groups, still persists informally. The academic quality in each of the three university groups differs substantially, together with student satisfaction and faculty output.

The new ANC government in its first phase had raised expectations of fast delivery and equalization. Houses, jobs, education, and health were to be made available ensuring a "better life for all," as the slogan read. Indeed, many run-down townships received electricity, clean water, and sanitation in small RDP (Reconstruction and Development Program) houses for the first time. More than two million houses have been delivered, more than fourteen million social assistance grants are paid out on time each month, and large percentages of those formerly excluded moved into a comfortable middle-class existence, particularly through an expanding civil service. With 3.72 million officials, South Africa has an oversized civil service, which totals 22.6 percent of the labor force and is said to outnumber those employed by its U.S. counterpart, which has six times the population (315 million). According to a parliamentary reply by the Minister of Public Service and Administration, the SA public service is also top-heavy. In 2013, the SA public service designated 34 ministers, 33 deputy ministers, 159 directors-general, and 642 deputy directors-general (Freedom Front Party, e-newsletter, 353, May 2013). Salaries, luxury car and travel allowances, and in some instances even bodyguards of these top echelons compare well with those in developed states. But all these "improvements" could not match the overambitious promises that were made and the optimistic future predicted. Demand outstripped supply. The noble goals faltered on a reality of limited resources, unqualified civil servants, and entrenched habits of doing things, regardless of the intentions of government. In a culture of promised entitlement, hopes remained unfulfilled, which created resentment and the search for scapegoats. South Africa still remains a highly unequal society.

Many analysts point to the governing similarities between the old apartheid rulers and the new black elite in greed, nepotism, corruption, underhanded dealings, control of the judiciary, and infiltration of party loyalists into strategic positions. Ken Owen (2012: 47) writes, "I watch with equanimity, even amusement, as South Africa under the African National Congress government blunders along the same path of folly as it did under the National Party." Owen argues that a sense of victimhood and envy of richer communities makes "black South Africans rail in much the same terms against white South Africans" as some apartheid Afrikaners railed against wealthier "Jews and the English" fifty years earlier. While undoubtedly correct, the analogy overlooks that apartheid nationalists initially looked after a relatively small constituency of poor whites while the ANC has to satisfy a huge poor majority. The ANC can also claim democratic support for their ethnic nepotism, while Afrikaner nationalists were elected by a racial minority.

Reflections on Mandela

The image of postapartheid South Africa is inextricably linked to Nelson Mandela. Although he withdrew from active politics after a one-term presidency (1994–1999), he remained the moral conscience internally and a principled defender of human rights externally. Despite numerous biographies (among whom Sampson 2004 and Lodge 2008, stand out) published so far and many more likely to appear, why Mandela has emerged as the truly global icon still remains to be explained. Bitterly opposed ideological foes praise Mandela. From the Iranian regime to the Israeli prime minister, from Cuba's Castro to the Bush administration, Mandela is unequivocally endorsed without reservation. When the savvy former German foreign minister Joschka Fischer was asked who among all the international personalities had impressed him most during his time in office, the interviewer expected him to name Bill Clinton. No; Fisher insisted on Mandela and Pope Paul II (*Der Spiegel*, July 10, 2006). Yet Mandela was no populist ideologue who mesmerized masses. Scarcely a personality cult has developed around him in South Africa. Mandela had subjected himself consciously to the organizational discipline and dictates of the ANC. Like the TRC, Mandela's glowing reputation is much greater abroad than among his own ranks at home. In the United States, Hollywood celebrities, rock stars and corporate executives heavily paid to have their picture taken with the obliging visitor. Thus Mandela became indispensable as the unabashed South African fundraiser for the ANC. Since few would dare to turn down Mandela's often only vaguely specified requests for contributions, he could act as the generous benefactor to many worthy and unworthy causes, including a problematic contribution of one million rands to a financially troubled Zuma in 2005. At the same time the many hangers-on exploited the Mandela name, including his trusted personal lawyer, who sold forged Mandela paintings. Throughout, however, Mandela never indulged himself from these funds.

Internationally, Mandela's iconic status pressed the warring factions into a power-sharing constitution in Burundi, although the civil war did not cease. Before his retirement, Mandela continued to lead by example whether on AIDS education or as the lone critic of a Nigerian military dictatorship when nobody dared to follow him. His successor, Thabo Mbeki, supported the Nigerian military strongman Sani Abacha after the execution of the Ogoni activist Ken Saro-Wiwa. Mandela also intervened successfully in the long-simmering Lockerbie bombing, by sending his chief of staff, Jakes Gerwal, to work out a deal with Gadhafi in Libya.

Why a leader appeals to followers is a useful route for assessment. Followers often project subconscious desires onto romanticized leaders. Mandela has been mythologized and made into a magician, from triggering rugby victories (as portrayed in the Hollywood film *Invictus*) to preventing racial wars. When *The Economist* (October 20, 2012, p. 11) editorializes about a Mandela "whose extraordinary magnanimity helped avert a racial bloodbath," it implies that without Madiba, blacks would have taken revenge on their white oppressors. However, all things considered, there was relatively little racially motivated violence against whites by the black majority. It was the potentially dangerous white right wing that was appeased by Mandela's conciliatory gestures. Above all, Mandela calmed the interparty animosities between the ANC and Inkatha by practicing inclusiveness and preaching forgiveness. Mandela took great risks with upholding the principles he believed in. When he exhorted the crowd at a mass rally in Durban to "throw your weapons into the sea," several thousands walked out in protest. Mandela's historic contribution lies in risking to start negotiations with his adversary, when such initiatives were unpopular among his own comrades. Alleviating white fears about black revenge and black suspicion of collaboration simultaneously was no easy task. Mandela grasped the historical moment as a true leader. After Mandela's death in December 2013, the government as well as the opposition invoked Mandela's legacy in support of their criticism of each other. Others use his name to exalt South Africa's image. After an African summit in Washington in 2014, the South African ambassador, Ebrahim Rasool, declared South Africa "a moral superpower" by teaching the world a lesson how to transform a seemingly escalating racial confrontation into nonracial reconciliation. One may doubt this ambitious label for the current state of affairs, because it reflects more of a future ideal than present reality.

Everybody knew that Thabo Mbeki was not Mandela's first choice as his successor in 1998. It was Cyril Ramaphosa, the popular leader of the NUM and ANC chief negotiator with the Afrikaner nationalists, later turned billionaire businessman, and finally overwhelmingly elected ANC vice-president on a Zuma slate in December 2012. Mandela always subjected himself to organizational discipline and adhered to the narrow choice of ANC structures. He subsequently praised Mbeki as "the best president South Africa ever had." In turn, Mbeki basked in Mandela's glory but simultaneously resented operating in his shadow. Insiders knew about their policy differences and private spats to the extent that an annoyed President Mbeki at one stage would not take phone calls from his predecessor for several weeks. It was also reported that a retired Mandela conducted sensitive conversations in his garden because he suspected his residence to be bugged.

Apart from this journalistic obsession with personalities, the more politically informed hold an image of a country struggling with the world's highest HIV infection rate and riddled with crime and corruption. Others point to "reracialization" for a controversial affirmative action policy that motivates many members of minorities to emigrate. They raise the specter of Zimbabwe into which the liberated South is supposed to descend eventually, especially as the ANC government stubbornly refuses to act against or even condemn the atrocities of the Mugabe regime. The informed left-liberals, on the other hand, point to the widening inequality between a small nonracial economic elite, still largely dominated by whites, and a vast impoverished underclass, almost exclusively composed of an unemployed and undereducated African youth. A fragile democracy rooted in such disparities of life-chances is supposed to be unstable and threatened by definition.

South African and international business, on the contrary, praise the neoliberal policies of the postapartheid government. Redistribution and a leveling of inequality require a growing economy, to which fiscal discipline, prudent privatization of state assets, and unpopular market-oriented policies are essential foundations. Once-powerful unions are now seen as special interest groups who should not be allowed to dictate labor policies and wage levels. State subsidies to business for youth employment—normal in Europe and even cautiously considered by the ANC government—are strongly opposed by the allied unions, who fear a cheaper "reserve army" of labor emerging. Even if centralization of decision making in party headquarters violates ANC tenets of participatory democracy and undermines the powers of parliament, a developing country needs a strong executive, one reads. The influential foreign media, from the *Wall Street Journal* to *The Economist* or the *Frankfurter Allgemeine*, initially lauded the progress South Africa has made in sociostructural reforms but more recently also diagnose a sad decline.

In many respects from an economic neoliberal market perspective, success is rightly celebrated. In 2010 South Africa was even invited to join the exclusive BRIC club (Brazil, Russia, India, China). Postapartheid legitimacy has opened the closed gates of Africa for South African business. The self-declared southern "engine of growth in the dark continent" is not yet half as resented as comparable U.S. multinationals in their backyard of Latin America. Since 1994, South African companies have invested an estimated several billions of dollars into the continent. Only eight of the top 100 firms listed on the Johannesburg Stock Exchange do not operate in Africa. The "development of underdevelopment" is also not confined to the export of raw materials, but includes retail, financial services, telecommunications, and transport companies. Unlike the sole quest for profit by other international competitors, the South African corporations rationalize their presence with an additional mission. In the words of an editorial in *Business Day* (July 23, 2006), "South African companies . . . can help stamp out corruption and inefficiencies which have come to mark some African economies." By implication, South Africa is free of this deficit. With this attitude of condescending superiority, the new southern colonizers are unlikely to be welcomed, particularly since they are often equally corrupt. They have learned the trade of making illicit deals during the long years of beating sanctions against the apartheid state. The habit is hard to shed.

For observers with a wider comparative global vision, the "miracle" of a negotiated revolution has long ended in South Africa. They nostalgically recall the moral authority that the former pariah state had acquired once it transformed itself peacefully from racial minority rule to a normal democracy. Nowhere else in the world had a dominant ruling minority negotiated itself out of power; nowhere else had a long-oppressed majority eschewed revenge and the temptation to turn the tables. Against all predictions of a bloody racial civil war, South Africa had taught the world a lesson in ethnoracial peacemaking. Israel/Palestine, Northern Ireland, or Sri Lanka could do well to heed the lessons, academics still argue. Yet the euphoria about South Africa has evaporated. Apartheid was a global morality play between good and evil. With the curtain closing, South Africa, like the rest of the continent, has also fallen off the map of brittle world attention. Like its neighbors, the country is mired in Africa-fatigue, beset with too many unsolvable problems, better to be ignored and left to itself unless the eager Chinese take over. In Africa, nationalism was viewed as the response to colonialism. However, the liberating nationalists frequently emulate colonial habits.

Frustrations with inequality and status differences have turned inward. Repressed aggressiveness often flares up in linguistic warfare. Legacies from the struggle period have moved into the courtroom or into crude verbal confrontations, even at the official level of state functionaries. An example of how the old and new rulers relate and communicate with each other is exemplified in a traffic incident. A heated confrontation between two cops (a white Afrikaner and a black traffic officer in a patrol car) and the bodyguards of Winnie Madikizela-Mandela in her silver Audi 6 in December 2010 made headlines when both parties laid charges against each other. The speeding Audi was pulled over. According to court testimony, the white cop was assaulted by one bodyguard: "He ran to me and pushed me with both hands very forcibly. He is quite a big guy, a bigger oke than me. He then told me we cannot search his vehicle, it was not apartheid any more. I then ran back to my vehicle to get a Taser gun and said: 'Listen I will taser you if you insult me again.' Then Mrs Mandela got out of the car and shouted: 'Who the fucking hell do you think you are?' Hey, she was more out of control than her bodyguard." Then Janie Odendaal, the traffic cop, replied: "I don't give a fuck who you are, you get back into the fucking car." The Solidarity union defended the policeman with the rationale that he stood up for the ordinary person: "It's a very lonely place to be if you're just a warrant officer and the whole system and political elite is against you" (M&G, December 16, 2010). However, instead of being lauded for implementing traffic laws regardless of status, the two policemen were suspended for the time being.

At least the large-scale political violence of the 1980s and early 1990s between the ANC and Inkatha has ceased. It has been replaced by ongoing xenophobic violence and smaller intraorganizational ANC violence. With the often violent suppression of protests and strikes, as evidenced in the shooting of thirty-four miners at the Marikana site in August 2012, and the high level of criminal violence, South Africa is still far from a reconciled society.

In Mpumalanga, South Africa's poorest province, which has the highest percentage of ANC voters countrywide, even the stakes in local government elections are so high that several dozen politicians have been killed between 1998 and 2013 in internecine ANC rivalry. Some suspects have been arrested at various times, and the national police commissioner has appointed a twelve-man team to investigate, but the feuds are unlikely to result in successful prosecutions. The administration of the neighboring bankrupt Limpopo province has been taken over by the national government. The ANC Youth League, before its expulsion from the ANC under Julius Malema's guidance, has vowed to make the province ungovernable, "as long as the occupation persists." It is also the area where witchcraft and ongoing muti killings make regular headlines. In North West Province, a report by an ANC team set up to revive ANC structures states that 90 percent of municipalities under ANC control are dysfunctional because of political infighting. "Internal organizational battles are simply transferred to councils, where groups pushed for controls of municipalities and eventually for the resources to fight their battles in the organization" (ST, February 13, 2011). The potential for fast enrichment through tenders and connectedness fuel the rifts. The Black Economic Empowerment (BEE) bourgeoisie uses its capital to buy into the political class. In the end they fuse. The report just cited states, "ANC conferences are becoming reduced to political stock exchanges, where those with disposable cash or other tradable instruments can exercise a choice of leadership for themselves in the ANC, whether they are inside or outside."

In the run up to the local government elections in May 2011, street clashes between frustrated slum dwellers and police escalated. What the media reported as "service delivery protests" were battles about who gets their hands in the till, because community sentiments were frequently ignored by the upper ANC echelons. As COSATU general secretary Zwelenzima Vavi (CT, April 4, 2011) admonished, "Popular candidates favoured by communities were replaced by sycophants who will defend those who put them there when they want tenders. People have been nominated but they have no skills to do the jobs." Desmond Tutu, the outspoken moral compass in a swamp of political immorality, has emphasized that the new black elite still represents a psychologically "wounded" people. Assigned racial inferiority leaves its mark, for both the racializer and the racialized. Low self-esteem manifests itself in the obscene quest for conspicuous consumption. Despite the philosophical and idealistic sermons of leaders, writes

Stephen Ellis (2012: 295), "liberation became largely reduced to its crudest material aspect. For many South Africans, it came to mean aspiring to the standard of living that was formerly the preserve of whites." A rapacious bourgeoisie, connected with the new power holders and intent on looting the state rather than producing its own wealth, triggered resistance.

A newly constituted Democratic Left Front (DLF) thrives to distinguish itself from the ANC-COSATU–SACP alliance by emphasizing its anticapitalist goals. The ANC is accused of merely managing capitalism but not transforming it. Neoliberal market-led models, social democracy, and African economic empowerment are considered mere variants of the same corrupt system in perpetual crisis. Grassroots democracy from below, not an authoritarian vanguard from above, is heralded as the most effective weapon against technocratic politicians serving the market and the power of capital. "The people" should be liberated from being passive recipients of benefits from a coercive state apparatus to assuming the leadership role of social change. A people-driven vision of a better life will resurrect the "stolen dream." However, like everywhere else, the noble dream of "real liberation" from capitalism remains wishful thinking for the time being.

At least these public intellectuals on the "ultra left" (Mbeki) have eschewed the safety of silence that marked the ANC alliance when it squandered liberation ideals they should have guarded. None of the ANC ethics czars protested against the corrupt arms deal; none raised their voice when their own comrade of integrity, Andrew Feinstein, was dismissed for insisting on scrutiny. No prominent ANC leader publicly contradicted Thabo Mbeki and his obsequious health minister for the lunacy of the then-prevailing HIV/AIDS denial. On the contrary, they even endured with silence the ridiculing reprimand of Mandela when he raised the controversial issue. The editor of the SA *Sunday Times* vividly recalls that moment:

> Mbeki will not be missed. On hearing these comments my mind raced back to 2001 when Mbeki summoned Nelson Mandela to a national executive committee meeting for a dressing down. Mandela's sin was that he had become increasingly vocal on issues of HIV/Aids, warning in his utterances that the disease would claim more lives than World War 1 and World War 2 combined if we did not treat it as the emergency it was. At this time Mbeki was at the peak of his Aids denialism and saw Mandela's entering the debate as a personal affront. The then 83-year-old Mandela was summoned to be put in his place. One after the other, Mbeki's Rottweilers sank their teeth into the world's greatest statesman. They humiliated him and made him feel tiny. A shameful display of power. Those with a conscience sat there silently as this ugly fest was going on.
> Makhanya, ST, September 28, 2008.

Even to this day, most party officials do not question the continued tolerance, if not outright support, of Mugabe by Pretoria. Unable to comprehend how

South Africa's moral high ground has been lost by shady deals with tyrannical regimes the world over, human rights–conscious commentators rightly view silence as complicity. Jacob Dlamini (*The Weekender*, October 24, 2007) has compared the silence of those who complied with the conformity pressure by Mbeki with the purges by Stalin. Stalin's victims, loyal communists, had convinced themselves that their fate was in the interest of the party and that the leader knew best what was good for the cause. However, postapartheid South Africa did not have show trials or the Stalinist personality cult. The fear of leadership ire sprang from opportunism rather than fear of life or banning to a gulag.

What continues in the Soviet tradition, where many exiles were educated, is a mindset of eternal warfare, spies trying to sabotage, and sinister "third forces" planning to overthrow an insecure regime. "Politics-as-war" negates the rhetoric of reconciliation and nation building. The language of mobilization emulates the language of warfare. Cadres are deployed; a legitimate political opposition is "targeted," often violently, when political rivals try to invade the turf of the established. The foot soldiers guard the space for public demonstrations jealously. They claim a monopoly of street protests. As Njabulo Ndebele (CP, August 26, 2012) has observed, "Cosatu and some of its unions are so used to dominating the space of public demonstrations that they could not tolerate it being occupied by a DA that wanted to deliver, in a demonstration, a memorandum to the emperor of all unions. They would teach the DA a lesson in violence. Cosatu's followers attacked the DA demonstrators with rocks and stones, drawing much blood." If no opposition is visible, cities not ruled by the ANC are trashed, or infrastructure developments created by the opposition are vandalized. Helen Zille (*SA Today*, August 26, 2012), the DA former mayor of Cape Town and later premier of the Western Cape, calculates, "Budgets would stretch much further if the City did not have to spend R2 out of every R3 of capital expenditure on fixing vandalised property." Where a sense of ownership is missing, frustration about real misery is released on symbolic substitutes.

Once an anticolonial liberation movement succeeds and finally assumes power in a new democracy, one would expect it to redefine itself as a normal political party, competing in free elections. However, such a switch is fraught with obstacles and often resisted. The main reason for the reluctance is losing the moral monopoly of a just cause. As an interest-based party, South Africa's liberation government, the ANC, jettisons the notion of a "broad church" and abandons an "all-class alliance." Instead, waiving the record of liberation facilitates branding competitors as "counterrevolutionaries." In a similar vein, Zimbabwe's President Robert Mugabe asserts that his anticolonial victory should "not be sacrificed with a cross on a ballot." Yet a liberation democracy can flourish only on the basis of equally valid claims to power by all groups adhering to an agreed-upon constitution. Party and state are increasingly treated as synonymous. With a split ruling party, both factions attack state institutions and even the constitution when it stands in a faction's way to realize its version of the "national revolution."

In a probe of the acute disillusionment two decades after liberation, not one event but an accumulation of moral turnarounds can be identified. They raised eyebrows, even among those who once were staunch supporters of "the progressive forces." Not all moral turnarounds can be attributed to the shortsightedness of leaders. Many deficits derived from conditions that the new power holders had inherited. However, the decline of the South African image coincided with Thabo Mkeki's irrational autocracy and Jacob's Zuma's antics as president. Nowadays much of the demise is blamed on a weak, indecisive, and corrupt President Zuma. However, the policy failures started much earlier, when Thabo Mbeki ran the government during Mandela's passive presidency.

A rough ranking of the importance of moral turning points presents the following picture, starting with the most serious blotches on the South African image. Six trends and events can be discerned that contributed to the loss of moral capital since 1994: HIV/AIDS denial; accelerating crime; corruption; reracialization combined with political nepotism; elite perks and conspicuous consumption; and support for Mugabe's Zimbabwe.

Patriarchy, Sexual Violence, and HIV/AIDS

HIV/AIDS as an initial taboo of discussion followed by denial based on Mbeki's unscientific theories and his reluctant and cavalier actions against silent and preventable mass death must count as the most serious failure. An entire cabinet colluded with this lunacy by keeping silent. At the International AIDS conference in Toronto in August 2006, the UN special envoy on AIDS, Stephen Lewis, castigated South Africa as the only country in Africa whose government was still "obtuse, dilatory and negligent about rolling out treatment." Lewis labeled the South African theories "more worthy of a lunatic fringe than of a concerned and passionate state." In 2006, this tragic state of affairs was highlighted by Jacob Zuma having unprotected sex with an HIV-positive woman and publicly stating that a shower afterward minimized the danger of infection.

South Africa, which has less than 1 percent of the world's population, now bears 17 percent of the world's burden of HIV infection in the 15-to-49 age group. With nearly six million infected, South Africa has more HIV-positive people than any other nation. The global adult prevalence rate stands at 0.8 percent (*The Economist*, March 10, 2012). South Africa's foremost AIDS researcher, Nicoli Nattrass (*The Aids Conspiracy*, Columbia University Press, 2012: 89) reckons "about 180,000 new HIV infections and 333,000 deaths could have been prevented over the term of the Mbeki presidency." The Cape Town playwright Mike van Graan (CT, February 28, 2007) compares this silent genocide to Idi Amin's eight-year reign of terror in Uganda, where an estimated 400,000 people were murdered, close to the number of South African victims who could still be alive had they been given access to the lifesaving drugs when they needed them. Van Graan writes, "The perpetrators of this genocide of neglect do not wear battle fatigues, but designer suits. Their weapons of mass destruction are not machetes and machine guns, but denialism and intellectual arrogance." The South African cabinet, supposedly a group of independently minded individuals, have confined themselves to their resorts without breaching cabinet solidarity with their incompetent health colleague and misguided president. Were it not for the civil society activism of the *Treatment Action Committee* (TAC) under its founder, Zackie Achmat, or the educational campaign of satirist Pieter-Dirk Uys, the life-and-death struggle of millions would not have embarrassed an unconcerned government. One also has to note that so far nobody has been held accountable for this mass crime. While some have called it genocide, it lacked the intent that is an essential part of the genocide definition. However, it was genocide by neglect. When Mbeki was forced to resign as president in 2009, it was not because of his record on AIDS, but because of his dispute with his more popular rival Zuma.

Unlike in the West, where twice as many men as women are infected, women bear the brunt of the disaster in Africa because of the mostly heterosexual transmission. In a patriarchal, promiscuous tradition, women are unable to enforce responsible male sexual behavior. Because of unequal power relations, sexual violence against women and children is rampant. However, compared with the situation before 2006, there has been a marked improvement in AIDS awareness, testing, condom use, and the provision of antiretrovirals, though the victimization of women and children remains high. The efficient delivery and administration of vital drugs to a million people under difficult circumstances is now considered exemplary in Africa.

In February 2013, after a particularly gruesome gang rape and murder of 17-year-old Anene Booysen in Bredasdorp, the media published police statistics that 64,514 sexual crimes were reported to police in 2012. (CT, February 5, 2013). However, only one in twenty-five rapes are reported, according to the Medical Research Council. SA sexual violence ranks highest in Africa and occurs 100 times more than similar attacks in Germany or Canada. Unique in many SA rape cases is the frequent mutilation of the body in a culture where men feel they have a right to the female body. The rural *ukuthwala* tradition of abduction of young women by powerful men has sanctioned this patriarchal possession. Often the rapes are acts of revenge by rejected boyfriends, not strangers. The unemployed men feel emasculated by the empowerment of women, while they lost their traditional role as breadwinners. Emotional poverty, absence of care and intimacy in childhood, and frequent childhood sexual abuse of the rapists themselves combine with drug and alcohol in a toxic mix of bored despair.

Referring to Oscar Pistorius's murder of his girlfriend, Reeva Steenkamp, the SA journalist Eusebius McKaiser (*New York Times* [NYT], February 20, 2013) has commented that the case of the blade runner "is actually more typically South African than the exceptional story of this life might suggest." McKaiser rejects the notion that sexual violence is caused by poverty and points to the normalization of violence by South Africa's apartheid past: "It has created a paranoid nation obsessed with the threat of crime, where those with the means arm themselves heavily and shut themselves into gated communities." One has of course to be reminded that the United States too has a record of regular random shootings and an obsession with guns. Another credible hypothesis holds hard-core sports, such as rugby and U.S. football, responsible for the brutalization of young men in a macho culture.

Lesbians rank at the top as targets for homophobic assailants. South Africa has a shameful record of "corrective rape," better named lesphobic rape, the vicious practice of sexually assaulting lesbians to "cure" their sexual orientation. Township opinion makers and the ANC leadership as a whole have been slow in launching an education campaign, publicly condemning homophobic attacks as hate crime. Not surprisingly, even the police reflect a widespread homophobic sentiment in the population at large. Annual gay parades in Cape Town are organized to market the city for global tourists, but on the ground reality speaks a different language. Foreigners who flee their own homophobic environment for constitutionally protected gay rights in South Africa soon learn the difference. A Congolese refugee claimant, Junior Mayema (M&G, March 8, 2013, p. 25), reports, "Last year I was attacked on the street in Salt River in an incident that was clearly motivated by homophobic hate. With my face bloody and bruised, I went straight to a police station, but I was told to go away. They said they could not help me because I was not South African: this despite my temporary refugee papers. For a Burundian friend it was even worse: she was beaten up by the security guards at the home affairs department's refugee reception office in Cape Town. This just added to her humiliation because she is a transgendered woman and was not acceptable in either the 'male' or 'female' queue."

At the turn of the century, 39 percent of teenage girls report being forced to have sex (SA Health Review, 2001). Sexual abuse hearings by a parliamentary task team, pushed by MPs Cas Salojee and Pregs Govender, revealed that more than half a million children are violated annually. A third of all rapes were gang rapes. Forty-one percent of reported rape victims were under 18 and 15 percent under 12 years of age. Almost half of the sexual assaults reported were also committed by offenders under 18 years of age. Most shockingly, a third of raped schoolgoing girls were raped by teachers. A proclaimed "Child Protection Week," self-defense courses, stricter harassment policies, and other school safety measures made some difference, but the environment in some township schools is still unsafe. The education minister at the time spoke about reintroducing same-sex schools in some areas, against the opposition of the teachers' union. The parliamentary inquiry also showed widespread ignorance: "Up to 30% of sexually active teenagers did not use condoms, with most believing that they do not prevent HIV infection, while 14% believed sex with a virgin could cure them." Moreover, according to Govender, "it is frightening that those who said, yes, they did think they had AIDS, were also likely to say they would spread it deliberately." Infected people are often stigmatized by their communities. However, HIV testing is now encouraged, so most infected people now know of or do not want to know their status. The 2001 Health Review reported that fewer than 10 percent of people know that they are HIV positive, only 0.5 percent believe that someone in their family has HIV, and 92 percent who test positive are unable to tell their partners for fear of being rejected.

But this bleak picture at the turn of the century has changed for the better through public awareness campaigns. The most striking aspect now is not the still high HIV infection rate, but its differential spread in different population groups. In Cape Town six times more Africans (19.9 percent) are stricken than Coloured people (3.2 percent) and forty times more than whites (0.5 percent) in the same 15-to-49 age group, according to the 2005 Human Sciences Research Council (HSRC) representative survey. Neither poverty nor the number of partners accounts for the difference. Neither multiple partners for what has been labeled "survival sex" nor the provision of luxuries ("consumer sex") explains the ethnic group difference. Analysts of the survey, such as Chris Kenyon and Motasim Badri (CT, February 23, 2009), conclude, "There was no tendency for richer or poorer persons (men or women) in any ethnic group to have more partners." Multiple partnerships are flaunted in the SA media among whites and blacks alike, with whites perhaps more circumspect about their illicit affairs. President Zuma practices polygamy plus adultery openly in the name of Zulu tradition.

As is well known, the crucial variable is the *concurrent* versus the *serial* sexual relationships. Simultaneous partnership locks participants into infectious networks and puts them at much higher risk. Everywhere the multiplying concurrency combined with the lack of awareness of the concomitant risks fuels the striking ethnic difference. Yet a change of attitude along Uganda's once-successful "zero-grazing" mobilization is hardly triggered when the revered political leaders themselves proudly practice the opposite. Real African men, so the image suggests, keep a string of simultaneous girlfriends. The Zimbabwean journalist Busani Bafana (M&G, March 20, 2009) suggests that in Africa mistresses are part of a successful man's curriculum vitae (CV): "Having a mistress is rather like wearing a badge of honour, adding to the man's social standing."

In South Africa marriage rates in the same age group also differ substantially according to ethnicity. More than double the percentage of white people (67 percent) between 25 and 34 are married or living together, compared with 31 percent of black people. The reasons for this discrepancy are unclear but probably result from the greater poverty, the expectation of lobola payment, and the migratory labor system which fractured African society. The disempowered women turn out to be the main victims of male promiscuity. They are disproportionally infected at a younger age, because they are seldom in a position to insist on safe sex. It is not reinforcing racist stereotypes, as Thabo Mbeki opined, to blame such differences for women's vulnerability.

There is no space here to analyze the complex reasons for the long HIV/AIDS denial by office holders, dependent on party patronage, and the stubbornness of a misleading president and health minister, who propagated beetroots and garlic as the best antidote for HIV. The reputed biographer of Mbeki, Mark Gevisser (2007), has alluded to Mbeki's "own paranoia, the consequence of his particularly difficult history." The other reasons Gevisser (Letter to the Editor, BD, March 22, 2002, p 8) lists "range from a valid abhorrence toward the profiteering of Big Pharma, to Mbeki's need to be a prophet in the wilderness; from a reading of race politics which sees the western world as using AIDS to pathologize African male sexuality, to a sense of paralysis and denial that permeates the ANC when it is forced to face up to the fact that the country it so gloriously liberated is now dying.' Fortunately, the pressure from civil society, particularly the TAC under Zackie Achmat, has succeeded in reversing this trend since 2006.

Even the ANC's breakaway opposition Congress of the People (COPE) justified the neglect of the HIV pandemic with apartheid faults. COPE founder Mosiuoa Lekota (*The Weekender*, February 28, 2009, p. 6) says with hindsight, "We had to do it, given the history of pharmaceuticals under apartheid, where many chemicals were distributed in this country using black sections of the public as guinea pigs." Even if the assumed abuse during the past is correct, the ANC in power had the means to ensure that the new drugs met the highest safety standards and were not different from the medicine used to combat mother-to-child transmission in the West.

Dramatically increased condom use among South African young men aged 16 to 24—from 20 percent in 1959 to 75 percent in 2009—has finally reduced the infection rate, although nine hundred South Africans continue to contract the virus every day (*The Economist*, March 10, 2012, p. 42). Together with 1.5 million who now receive free antiretrovirals, the life expectancy has also begun to climb from 54 in 2005 (down from 63 in 1990) to 58 in 2010.

Crime and Punishment

You did what you did, because you were responsible. . . . Mourning as we are, let us take note of the fact that whatever happened, represents the best of policing.
—Riah Phiyega, national police commissioner, four days after the shooting of thirty-four miners at Marikana, August 2012

The high crime rate affects the quality of life of every South African. Surprisingly, most have become used to the mental stress of living in fortified dwellings or being reluctant to walk the streets after darkness. For the country as a whole, the hidden costs of crime lie in the continuing emigration of skilled professionals, both white and black. The quiet exodus of valuable human capital is ignored by the government. Instead of trying to retain this precious asset or lure emigrants back with incentives, some cabinet ministers even encouraged the departure of people "who whine and don't like the new order." Moreover, the South African emigrants seldom serve as "good will ambassadors."

The slow exodus of young professionals with ready options abroad is to be expected when at every dinner conversation somebody tells a story of a nearby robbery and break-in. Among the 15,000 annual murders, mostly in black townships without publicity, some groups stand out as particularly vulnerable. Farmers have endured highly publicized attacks. While organized syndicates, like everywhere else, are responsible for the more spectacular crimes of hijacking and transit heists, farmers are disproportional victims of rural insecurity. J. M. Coetzee's brilliant novel *Disgrace* highlights this brutalization. Whether relics of feudal labor relations or slow land redistribution is to blame for these tragedies is fiercely debated.

The doyen of South African journalists, Allister Sparks ("Crime's Became a Routine Part of Life," CT, February 4, 2007), has rightly connected the persistent high crime rate with "the ethical erosion, the rampant self-enrichment culture" that has corrupted the political process at every level. When 77 percent of 16- to 25-year-olds say that their main ambition in life is to make more money; when there is hardly any struggle hero left who has not become a multimillion-rand tycoon through black empowerment deals in a very short time; when the conspicuous consumption and high life of this black and white elite is celebrated by the media ad nauseam, it is not surprising that the relatively deprived also desire a share through robbery. Sparks reiterates an old sociological insight that—contrary to conventional wisdom and government rhetoric—crime waves do not result from poverty and unemployment: "The really poor don't carry out cash-in-transit heists, big hold ups or the blowing up of ATMs. Nor do they shoot the project manager of Business Against Crime." The homeless on street corners beg the drivers of fancy cars but do not hijack their vehicles. Most shack dwellers in informal settlements merely feel abandoned. Most fatalistically strive for survival and meaning through some simplistic religion or other addictive hallucinations.

Yet out of the anomie and destruction of community springs organized crime. The abandoned are easy recruits for well-heeled syndicates. With the social fabric of caring families long destroyed, gangs form as emotional substitutes. Their members are no longer shamed by traditional values, but governed by the new value system of greed and instant wealth. The illegal robbery by mafia-type gangsterism corresponds to the legal enrichment by well-connected state agents, including a poorly paid, poorly trained, and partially corrupt police. Therefore, putting more police on the beat will not necessarily decrease crime, although the professionalization of law enforcement and a reform of a dysfunctional justice system would help.

Gang members who tasted the good life are also not deterred by stricter laws or mandatory sentencing. The overcrowded prison system does not rehabilitate, but merely toughens hard-core deviants. Nor would the death penalty—which a majority of South Africans advocate—lower the murder rate, though it would save the state some prison costs. Blaming an indulgent human rights culture for the malaise misses the point of the much deeper erosion of the social fabric and value system. Unqualified teachers who casually neglect their socializing duty in many township schools contribute to the root causes of crime. An authoritarian school system that richly rewards a few winners but abandons the rest to low self-esteem conditions criminals to succeed outside overvalued credentials. If the low achievers cannot receive the public recognition that the class of the new rich has allocated itself in abundance, not even symbolically by the party that claims to be their representative, then many will steal the dream by force.

Like Sparks, the human rights activist Rhoda Kadalie ("Blind Lead the Blind Through a Moral Wasteland," 3D, February 8, 2007) has linked the corruption among the political haves directly to the crime of the antipolitical have-nots: "The growth of the corruption industry among political 'gangsters' set the context for gangsters who constantly explore ways to buck the system. What we see is low-intensity warfare between criminals who are angry and a government that does not give a toss about its citizens." While true for the cynical moral climate the political class has facilitated, this rational explanation ignores the drug addiction that springs from the same social breakdown. The 40 percent of rape victims who are children are abused by perpetrators who are out of a normal state of mind when committing their horrors. Seventy percent of robberies and housebreakings are estimated to be related to drug use. Yet as in most societies, South Africa treats drug addiction not as a medical but as a criminal problem. In addition to the trade in a multitude of hard drugs as a source of instant wealth, the relatively cheap alcohol available in the country has resulted in high levels of addiction. Many children of farm laborers in the Western Cape, paid by the "dop-system" of free wine in the past, still suffer from the legacy of fetal alcohol syndrome. The extraordinarily high rate of domestic crime and spousal abuse is linked to these structural conditions of poverty and life chances denied, of which the moral breakdown is merely a symptom.

Many South Africans advocate stricter deterrence. But a broken prison and police system often merely brutalizes. The president of the South African Prisoners' Organization for Human Rights, Golden Miles Budhu, claims that almost every warder in the prison system accepts or demands bribes. The official ratio of the poorly paid warders to prisoners is set at 1:10, but in the grossly overcrowded system, it often amounts to 1:50. Not only are prisoners at risk of assault from other inmates; warders and prisoners exist in a permanent state of warfare. When a warder is attacked, collective punishment and torture are exacted. In a famous case in St. Albans Prison in Port Elizabeth, 273 inmates laid charges against the minister of correctional services after a widely publicized incident. After a warder was stabbed, inmates were compelled to lie naked on the wet cement floor of a corridor, where about a dozen female warders walked over them and kicked them in the genitals. After being beaten with electrically charged batons, the prisoners wet and soiled themselves and were returned to their cells in that state. In another torture method, a gas mask is put on the shackled inmate to stifle screams when the inmate is treated with electric shocks, beaten, or put under cold showers. It is generally assumed that the SA police regularly beat information out of uncooperative suspects. The average recent annual rate of death from unnatural causes in the prison system was 55, while the death of people in police custody or during arrests has doubled from 250 in 2004 with a peak of 568 in 2008–2009. In March 2013, Gareth Newham of the Institute for Security Studies reported to Parliament's portfolio on police that cases of police brutality increased from 416 in 2002 to 1,722 in 2012, and civil claims against the police had doubled in the past two years to 14,8 billion rand In a country plagued by a high common crime rate and with a majority clamoring for the return of capital punishment, no public outcry over such human rights violations has initially been registered. This changed with the Marikana massacre, further reinforced by the TV exposure of an incident in 2013 when a Mozambican taxi driver was chained to a police vehicle and killed by nine policemen. Previously, a shoot-to-kill policy was officially encouraged. A crack police tactical response team (TRT), created by police commissioner Bheki Cele in 2009, was exhorted by the former deputy police minister Fikile Mbalula, that the TRT's role is "not to negotiate, but to fight." The *Weekend Argus* (January 31, 2009) front page headline reads, "Cops Praised for Killing 8 Robbers," quoting the provincial minister applauding police for "reaching for their guns, shooting to kill and sending criminals to the nearest cemetery" after they gunned down eight suspected robbers in a heist in Durban. A member of the SA Human Rights Commission, Danny Titus, after investigating the fatal shooting of a peaceful protester, not only reported "excessive force" but also commented, "After the shoot-to-kill policy, we have seen an increase in the arrogance of the police. We saw it first with Jackie Selebi with his finished and klaar (clear), statement, then with Bheki Cele" (CT, October 1, 2012). Titus said he believed the police saw the commission "as a bunch of sissies." While such tensions exist the world over, there are few democratic countries in which a police force shoots thirty-four striking miners and is advised by the head cop that they do not have to feel sorry about this since they merely defended themselves against an aggressive mob. An Institute of Race Relations report found that of 378 assaults reported to the Independent Complaints Directorate (ICD) between 2008 and 2009, only six police officers had been prosecuted successfully. Since police officers are frequently familiar with prosecutors, the prescribed process is easily circumvented. In addition, police unions undermine the disciplinary powers of senior officers. The report recommends that high-ranking officers be held accountable for criminal behavior within their stations.

Corruption and Consumption

Little did we know that our own people would be as corrupt as the
apartheid regime, and that is one of the things that has really hurt us.
—Nelson Mandela

No state bureaucracy anywhere can be said to be free of corruption. However, countries differ widely in the degree of embezzlement of public funds, the amount and frequency of bribery, the rigor with which corruption is combated, how whistle blowers are protected against reprisals, or the ease with which a kleptocracy is tolerated and institutionalized. Democracies based on identity politics are particularly prone to corruption. When voters choose parties according to ethnoracial affinity rather than performance or ideology, they do not punish their group for corruption. Corrupt politicians are reelected again and again, because they represent their own group identity versus outsiders who cannot be trusted. Deserting one's own group leaders would mean a symbolic break with a cherished identity. South Africa, with massive ethnic voting and a small "floating vote" confined to an educated elite, occupies a prominent place in the league of identity politics. Therefore it matters little whether a ruling party loses or retains the "moral high ground." The unpredictability of a corrupt government and waste of resources may spook foreign investors or civic society watchdogs but not the local electorate. "Naked emperors," exposed by breathtaking scandals almost every month, can still rely on the loyalty of their followers. The culprits need not even refute the accusations of their opposition. They simply ignore the revelations of media pundits. At the most, the accused deny knowledge of the alleged sins or promise to institute an independent (but rigged) commission to investigate until the fickle public opinion has shifted to new crimes. Shrewd culprits even join the outrage. They promise particular vigilance and drives for integrity as a priority in the future. What more could the loyal following want?

In the 2014 perceived corruption index of the Berlin-based "Transparency International," South Africa ranks 67 among 175 countries, ranging from a relatively clean record of New Zealand, Denmark, Finland, Sweden, and Singapore to a bottom ranking of Somalia and North Korea. What distinguishes South Africa is the alleged involvement of top officials, from parliamentarians to national police chiefs and to heads of public corporations, who once were held up as icons of integrity in a noble struggle of liberation. President Zuma had 783 charges of corruption, fraud, money laundering, and racketeering against him dropped under a legal-technical pretext in 2009, although the acting national director of public prosecutions, Mokotedi Mpshe, remained convinced that convictions on the charges could be secured. The former editor of the *Mail and Guardian* calculates that "over 30% of the members of the new national executive of the ruling party have malfeasant marks over their heads" (Ferial Haffajee, "History Will Not Absolve Us," M&G, January 21, 2008).

It is highly doubtful indeed whether a liberated South Africa, surrounded by friendly states and beset by serious problems of internal security and massive poverty, needed to refurbish an inherited army with new submarines, corvettes, attack helicopters, and other expensive status symbols for external defense. Instead of spending billions on foreign arms purchases, rationalized with job creation and controversial offset agreements, the funds would have been better allocated for a professional police force and defunct justice system, an effective coast guard for protecting marine resources, and poverty alleviation in general. The rationale of R30 billion spent on arms did not create R110 billion in offsets, nor did the promised 65,000 jobs materialize. As the indefatigable antiarms campaigner Terry Crawford-Browne has castigated the waste decades later, "The warships are out of action, awaiting repairs and/or new engines. The warplanes are out of action because SA doesn't have enough pilots to fly them, mechanics to maintain them and even the money to fuel them" (CT, January 24, 2013). The main profiteers were the European suppliers (BAE, Ferrostaal, and Thyssen/Krupp) of the "toys for the boys" and the middlemen who expected and received appropriate rewards for "facilitating" the contracts.

As could be expected in the murky arms business, accusation of bribery, nepotism, and cronyism followed suit. The ANC's chief parliamentary whip, Tony Yengeni, was finally suspended and convicted, but not until the party had demoted Andrew Feinstein, its own able representative with integrity at the Public Accounts Committee, for insisting on a thorough investigation of the scandal. The chair of the oversight committee, Gavin Woods of the IFP, also resigned in disillusionment a year later. Although a 380-page report of an official investigation into the strategic defense package cleared the government of all responsibility for the "irregularities and improprieties discovered," it failed to defuse the controversy. Patricia de Lille of the rival PAC at the time called the probe a whitewash. The company owned by the brother of the chief of acquisitions, Shabir Shaik, as well as the former Defense Minister, Joe Modise, was implicated in conflict of interest irregularities. By circumventing a rigorous investigation into the "improprieties" by Judge Willem Heath, it is generally assumed that the government failed to uphold required standards of accountability and transparency. Half a dozen books, among them Terry Crawford-Browne's *Eye on the Money* (2007) and *Eye on the Diamonds* (2012), Paul Holden and Hennie van Vuuren's *The Devil in the Detail: How the Arms Deal Changed Everything* (2011), and Raenette Talijaard's *Up in Arms* (2012), have detailed the murky case, which is still before the courts on appeal. The arms deal reinforced the widely held impression of "dirty politics," so that half of South African voters now believe that the new politicians are as corrupt as or more corrupt than their apartheid predecessors. Having inherited its own arms industry from the previous regime, the postapartheid government is also known to have exported arms clandestinely to several conflict areas in Africa and Asia in contravention of proclaimed policy.

Corruption of high-ranking officials pervades all public sectors and includes massive accounting fraud, tender allocations, and patronage appointments. This patronage is openly admitted in the ANC's policy of cadre deployment. Instead of creating a depoliticized professional civil service loyal to every legitimate government, South Africa created a class of bureaucrats that were loyal cadres of the ruling party, regardless of competence. Perhaps South Africa can take a leaf out of the Chinese Communist Party, which rewards performance, not only loyalty, let alone popularity. Only "model" students are allowed to join the party, which has evolved into a more meritocratic organization over time. Chinese civil servants are required to pass an exam, although runaway corruption has not ceased.

In South Africa, while the justice system is much more in the open now than it was during the apartheid period the system is frequently incapacitated to deal with ordinary crime, let alone sophisticated white-collar corruption. A famous cartoon depicts a small boy announcing to his father that he considers a career in organized crime. The father earnestly replies with the question, "Government or private sector?"

Corruption is not confined to politicians or a specific ethnicity. Three years after the soccer world cup in South Africa, half a dozen leading (white-owned) construction firms were accused of rigging tender bids and exchanging kickbacks for building several new stadiums and the Gauteng train. Some of the executives received pay packages of R500,000 a month. The state and taxpayer were robbed of billions which could have been spent on poverty reduction.

The political analyst Moeletsi Mbeki ("Corruption and Dependence: South Africa's Road to Ruin or Salvation," *Open Democracy*, March 31, 2011) has observed, "South Africa's First Family has been in power for less than two years and already sports iron ore prospecting rights in an existing iron ore mine, oil wells in the Congo, shipping businesses, gold mines and is soon to acquire billions worth of shares in South Africa's largest steel maker Arcelor Mittal to name but a few businesses Zuma's family is engaged in since he became President in 2009." Since 2012 the media and opposition parties have questioned the millions of taxpayers' funds spent on "renovating" Zuma's private homestead, Nkandla, without receiving an accounting beyond "for security reasons."

Like a church congregation gone astray, the ANC too should not be blamed. "When leaders make mistakes, it is not the ANC but the leaders," NUM president Senzeni Zokwana asserts (SI, January 5, 2014). The popular critique of Zuma over his waste of public money for his private residence at Nkandla implies that a post-Zuma regime will not commit such crimes. Yet the ruling ANC faction closed ranks around the president when the reported expenditures for luxuries escalated from R27 million in 2009 to more than 200 million in 2012 and finally 246 million in the Public Protector's (PP) report in 2014. The impeccable integrity of PP Thuli Madonsela was rubbished by a whole coterie of cabinet ministers with Blade Nzimande, the leader of the SACP, crowning the rejection with the racialized comment of "white people's lies." Even the usually loyal ANC apologist Pallo Jordan found it "shocking" that for three years none of Zuma's inner circle warned him about the unfolding scandal to which Zuma claimed obliviousness. Mondli Makhanya (CP, March 23, 2014) rightly referred to the ANC response as "a reflection of the morality of the entire ANC leadership." The collective elevated a corrupt Zuma with shady friends into power: "None of them will question the morality of the man who prioritized his comfort above ethics and the laws of the land" (ibid.). Beyond shame, one has to conclude that these predators will continue in the same vein after Zuma has been ousted. They will spin their power with a democratic victory by an ignorant electorate. If necessary, even religion is invoked to legitimize the ruling party. ANC secretary general Gwede Mantashe, a leading member of the Communist Party and presumably an atheist, unashamedly invokes God when electioneering in a church: "We ask for prayers. Do not just pray for government; pray for the ANC. The ANC is a tool in the hands of God to change people's lives. It is not because of the ANC's ways that we are in government. . . . It is through God's will" (M&G, March 20, 2014, p. 31). The blasphemy in claiming divine legitimacy notwithstanding, the brazen manipulation of a religious voting public once more testifies to the moral bankruptcy of a movement that has lost its way.

Njabulo Ndebele (CP, June 17, 2012) portrays Zuma as the emperor without clothes and castigates him for saying that there was nothing wrong with politicians doing business with government: "President Zuma doesn't seem to have a clue about the fundamental conflict of interest. Chancellor House [the ANC investment agency] is the most visible and most disconcerting symbol of this. Is it any wonder then that tender fraud has spread like contagion across the country?"

The 2009 decision by the Directorate for Priority Crime Investigations to discontinue the probe into the arms deal in which various ANC leaders were implicated obviously cast doubt about how seriously corruption is tackled when the suspect head of state is exempted from scrutiny. Nevertheless, President Zuma in a written reply to a parliamentary question pronounced, "This decision does not impact in any way on government's fight against corruption which has in fact intensified." Allister Sparks (BD, February 4, 2009) comments on the ruthless mentality as revealing "a contempt for the judicial system by a ruling group so obsessed in its determination to stop the case against Zuma and ram him into the presidency that it is prepared to pervert the most precious institutions of the democracy so many South Africans fought for so long and at such costs to achieve."

However, in 2012, forced by court orders, Zuma has established the Serenti commission to probe the murky arms deal. Few believe that the body, chaired by a retired judge, will get to the bottom of the affair and several Zuma critics have resigned from the commission in the meantime. Already editorials (CT, October 23, 2012) warn, "Credibility will have to be earned, and it will only be earned if South Africans are privy to its workings and in a position to judge for themselves. Bluntly put, the commission must do as much of its work as possible in public. Reporting to the president without accounting at the same time to South Africa travesties the spirit in which the announcement of the commission was received. Worse, it will feed a growing perception that a credulous public has been conned yet again."

It is worthwhile to note that both powerful sections of business and outspoken ANC leaders as well as COSATU officials (such as Zwelinzima Vavi) who initially supported Zuma with militant rhetoric turned equally ferociously against him. Corporate South Africa, which expected to be able to control the presidency, began to worry about his inconsistent style and the destabilizing impression of a leaderless economy. In April 2012, Reuel Khoza, the chairman of South Africa's Nedbank, warned that the country's democracy is under threat from a "strange breed" of political leaders who appear to be incapable of dealing with the demands of modern-day governance and leadership. Other influential business and media voices had long before expressed similar warnings about a corrupt and incompetent state under Zuma's watch. At the same time, South Africa was repeatedly downgraded by international investment agencies.

A typical outcome of a forensic audit was the 2012 report for the municipality of eThekwini (Durban), South Africa's second largest city. A sharp rise to more than R1,3 billion of irregular expenditure was identified. The report recommends disciplinary action for several department heads and ten city councilors. A total of 123 employees were found involved in business dealings with their employer, in addition to thirty-eight staff members already implicated in the auditor-general's report for the previous year. The mayor, James Nxumalo, commented that "the report does not signal a crisis. It is a wake-up call to arrest toxic practices" (BD, February 9, 2012). However, there is no evidence that disciplinary action was taken against the coterie of corrupt individuals identified the year before. The COSATU provincial secretary rightly commented, "What this reveals is the extent of rot in our communities, but also the type of cadre we have when we do deployment" (BD, February 9, 2012). With the exception of Cape Town, which is run by the opposition DA party, many municipalities show a similar chaotic record of unabashed mismanagement. In 2012 only three out of three dozen national government departments received a clean audit. The Johannesburg *Star* ("The High Price of Stability," January 18, 2012) editorialized, "The situation at the Department of Public Works, which is responsible for billions of rand in public property was so appalling that Novembe could not form an opinion. This is the department that could not account for state assets; it is the cash cow of thieves. It has had six directors-general, including some in an acting capacity, in the past three years." Willie Hofmeyer, a longtime ANC activist and the former Special Investigating Unit head, estimated that the state lost R30 billion to corruption each year. In February 2012 he reckoned that the president's goal of 100 offenders being convicted by 2014 was "very ambitious," as there had been only "about five" corruption convictions in the ten years up to April 2010 (BD, February 22, 2012). The lack of prosecutions is a result not only of political interference, but of the dearth of anticorruption capacity in the judicial system.

Once opportunism alone has invaded policy making, ethical considerations have been given short shrift and moral corruption has expanded as well. South African government in collusion with business has abdicated adherence to principles and is geared to economic interest only. Examples abound. The government refused a visa to the Dalai Lama because it did not want to risk Chinese displeasure. Cyril Ramaphosa, the chairman of mobile-network conglomerate MTN with a license in Iran, has to defend himself against the charge of rival Turkcell that it paid bribes and encouraged South Africa to back Iran's nuclear plans. At the Security Council in 2008, South Africa did not support sanctions against two widely known violators of human rights, Sudan and Myanmar (Burma), for opportunistic economic reasons.

The self-allocation of disproportionately large salaries and perks by state officials, managers of public corporations, and private-sector executives in the face of widening income gaps tainted the image of liberation early on. The high lifestyle and conspicuous consumption at the top has created at the bottom an atmosphere of emulation on the one hand and necessarily disappointed expectations on the other. When leaders do not set an example of modesty in accordance with their impoverished constituency which they are supposed to serve, they encourage cynical alienation. One of the South African mysteries remains why so far no major movement has emerged to exploit these disparities apart from the populist ANC youth leader Malema, who practices the same conspicuous consumption as the maligned elders. The "comrades in business" (Adam, Slabbert, and Moodley, 1997) legitimate their lifestyle with the slogans "We did not liberate ourselves to remain poor" and "Blacks should not be ashamed to be filthy rich." It is this crass and callous materialism that above all characterizes the postapartheid order, which was supposed to transcend commodity fetishization.

Among the many examples of waste in the face of abject poverty, the travel style of the president and his coterie of officials illustrates the insensitivity of the new elite. In 2010 the defense minister told Parliament that the costs of chartering flights for the VIP service had jumped from R3.6 million in 2009 to R16.9 million in 2010. A year later the ministry announced that two new luxury jets had been leased, because "the safety of the country's political principals cannot be measured in rands and cents." When asked why savings through the use of commercial flights cannot be maximized, the spokesperson replied, "The president cannot be expected to sit on a commercial South African Airways [SAA] flight reading confidential documents" (CT, April 5, 2011). It was also argued that the large entourages of the president required separate planes. In January 2012, again a second luxury aircraft was hired to "shadow" President Zuma's Boeing Business Jet when he flew to New York, as a backup in case of mechanical failures of the just-overhauled presidential jet.

The lifestyle of the political elite encourages rich underlings to be inventive as well, particularly in gender relations that show some of the most perverse features, resembling Berlusconi-type scandals. The leadership's example has enticed other women on the prowl for politically powerful dates. Nikiwe Bikitsha (M&G, January 21, 2011) noticed, "I was astounded by the number of young and scantily clad women who attended the ANC's gala dinner in Polokwane two weeks ago, who appeared as if on exhibition in a manner that I found quite debasing." Obscene birthday splashes by newly rich tycoons (such as Kenny Kunene) with prominent ANC friends, eating Sushi from the body of blondes sprawled over luxury cars, forces the ANC secretary general Gwede Mantashe to proclaim, "We further reiterate our condemnation to the act of serving sushi on a woman's body, as this act is anti-ANC and anti-revolutionary. This act is defamatory, insensitive and undermining of women's integrity" (CT, February 1, 2011). More apt is the comment by Ken Owen (2012): "It said a great deal about the racial fantasies of sex and power in the minds of the new elite. They have gone from deprivation to depravity in a single leap."

Yet apart from the three state-controlled TV channels, South Africa enjoys a remarkably robust media debate and a truly free press, comparable to and even better than most parochial U.S. counterparts. When the government nonetheless receives a relatively free ride locally, it is more a result of the self-censorship of some journalists than official pressure to toe the line. Since 2014, several ANC critical daylies, such as the liberal *Cape Times*, have been bought by ANC friendly tycoons and several of their best staff and columnists have been terminated or left on their own. Others, such as daily *New Age*, owned by the Indian Gupta clan, have long been mouthpieces of the government. Under commercial pressure to please media corporations with good ratings and circulation figures, black and white journalists have depoliticized the country with focusing on celebrity cults, crime stories, accidents, sex scandals, and sport entertainment. This Americanization of SA media culture could not be imagined during the politicized anti-apartheid struggle. Serious criticism is also easily racialized and thereby discredited as originating from die-hard apartheid supporters. Many potential black critics on the other hand have been co-opted by state patronage. Many of the relatively few black academics have been poached with vastly higher remuneration in private corporations.

In this climate of voluntary compliance, state repression is not needed. South Africa has so far adhered to its admired constitution, guarded by an independent judiciary, although the courts have come under increasing criticism by the government. South African constitutionalism has not been tested in a real crisis when a government is threatened by a loss of power. Whether South Africa then reverts to the authoritarianism of the old order, adopts Zimbabwe-style repression, possibly in alliance with sections of big business interested in stability, or remains true to its liberatory democratic vision remains to be seen.

Among the five most important triggers of the Arab spring—youth unemployment, soaring food and living costs, rampant corruption, political repression, and widespread human rights violations—South Africa shows ample evidence of the first three but lacks the stifling atmosphere of a tyrannical police state. As long as a free media castigates an incompetent and corrupt government, not all is lost. People violated by state agents can seek recourse from independent courts. Regular elections are not rigged, as they were in the old Arab states. Frustrated people can and do protest in the streets as well as through ballots, albeit more by abstentions than by voting for opposition parties. Above all, the South African regime change has restored the dignity of the formerly disenfranchised. They are no longer humiliated officially and socially. Although half of the black population is marginalized in the neglected informal settlements and shantytowns, they can still participate in liberation symbolically. They may be shot by an inept police force during protests, but it is their own police and not the "boers" who brutalize them; it is their own SACP, who rhetorically elevates their poverty as the party's cause in the alliance. As Thomas Friedman (NYT, February 1,

2012) has observed, "Humiliation is the single most underestimated force in politics. People will absorb hardship, hunger and pain. They will be grateful for jobs, cars and benefits. But if you force people to live indefinitely inside a rigged game that is flaunted in their face or make them feel like cattle that can be passed by one leader to his son or one politician to another, eventually they'll explode. These are the emotions that sparked the uprisings in Cairo and Moscow."

Reracialization, Affirmative Action, and Black Economic Empowerment

Reracialization through ill-conceived affirmative action undermined the genuine good will after liberation. Instead of basing preferential treatment on criteria of class and disadvantaged educational background, as Kanya Adam (2000) has argued in *The Colour of Business*, the policy perpetuated racial identities and pitted the old racialized groups against each other. However, there can be little argument against institutional redress for the formerly disadvantaged. It should also be uncontroversial that special efforts have to be made to broaden diversity, to mentor individuals, and to monitor progress. But do these goals require mechanically applied racial quotas? While some preferential treatment of formerly disadvantaged people is clearly necessary, the way in which this principle is applied in practice twenty years after apartheid is being questioned.

Black Economic Empowerment (BEE) was invented to co-opt the emerging black bourgeoisie into the system. It emulated the famous decision by Anglo American in 1963, threatened with nationalization of the mines by the Afrikaner government, to give Afrikaners a stake in the industry by setting up *Gencor*, an Afrikaner mining house. As everyone agrees, BEE has only benefited a small elite of well-connected individuals who unabashedly became millionaires overnight. As Raymond Louw, the editor of the former *Rand Daily Mail*, has commented in his *SA Report* (vol. 28, 36, September 10, 2010), "The newly rich black capitalists have not on the whole displayed much talent in creating wealth, concentrating instead by demanding as large a share as possible of existing wealth generated by their white counterparts. In doing so, these new capitalists have not endeared themselves to their kinfolk in the working class or in the ranks of the unemployed. As the beneficiaries of black empowerment their greatest talent seems to be their ability to exploit their connectivity with the ruling ANC." Instead of broad-based black empowerment through training and mentoring programs of poorly educated workers in all groups, the mere racial bean counting, as Wilmot James has argued, encourages tokenism and "fronting" without generating new skills. Racial quotas not only perpetuate the old apartheid perceptions but reinforce racial intergroup competition and distrust. Racial antagonism is directly fostered by the current implementation of "representivity" according to *national* group ratios (80 percent Africans, 9 percent Coloureds, 2 percent Indians, 9 percent whites) rather than local or provincial conditions.

The ANC national implementation of "representivity" disadvantages Indians in Natal and Coloureds, the majority population (56 percent) in the Western Cape. The exiled ANC activist and subsequent senior civil servant Horst Kleinschmidt diagnoses the problem succinctly, based on his own experience: "In the civil service, unhappily, affirmative action, transformation, cronyism and 'tenderpreneurship' have become the direct enemies, not only of an accountable government but of the non-racial goal. The ANC leaders who now lack commitment to promote non-racialism have allowed powerful fiefdoms of African nationalism to triumph in much of the civil service" (personal interview and CT, March 21, 2011). Kleinschmidt, who was an effective head of the fisheries section of the Department of Environment and Tourism for five years (2000–2005), conveys how transformation worked in practice: "The leadership would come from Pretoria and address the fisheries component of the staff in Cape Town and pronounce 'There are 176 too many Coloureds in the fisheries section, besides the 250 too many whites.' I was told that I could employ 1.5 more Indians, as they, apparently, were under-represented. I reported these narrow-minded zealots to my administrative and political seniors, but there was no appetite to check such excesses. A concern to balance the need for transformation with qualifications, competence and regional demographic factors, let alone experience, was dismissed as disguised white racism" (CT, March 21, 2011). In many sectors of the civil service, Africans were appointed regardless of competence: "Job applications of white people were routinely thrown into the waste bin. Coloured candidates were passed over even when they presented the best first, second and third choice before us. . . . I was made to understand that their PhDs and related experience counted for naught. . . . As for the coloureds, more subtle hints were offered: they did not support us in the struggle, so why should they get jobs, I was told during the tea break." Allocating jobs, promotions, or any other scarce resources on the basis of connections or party attitudes amounts to political nepotism. Although common in many societies, conflict-of-interest prescriptions are set aside in South Africa with reference to the promotion of historically disadvantaged groups. Under this principle, additional privilege of already privileged power holders can be celebrated as earned and justified.

Interethnic hostility by Africans against Indians has again emerged in Natal. Indians, viewed as educationally and economically advantaged, are accused of not voting for the ANC but nevertheless being rewarded. Sheer envy and greed fuel animosity, not helped by a minority of wealthy Indians flaunting their fancy cars and better houses or depicted as treating African employees shabbily. Disgruntled high-profile black business people in the construction industry who felt shortchanged by tender allocations of the ANC provincial government want Indians excluded from bidding for all government contracts. They formed an organization, Imbumbwa, which lobbies the ANC in this regard. At the end of 2013, another organization, Mazibuye, claiming 10,000 members, circulated pamphlets in isiZulu that advocates all Indians being dropped from affirmative action and BEE programs. Indians, who in the majority entered the country as semislaves in the indentured labor system at the end of the nineteenth century, are now ironically portrayed as slaveholders by the "sons of the soil." A spokesperson of Mazibuye, Zweli Sangweni, proclaims that very angry people "are tired of being enslaved by Indians in their own land" (CP, January 12, 2014). He threatens a civil war breaking out in KwaZulu-Natal and boycotting the ANC in elections, if the government does not agree to the racist demands. In this agitation of envy, homogeneous Indians "earn five times more than Africans, . . . are better skilled and do not suffer from unemployment . . . and almost all business establishments once owned by whites are now Indian-owned" (Sandweni, SI, January 26, 2014, 17). The demagogue draws a sharp class line and allocates eternal alien status to fourth-generation immigrants when he asserts that "Indians cannot under any circumstances share a socio-economic classification with the indigenous African people in South Africa, because they do not experience abject poverty like Africans, simply because they are in the diaspora" (ibid.). Diaspora implies a minority that does not and can never belong.

While in the past Afrikaner nationalists and English colonialists aspired to get rid of "nonassimilable" Indian competition, now some blacks take up the grudge. Should the ANC blockage of tribalism break down and the noble vision of nonracialism erode further, it is not inconceivable that a similar fate befalls Indian South Africans, as faced by their wealthier counterparts under Idi Amin in Uganda four decades earlier. The very xenophobic agitation and visible animosity against a better-off minority make many of its younger professional members already contemplate emigration, similar to the smaller Jewish minority of once 160,000, of which now only half are left in the country.

The close cooperation of many prominent Indians with the ANC in the anti-apartheid struggle will be a forgotten segment of history. In contrast, the even closer ongoing dealings of the current ANC elite with Indians are frequently tainted by corruption and scandal. Obscene spectacles like the bribing Gupta family being allowed to land its private planes at a military airport base for a wedding with racist overtones by the visiting guests and a Shaik brother benefiting from an arms deal and receiving preferential treatment after conviction have fueled perceptions of fraud and collusion rather than common intergroup solidarity. The real victims of the stereotypic perceptions of callous Indian exploiters will be, as in the 1949 riots, the many poor Indians in lower income suburbs, such as Chatsworth, who eke out a living with perseverance and pride in the better education of their children. It is the one portable asset that an insecure minority cultivates. Not only does the agitator ignore these important class distinctions in a heterogeneous community; he also pretends to act on behalf of the poor constituency while self-enrichment is the real goal. This is evident in the claim of patronage that only ANC supporters deserve state contracts. As a local analyst (Imraan Buccus, SI, January 26, 2014) has pointed out in the case of another racial chauvinist and Mazibuye founder, "Mfeka has an eye for lucrative tenders, but his forum likes to present itself as an initiative of poor African people. This claim has been roundly rejected by the 'poor people's movement.'" Despite the fact that that it is only a small vociferous minority among Natal black people who openly express these views, anti-Indian sentiment resonates in many parts of the country and could easily gain more support, given the neglect of the poor by the Zuma government and decline of the ANC nontribal tradition.

The new black capitalists also often treat their workers in ways attributed to their white counterparts in the past. The bankrupt gold producer Aurora, owned by Nelson Mandela's grandson Zondwa Mandela, Zuma's nephew Khulubuse Zuma, and Zuma's former legal advisor Michael Hulley, failed to pay outstanding salaries to workers. The workers threatened not to vote in the coming elections in protest against their dire circumstances. COSATU assailed as "shocking" the failure of the ANC in Limpopo to pay its workers' salaries. "We expect the ANC to lead a program for transformation of society and to fight for the improvement of working and living conditions of our people," said COSATU's provincial secretary. The general secretary of the union federation goes further and concludes, "If we can't change the direction, we must be honest with ourselves that the movement is gone. It has been taken over by individual interests and greed" (Vavi, BD, April 6, 2011). There is little indication indeed that the ANC is willing to reform or capable of reforming itself from within, despite resolutions to the contrary. Once graft is embedded in institutions, the predatory state carries on, regardless of the warnings of individuals. As long as state and party are seen as synonymous, the logic of identical power holders in both realms leads to this unholy fusion.

Descent into Zimbabwe?

The government's resignative passivity toward Zimbabwe in light of the gross human rights violations of the Mugabe regime has tainted South Africa. The Zimbabwe reversal of a once-promising model of colonial reconciliation haunts South Africa. The land seizures in Zimbabwe find some tacit approval in South Africa, which paradoxically led to particular harsh state actions against squatter invasions that threatened the desired investment climate. How much investment was withheld and how much doubt about the future of South Africa was created by developments in Zimbabwe are impossible to calculate. One of the unique assets that postapartheid South Africa had acquired was the soft power of a negotiated constitution. Instead of protecting its brand name of a model of racial reconciliation—as any sensible company would do—it squandered it. Although Zuma seems to be less mesmerized by Mugabe than Mbeki was, the SA government is oblivious to this damage.

On the same day when the front pages of most SA newspapers showed the bloodied faces of a beaten-up Zimbabwean opposition leader, the ANC issued an inane statement about the "alleged" assault, urging all parties to settle their

differences lawfully. The African Union (AU) and Southern African Development Community (SADC) likewise cannot bring themselves to condemn their
fellow member state that makes a mockery of their much-touted commitment
to good governance and self-policing. When the regional court that SADC had
created for aggrieved citizens ruled against the Zimbabwean government, the
SADC heads of state simply abolished the court in 2012.

The official South African refusal to condemn human rights abuses in Zimbabwe, let alone decisively intervene, has led to the perception that South Africa
itself could head along the same road of autocratic rule should the ANC ever lose
its majority support. Mondli Makhanya, of the *SA Sunday Times*, speculates in
the wake of the sham 2008 Zimbabwean elections, "In South Africa some ask,
could it happen here?" Columnist Justice Malala warns, "When, one day, we
open our eyes and our mouths, our children will not have a country to live
in. This country will be a Zimbabwe because we allowed Mbeki and his cronies
to rape it." In the eyes of the foreign observers, Zimbabwe simply highlights all
the SA shortcomings. In the *New York Times* (July 3, 2008), columnist Roger
Cohen concludes his assessment of Zimbabwe with the following: "Mbeki must
consider the blood that has flowed from his myopia and now tarnishes his
legacy." Jeffrey Simpson (G&M, July 4, 2008) asserts, "Nelson Mandela's moral
leadership has disappeared from today's South African government." The *New
York Times* columnist Thomas Friedman (July 16, 2008) concludes, "But when
it comes to pure, rancid moral corruption, no one can top South Africa's president, Thabo Mbeki." Johannesburg's *Business Day* (August 5, 2008) editorializes,
"Put simply, we are faced with a choice between a constitutional democracy
where the rule of law prevails, and a system where state institutions are beholden
to the ruling party or whichever faction's threats can instill the most fear in the
population."

Speculation as to why South Africa adopted a policy of ineffectual "quiet
diplomacy" (which was heavily criticized when advocated vis-à-vis the apartheid regime) ranges from solidarity with liberation leaders elsewhere to anxiety
about stirring up the lingering land question in South Africa itself. Historically,
the Moscow-oriented ANC was traditionally aligned with Zimbabwe African
People's Union (ZAPU), the initial rival of the Bejing-supported Zimbabwe
African National Union (ZANU) before their forced merger. More than historical solidarity, it would seem that the precedent-setting ousting of a liberation
leader by a union-based new party motivated ANC support for Mugabe. Some
ANC leaders also seriously believe in the conspiracy theory of a Western-
initiated attempt to recolonize Africa, with South Africa the next target, when
in reality the South African president was courted as an ally and a great hope
for Africa before his moral delegitimation on Zimbabwe. An editorial in *Business Day* (March 27, 2002) comments, "The people around Mbeki have a limit-
less capacity so see a conspiracy in everything," as when earlier the minister of
police publicly announced that a plot to overthrow the president by three well-
respected ANC leaders was being investigated. The plot turned out to be a hoax.

Although the South African Left, in the form of the SACP and COSATU, has condemned Zimbabwe, it has not advocated a concrete policy of intervention. Moreover, only a few ANC luminaries (such as Kader Asmal and Trevor Manuel) belatedly voiced dissent on a policy that clearly harmed the South African image abroad. For example, the *New York Times* (June 24, 2008) editorialized, "Instead of defending Zimbabwe's people and their right to democratic change, he [Mbeki] has shamefully chosen to protect Mr. Mugabe."

Zimbabwe presented a litmus test about the avowed commitment to good governance as a precondition for more direct investment and Western development assistance. The ANC has failed this test, and out of free choice. When a simple and at least clear moral disassociation from tyranny in a neighboring country was called for as confirmation of South Africa's commitment to good governance, ANC cabinet ministers sheepishly responded that their country should not be held responsible and penalized for conditions in Zimbabwe. A leadership paranoid about alleged Western recolonization and obsessed with racial slights has refused to uphold universally endorsed democratic principles and human rights. The ANC stance undermined the assurance that South Africa would never follow the Zimbabwe example, with far-reaching implications for the trust of minorities and foreign investors in the future of the country.

Yet we still adhere to the hypothesis that South Africa is unlikely to turn into another Zimbabwe for several reasons. First, between 1984 and 1995, Zimbabwe lacked a formal political opposition, whereas South African politics were always contested by organized multiple black and white forces despite ANC dominance. Democratic rivalry and debate were not only institutionalized but also widely internalized as normal. Second, a strong SA civil society, particularly an independently powerful business community, influenced SA lawmaking in contrast to the weak and discredited white farmers' lobby in Zimbabwe. South Africa settled its contentious land question through a special Land Court rather than through state edicts. In the urbanized and industrialized South, literacy rates far surpass the rural underdevelopment in Zimbabwe. Third, with a 20 percent ratio of long-established minority residents (whites, Indians, and Coloureds) compared with less than 1 percent of more recent implants in Zimbabwe, minorities in South Africa exercise more power economically, politically, and ideologically, guaranteeing a plurality of voices and interests. This is absent in Zimbabwe. Finally, South Africa lacks an ethnically homogeneous army that an autocratic ruler could use to retain power. The heterogeneous South African security establishment, both the military and the police, does not lend itself to the suppression of rival groups as the mainly Shona army did with the Ndebele minority in Zimbabwe or, in 2008, the Kikuyu police in Kenya.

In short, in contrast to the modern South African economy, Zimbabwe is marginal and underdeveloped. Multiple influential South African interest groups would combat the demise into arbitrariness according to the whims of a dictator. Ironically, the new and internationally connected black bourgeoisie would most likely be in the forefront of preserving at least a semblance of democratic legitimacy. In the urban South African economy, land ownership is less important than in a country where two-thirds of the population still live in rural areas. Above all, the ANC has a long democratic history, different from ZANU. While critics have warned about the danger of "Zanufication" (Jeremy Cronin), the very awareness of those tendencies testifies to a rights culture, a vibrant civic society, and an entrenched constitutionalism in South Africa that even a determined dictatorial clique would have difficulty eliminating.

Rather than being threatened by a potential dictatorship, South Africa faces the opposite danger: anarchy. If the ANC hegemony is broken and the political class further fragments, particularly in the context of a declining growth rate and accelerating inequality, this could happen. The political analyst Moeletsi Mbeki has predicted that the government could face a Tunisia-style revolt in about 2020. Around this time the Chinese mineral-based industrialization would ebb and South Africa would no longer be able to sustain the welfare programs "it uses to placate the black poor and get their votes"(BD, February 16, 2011). Fifteen million recipients of social grants are currently supported by only five million taxpayers. Given increasing public service protests per year, often violently suppressed by police, the upheavals could escalate much earlier. Adding to these local disruptions the frequent national wage strikes with which marginalized unions flex their muscle, a sudden mass protest movement emerging can no longer be excluded. When the ANC spokesman contradicted Moletsi Mbeki with "our fledgling constitutional democracy cannot be equated with tyranny or stagnation," he rightly retorted, "People don't eat democracy" (BD, February 16, 2011). While townships burn and poor protesters battle riot police, predictions of a Tunisia-style revolt are dismissed as a delusion because of South Africa's constitutional democracy. The ANC turns blind and immediately racializes the prospect. "If there will be any revolt in South Africa, it will not be against the ANC government, but against white monopoly capitalists who continue to extract our resources, massively profit, whilst our people remain without jobs and living in poverty," said African National Congress Youth League (ANCYL) spokesperson Floyd Shivambu. The growing EFF inveighs against both white and black capitalists as well as the current ANC.

Popular Sentiment versus
a Liberal Constitution

South African civil society organizations lament the violation of the constitution by xenophobia. All government critics rally behind the defense of the constitution but ignore that the constitution does not resonate with a substantial section of the population. Crain Soudien (2012: 243) asks the pertinent question, "How does one make constitutionalism the very air which we breathe?" Soudien perceptively highlights a "key point" about the new South Africa: the transition to democracy "was not framed as an experience of public education. It was not seen as an opportunity for the new state to open up for public debate the nature of the new social order it sought to create." While the public was invited to comment on the constitutional draft, the feedback was ignored and most of the many written submissions were not even opened, let alone incorporated in the deliberations. "What happened instead was that the responsibility for imagining and then making the new social order was ceded to the state" (243). When Parliament constituted itself as the public, narrow party political interests took over and the debate was reduced to bargaining about envisaged party advantages. Shutting out the public from nominating and choosing its political representatives in a closed electoral system constituted one of the deplorable outcomes of this process. The SA electoral system allocates all control of elected representatives to party headquarters, not to specific constituencies. Proposed changes by the Slabbert Electoral Commission were rejected without debate.

Moreover, the progressive constitution was designed by an urban elite but remains meaningless for the poor and marginalized, who "cannot eat democracy." As a result, many disagree with some fundamental constitutional principles, such as gender equality, equality of sexual orientation, property rights, or the abolition of capital punishment. Even many of the better-educated and middle-class sections have become depoliticized and live without interest in public affairs. Many previously highly active ANC local branches have become dysfunctional, by default or design. Why has the government allowed this depoliticization to happen?

Those subscribing to the intentional design theory argue the more politicized and educated people are, the more they tend to drift into anti-ANC orientations and participate in service protests under present conditions. It is therefore in the interest of power holders to keep the township population uninvolved, oppose an "active citizenry," keep elected parliamentary representatives not accountable to constituencies, and ensure that delegates to party congresses are carefully selected and managed. The extent of this depoliticization is nonetheless surprising and remains unrecognized. Representative opinion surveys provide the astonishing evidence of the gap between constitutionalism with a supposed active citizenry and a contrary reality of depoliticization, or even antidemocratic tendencies for authoritarianism.

The periodic Afrobarometer, Round 5, for South Africa in late 2011 and released in fall 2012 surveyed a representative, random, probability sample of 2,400 South Africans in face-to-face interviews in the language of the respondent's choice. The survey with several hundred questions, coordinated by the Institute for Democracy in Africa (IDASA), yields an overall margin of error of +/−2 percent at a confidence level of 95 percent and is used here as the most reliable empirical evidence of national political attitudes and depoliticization. Unfortunately, no racial but only urban-rural, gender, and provincial breakdowns of the results are available. Yet one can safely assume that the figures for the black townships and informal settlements are likely to be less politically literate and more apolitical than the quoted total results indicate.

Only 42 percent of the general SA population declare to be "interested in public affairs" at all, 29 percent say that they never discuss political matters, and 65 percent admit that they "cannot really understand what is going on" in complicated politics. Only 11 percent declare themselves a member in a voluntary association or community group, 27 percent an active member in a religious group; fewer than 10 percent have complained to the media in the past year, participated in a protest march, or "gone on strike" (8 percent). In the Western Cape, 69 percent voted in the last national elections, but only 18 percent said that they attended a campaign meeting or rally, and 5 percent worked for a candidate or party. These figures represent a low level of involvement in politics and contradict the image of the engaged, active citizens as the norm.

Across the country an encouraging 90 percent consider elections to be "free and fair"; an equal number feel free "to say what you think" or "to join any political party." Close to 70 percent support a multiparty system, and 72 percent consider democracy "preferable." However, the popular understanding of democracy is questionable. While a multiparty system is widely supported, the role of opposition parties is viewed as concentrating "on cooperating with government and helping it to develop the country," 64 percent, while only half of that percentage want the opposition to be a watchdog that holds the government accountable. The nominal majority support for a liberal constitution, while not overwhelming, largely breaks down when juxtaposed with tempting authoritarian alternatives. On the question "If a non-elected government or leader could impose law and order and deliver houses and jobs: how willing or unwilling would you be to give up regular elections and live under such a government?" 63 percent declare willingness to jettison democracy under these conditions. Only in the Western Cape of all provinces is a slight majority (51 percent) "unwilling." Countrywide, a third of the adults agree, "Government is like a parent. It should decide what is good for us" or "government should be able to ban any organization that goes against its policies," and even more concede to government "the right to prevent the media from publishing things that it considers harmful." Thirty-eight percent agreed with the item "Government should be able to restrict access to information it sees fit, even if this allows it to cover up mistakes and corruption," while 48 percent would allow such restrictions only for information vital to national security.

A third of voters also support public nepotism in reply to "Leaders are obliged to help their home community or group first" (32 percent), compared with the stipulation that elected leaders "should represent everyone" (64 percent). For a relatively large percentage, the separation of powers between the three arms of a democratic administration has no meaning. More than a quarter (27 percent) would like to transfer more power to the president so that he could "pass laws without worrying about what parliament thinks." No intrinsic value is ascribed to democracy, unless it can deliver on pressing needs. The "most essential characteristic of democracy" is described as ensuring "job opportunities for all" (52 percent in the Western Cape), while multiparty competition, law and order, and media freedom rank far down. This is hardly surprising given that in a first response to the question about "the most important problem" the country faces, 45 percent mention "unemployment," followed by "crime and security" (8 percent), "housing" (8 percent), and "corruption" (5 percent). Xenophobia, foreigners, or immigration is mentioned by only 1 percent. Yet when asked about how well or badly government is handling various sectors, "managing immigration" is rated badly countrywide by 62 percent, in the Western Cape by 71 percent, and in Gauteng by 75 percent. "Badly" means allowing too many foreigners into the country.

South Africans do not trust each other, let alone "foreigners living here," which only 10 percent do "somewhat." "Generally speaking would you say that most people can be trusted or that you must be very careful in dealing with people?" elicits an 81 percent response in the "very careful" category. Yet paradoxically, trust in state institutions ("somewhat" and "a lot" combined) is expressed by majorities, with the SABC (South African Broadcasting Corporation) curiously leading (72 percent), the army (67 percent), courts of law (66 percent), president (62 percent), SARS (South African Revenue Service) (61 percent), ANC (61 percent), Parliament (56 percent), and the police (49 percent). At the same time and somewhat contradictorily, half of the interviewees accuse the police (52 percent), their local councilors (51 percent), and their member of Parliament (40 percent) of being involved in corruption ("most/all of them" combined). More disapprove (51 percent) than approve (40 percent) of the work of their local councilor. However, compliance to authority is stated by strong majorities: Courts are ascribed "the right to make decisions that people always have to abide by" (78 percent), police (74 percent), and tax authorities (72 percent), while 72 percent also state that one has to obey the government, "no matter whom you voted for."

A constitutional democracy provides rules and mechanisms to settle all conflicts peacefully. Force and violence have no place in settling differences, unless they are sanctioned by the laws of the land. Yet this basic rule of law is not recognized by substantial minorities. Twenty-five percent countrywide and 43 percent in the Western Cape agree with the statement, "In this country, it is sometimes necessary to use violence in support of a just cause." Only 68 percent countrywide and 52 percent in the Western Cape agree with "Use of violence is never justified in South African politics today." Obviously, the language of warfare ("cadres," "targeting the class enemy," threats of making Cape Town ungovernable, etc.) leaves its mark, deflating the rhetorical preaching of peace. The legacy of *la lutta continua* in the official "National Democratic Revolution" of liberation from inequality jars with the prescriptions of reasoned debates to reach a mutually acceptable compromise.

Once an anticolonial liberation movement succeeds and finally assumes power in a new democracy, one would expect it to redefine itself as a normal political party, competing in free elections. However, such a switch is fraught with disadvantages and resisted. The main reason for the reluctance is losing the moral monopoly of a just cause. As a mere interest-based party, South Africa's liberation government jettisons the notion of a "broad church" and abandons an "all-class alliance." Instead, waving the record of liberation facilitates branding competitors as "counterrevolutionaries." In a similar vein, Zimbabwe's President Robert Mugabe asserts that his anticolonial victory should "not be sacrificed with a cross on a ballot." Yet a liberation democracy can flourish only on the basis of equally valid claims to power by all groups adhering to an agreed-upon constitution. Much of the South African current political conflicts flows from this conundrum, where party and state are increasingly treated as synonymous. With a split ruling party, both factions attack state institutions and even the constitution when it stands in a faction's way to realize its version of the "national revolution." With a limited resonance and understanding of the constitution among a substantial minority, as demonstrated in the surveys cited, the constitution does not serve as the binding contract among the warring factions as it does in more mature democracies. Political education has a long way to go to achieve this literacy and unquestioned acceptance of binding rules. At the same time, as we have stated previously, the very political literacy about maladies and deficits of the current state of affairs is threatening to the ruling group and has therefore not been encouraged.

The one consistently progressive attitude and success of government rhetoric seem to be the expressed desirability of unity and national pride as South Africans. Primary identity based on subgroup membership clearly ranks second, if it is at all important. More than 90 percent "would want your children to think of themselves as South Africans" and believe "being South African is a very important part of how you see yourself." Other statements with agreement in the 80 percent range read, "People should realize we are South Africans first and stop thinking of themselves in terms of the group they belong to" or "It is desirable to create a united South African nation out of all the different groups who live in this country." An identical number of 83 percent also consider it "possible to create such a united South African nation." While the other representative SA opinion survey, the South African Reconciliation Barometer (SARB), comes to a similar conclusion about majority support for the desirability as well as possibility of national unity, it differs radically from the IDASA poll about subgroup association: "Only 11–14% generally respond that they think of themselves as South Africans first" (SARB 2011, sec. 5). The slightly different statements tested, combined with the concern with racial divisions and inequality, may have led the interpreters to the problematic conclusion that "South Africans continue to associate strongly with a range of social identity groups, rather than a single shared national identity." Even if a majority of respondents agree that belonging to one of these identity subgroups (race, ethnicity, and language) "makes them feel good about themselves," or makes them "feel important," or makes them "feel secure," such identification does not preclude equally important national identification. To juxtapose national identity with subgroup identity amounts to a doubtful dichotomy, since people embrace multiple identities simultaneously.

However, "the different groups who live in this country" do not include foreigners. The nationalist emphasis on "South Africans" needs the mirror image of the foreigner as well as a rather restricted right to become a citizen. A substantial minority would deny citizenship to a child born in South Africa to a non–South African parent according to Afrobarometer, and only 48 percent agree to the child's right of citizenship if the husband of a South African woman was born outside the country. Only 50 percent would allow citizenship to a "person from another country, who has lived and worked in South Africa for many years and wishes to make South Africa his or her home." A person "who wishes to hold dual citizenship" is rejected by 71 percent and approved by only 23 percent.

With this collective mindset of exclusion from a narrowly defined national community of citizens, South Africa remains a long way from harnessing the global skills of migrants, as Canada and other immigration countries do so successfully.

In conclusion, the end of the apartheid morality play has normalized South African politics. Pragmatic compromises, politics of expediency, and opportunism of shortsighted leaders have robbed the country of its former moral high ground in foreign perceptions, as outlined in the preceding text concerning trends and incidents. While to a certain extent inevitable in the pursuit of normal politics, much of the former moral capital was also squandered by questionable political choices. Prioritizing AIDS, combating crime and corruption energetically and efficiently, pressurizing rather than tolerating Mugabe, not wasting scarce resources on arms purchases and extraordinary civil servants' salaries, and above all addressing the gross inequality of a marginalized underclass would have generated a different South Africa, true to the liberation ideals. The costs of such moral losses are difficult to calculate but show up in higher emigration rates of skilled citizens, less confidence in the future by investors, less influence in the arenas of international diplomacy, and less internal stability and contentment in a society that was once envisaged as a model of harmony and reconciliation of unbridgeable divides.

Given the small and slow economic growth rate, how will the major SA power holders deal with spreading informal settlements, more street protests, and internecine strife? As one ventures into the hazardous prediction of the future of a country on the basis of past and current constellations, some broad trends can be discerned.

Starting with the Marikana disaster in August 2012, a new phenomenon of unrecognized, militant unionism emerged. The ANC-allied COSATU unions gradually lose their grip over the majority of the employed. They are tainted by their bonds to the political and economic establishment. COSATU's pension funds and investments by the ANC and ANC-connected figures do not escape the suspicion of the disenchanted poor. Increased class polarization is likely to occur. Even formerly revered ANC leaders, such as Ramaphosa, will not be able to dampen this disillusionment with a failed liberation, as long as the current inequality and neglect of the unemployed persists. Nor will the political liberal opposition, even though increasingly multiracial or in a coalition with smaller black parties, be able to unseat the ANC, given the political illiteracy. Disillusioned liberation voters will abstain rather than vote for the DA. An April 2013 cell phone survey of 3,000 respondents between the ages of 15 and 35 showed that 52 percent of blacks believed the absurd claim that the DA would bring back apartheid if the party were to gain power (M&G, April 19, 2013). Only if the DA, which now claims a 65 percent black membership, were to move from an essentially liberal, free enterprise–oriented center-right party to a social-democratic center-left party in alliance with broad union support would it have a chance to make electoral inroads. Such a constellation of "normal" European-style party politics would be predicated on the disintegration of the ANC "broad church" of an all-class party alliance. At this stage, this reorientation is unlikely, since both BEE business lobbies, communist and unionist, piggyback and benefit from a unified ANC state.

Since the economic crisis is likely to deepen with deteriorating labor relations, a declining currency, higher youth unemployment, social unrest, and general loss of confidence in the country, the fractured ANC in its current form will not be able to address these multiple challenges satisfactorily. Sooner or later the party as an "all-class alliance" will again split and eventually disintegrate. Such a scenario of uncertainty and escalating upheaval is more likely than a united, autocratic ANC preventing a democratic loss of power at all costs, as many analysts predict. Unconstitutional authoritarianism or emergency rule carries high costs of global legitimacy and also internal resistance, as the old National Party already had experienced. After two decades of democracy, abolishing the rule of law will not easily be tolerated. A plurality of interests in a modern economy backs democratic decision making. Nor will the country, as some pundits predict, easily slide into tribal civil war à la Kenya, given South Africa's history. The economic rationality and inventiveness to compromise, as demonstrated in the dismantling of apartheid, are likely to triumph. With a new party constellation, the fragile society will "muddle through," neither on a high nor on a low road. It is just a pity that the ideals of real liberation remain imagined.

*   *   *

Since 2013, several ANC critical books by disillusioned activists, journalists and academics have analysed similar themes as this chapter. See: Alex Boraine, *What's gone wrong? On the brink of a failed state* (Jonathan Ball 2014); Prince Mashele and Mzukisi Qobo, *The Fall of the ANC: What Next?* (Picador Africa 2014); Adam Habib, *South Africa's Suspended Revolution. Hopes and Prospects* (Wits University Press 2013).

II

Variations of Migration Policies: Africa, Germany, and Canada

5

Settler Colonialism

Referring to South Africa as a "settler society" is strongly resented by some descendants of such settlers. "We are not settlers" and "you should not use these SACP slogans," commented one Afrikaner colleague after reading a reference to the widely used concept in the academic literature. Mahmood Mamdani entitled his inaugural lecture at the University of Cape Town (UCT) intriguingly: "When Do Settlers Become Natives?" This is also the question in this chapter.

Waves of newcomers in foreign lands can be understood as collective migrancy. When the newcomers dispossess indigenes or set themselves up as a dominant group over local inhabitants, based on their so-called superior skills and knowledge, and exploit the natives, it amounts to colonialism. Independent of ethnicity, this applies to all alien intruders conquering an indigenous population, whether Protestants in Northern Ireland subordinating Catholics, Tutsis lording over Hutus in Rwanda and Burundi, Afro-American former slaves returning to Liberia, Jews settling in Palestine, or Europeans dominating most parts of South Asia and Africa and initially decimating the aboriginal populations of the Americas and Australia. These colonial migrants did not have to show a passport. They did not fill out an application to be admitted, but entered as "undocumented" invaders on the barrel of a gun.

However, should the Huguenots who escaped religious persecution in France to the Cape or the early Zionists who fled the pogroms in Eastern Europe to Palestine be measured with the same moral yardsticks as the slave-trading settlers or British cotton merchants, even if they dispossessed local inhabitants in the course of establishing themselves? Their original intent was not exploitation, but finding a sanctuary.

Historical background is important for understanding current xenophobic conflicts in Africa, because borders were drawn according to settler and colonial interests; African identity was shaped both in response and in resistance to colonialism. So the dream of a unified vision of a borderless continent in an "African Union" depends on the strength of regional nationalism in a continent of more than fifty sovereign states. Current disputes about "stolen land," ownership, and restitution also hinge on how historical migration is interpreted. The onetime-popular SA slogan "One settler, one bullet!" also hints at the potential of violence if problematic concepts gain legitimacy.

Two Types of Colonialism

It is analytically useful to distinguish between settler colonies and colonies of exploitation. While such stark distinctions obscure that the two types are frequently mixed and exploitation features prominently in settler societies as well, the differences yield insights that the all-embracing concept "colonialism" misses. How and where the fruits of exploitation are used or how the exploiters relate to the oppressed requires a more nuanced understanding. Settler colonialism can be defined as the forced and permanent intrusion of foreigners into another territory against the will of the indigenous population. Political domination of natives by the transplants distinguishes settler colonialism from normal transterritorial migration of people. Permanent movements of slaves or indentured laborers into other areas therefore do not fall into the category "settler societies."

Colonies of exploitation constitute the more common form of colonization. Imperial powers controlled a foreign territory through a relatively small group of administrators, soldiers, and missionaries. It is surprising how few European personnel were needed to control entire subcontinents of a billion subjects. In 1921, in India only 157,000 British were present, of whom 45,000 were women, 22,000 administrators, and 60,000 soldiers. Apart from the British officers, mostly Indians kept the native population compliant. Taking the example of Algeria, Pierre Bourdieu described this internalized colonization as "habituation." The colonial representatives returned home when their contracts ended. New European personnel replaced them, and they clearly perceived themselves as sojourners. Since very few European women—with the exception of nuns and "society ladies"—made the hazardous journey to the exotic colonies in Africa, many colonialists cohabited with native women or imported slaves. Portugal in particular encouraged such relationships. It provided the colonial administration with an additional source of loyal personnel in the form of a distinct mestizo class who looked down at the "uncivilized" rural population. Other colonial powers, such as France, pursued a policy of assimilation for a small, educated, native elite, who were even represented in the French Parliament. Britain generally frowned on social integration and preferred indirect rule and control through co-opted local traditional institutions. France and particularly Britain used colonial subjects as auxiliary forces in other colonies. The French "foreign legion" or the British "martial races" (such as Sikhs and Ghurkas) became notorious for brutality and fighting spirit.

In many instances, particularly in the climatically inhospitable West and Central Africa, the European colonizers hardly penetrated the hinterland outside the ports and major trading posts. Contact between the rural native population and the colonizers remained minimal and indirect. Goods and profits from the colonies were exported to the metropole. As long as the traditional institutions provided the expected services, slaves, markets, and access to the desired local products, the colonizers did not need to interact further.

Settler colonies differed from colonies of exploitation by attracting not only a larger population of European men and women but also foreigners who stayed as permanent residents. After many generations of emigrations, several million Europeans had settled in Algeria and South Africa. In South Africa they constituted 20 percent of the South African population at the start of apartheid in 1948. At the same time, there were 223,000 Europeans in Southern Rhodesia, the current-day Zimbabwe; 76,000 in Northern Rhodesia, the current-day Zambia; and 68,000 in Kenya. Members of the British upper classes and retired officers preferred to settle in the Kenyan Highlands, while Rhodesia was considered an area suitable for the rest. French settlers of barely a million constituted 11 percent of the population in Algeria before the war of independence (1958–1962), of which only 30,000 remained in Algeria after independence. Both France and Portugal under Salazar considered their colonial territory in Algeria, Angola, and Mozambique an "integral part" of the motherland before Mozambican and Angolan independence in 1974. About 220,000 Portuguese had settled in Angola, and Salazar wanted to boost Mozambique with more than 500,000 new emigrants before his overthrow in 1974. There is no fixed percentage that distinguishes settler colonies from territories of exploitation. The latter, with comparatively low numbers of settlers, were generally areas with infectious diseases (malaria) or climatically and agriculturally unattractive for European settlement.

Brutal treatment of natives can be found in both types of colonialism. The Belgian underdevelopment of the Congo under King Leopold and the German genocide of the rebelling Herero in Namibia by the Kaiser's imperial army (a forerunner of the Nazi atrocities, according to historian Helmut Bley) stand out as stark indictments of colonialism without settlers. However, under settler domination, "natives" were usually treated more harshly than under direct rule by a distant homeland. When the laws were made locally, settler interests prevailed without the mitigating influence of the Church or Crown abroad. Liberal public opinion in the metropole sometimes constrained colonial ruthlessness. Slavery was abolished through pressure from abroad. Therefore interests and attitudes of settlers and their sponsors abroad did not always coincide. Settlers were not mere agents of a mother country, but developed their own identity and interests. The cleavage widened when the metropole flirted with a less costly neocolonial option. Independence under native control directly threatened the settler political monopoly.

Only settler societies resisted decolonization with force. In the rest of European colonies, native sovereignty was granted relatively smoothly after World War II. This happened when investment in the homeland proved more profitable than in troublesome foreign areas that aspired to sovereignty. After the defeat of racial fascism, colonial racial domination by the victors became more difficult to justify. Gandhi's passive resistance served as a catalyst to the achievement of Indian independence. However, European settlers in Africa did not wish to see the ties with the mother country abandoned, and fierce strife ensued. Kenya's Mau Mau uprising, the ferocious Algerian war, the guerrilla war in Rhodesia between 1972 and 1980, the concurrent war of Frelimo in Mozambique against Rhodesian (South African)–supported Renamo, the People's Movement for the Liberation of Angola (MPLA) against the SA- and U.S.-supported National Union for the Total Independence of Angola (UNITA) movement in Angola and the South West African People's Organization (SWAPO) in Namibia against settler-backed forces, and finally the long anti-apartheid struggle testify to the clout of settlers. Algerian colons even threatened to overthrow de Gaulle by invading Paris. Britain could not squash Ian Smith's unilateral declaration of independence for Rhodesia in 1965 for fear of mutiny in the army. Sympathies for struggling kith and kin in the colonies remained strong. Yet military dependence on the metropole ultimately sealed the fate of the settlers once this support was withdrawn. In the Rhodesian case, the regional colonial power, South Africa, pulled the supporting plug in 1976. The enduring Northern Irish "troubles" provides another example of militarily dependent Protestant implants violently resisting their equal inclusion among the Irish natives in Britain's first colony.

Where the settlers were formally independent with their own strong army outside the jurisdiction of a metropole, as in South Africa and Israel, a different constellation emerged. Those settler states cannot be classified as mere client states that can be ordered at will to surrender. In fact the largest section of the original South African settlers, the Afrikaners, engaged in the first anticolonial war of the twentieth century against their British overlords on the African continent. Unlike the American war of independence, the Boers were ultimately defeated with a loss of 10 percent of their population in 1900. A strong nationalism, even more directed against imperial British domination than against the native population, had fueled a sense of ethnoracial self-determination, divorced from affinities to remote former homelands. South African theorists, particularly the late Harold Wolpe and the SA Communist Party, therefore developed the notion of "colonialism of a special type" or internal or domestic colonialism.

The settlers in Africa also faced a much stronger and better-organized native population than their counterparts in the Americas or Australia. African precolonial semistates were able to resist foreign intruders with various degrees of success and sometimes even blocked the permanent takeover of a country (Ethiopia) altogether. In the Americas, colonial conquest almost wiped out the native population, particularly the stateless hunting and gathering "First Nations" in North America. Colonial conquest almost exterminated the aborigines in Australia, but not the eleven percent Maoris in New Zealand. Cultural genocide and forced assimilation policies in residential schools, driven and aided by missionaries, accompanied settlement expansion. In South Africa, a similar fate of the more numerous Africans was, above all, prevented by the need for their labor. Much of the surplus extracted was not exported back to a metropole, as occurred in colonies of exploitation. Instead, the local reinvestment of mining profits laid the foundations for the only truly industrial economy in Africa. This economic interdependence decisively shaped intergroup relations to this day.

Founding Myths and Intergroup Attitudes

Historically, settler colonialism was neither confined to European countries nor solely derived from capitalist expansion. Unwelcome permanent migration of newcomers into alien territory, mostly by military conquest, forms part of human historical development until modern times. China's invasion of Tibet and the imposition of Chinese into the territory amounts to an Asian variant of settler colonialism. Like the French in Algeria or the Portuguese in Angola, China declared the subjugated area an "inseparable part of China" in 1999. The Tibetan occupation was even rationalized with the European colonial myth of modernization and the "civilizing mission." The Chinese argued that Buddhist Tibet was "even darker and more backward than medieval Europe" before Peking imposed direct rule. China objects to the Dalai Lama as head of Tibet's theocracy, in whom religious and secular power reside. This traditional political structure collides with Beijing's claim of political monopoly.

Stalin transplanted a significant number of ethnic Russians into the Baltic states as a deliberate strategy to wipe out Baltic ethnonationalism and export "scientific progress" to what he considered an ideologically backward hinterland. To this day official language use between the Russian implants and Baltic natives remains controversial and relationships between the two communities tense. Stalin's Tsarist predecessors had lured substantial numbers of Germans and Jews into underdeveloped Russia, only to return to Germany and Israel where higher living standards prevailed in the 1980s.

Black settler colonialism is often blamed as the source of strife in Liberia, where returning African American former slaves established themselves as a privileged ruling caste over the local population. Similarly, Tutsi minority dominance over Hutus in Rwanda and Burundi originates in the migration of herders in precolonial times, though exploited and exacerbated by European colonizers in deliberate divide-and-rule policies. The same can be said about the violent migration of the Ndebele, a section of the Zulu people, into Zimbabwe at the turn of the nineteenth century. Their conquest of the majority Shona, together with their dealings and subsequent resistance to the archimperialist

Cecil Rhodes, left a legacy of interethnic animosity, despite their common liberation struggle against the white Rhodesians during the 1970s. Otherwise Mugabe's North Korean–trained Fifth Brigade of Shona soldiers would not have been motivated to slaughter twenty thousand Ndebele ZAPU supporters in 1982, an atrocity *(Gukuharundi)* not officially recognized to this day. Much-resented Arab settlers in Zanzibar were the victims of genocidal massacres by locals in January 1964, when more than five thousand Arabs were killed, the sultan was overthrown, and Zanzibar merged with newly independent Tanzania as a semiautonomous region. After the United Nations ruled that the demand for independence by the Western Sahara should be decided by a referendum among its inhabitants, the occupying power, Morocco, transplanted Moroccans to outvote the real Saharawani residents of the area. (For a fuller treatment of most of these cases, see H. Adam, 2011.)

Settlers have to justify their intrusion not only to the natives but also to themselves. The "civilizing mission" and the "white man's burden" are well-known rationalizations. Most settler societies have cherished the myth of the empty land. Zionists openly propagated the well-known myth of "a land without people for a people without land," although two-thirds of the inhabitants of British Palestine were Arabs at the establishment of Israel in 1948. In Australia, the doctrine of *terra nullis* served until the early 1990s as the founding myth of the state, although an estimated 350,000 aborigines inhabited the land when Britain first established a penal colony. Only in 1992 did the High Court of Australia overturn the doctrine of *terra nullis* in the Mabo case. The subsequent passing of the "Native Title Act" (1993) reversed 100 years of legal reasoning that the natives did not own but merely resided and wandered upon the land. While recognizing distinct indigenous societies, the court avoided the crucial question of whether these aborigines exercised sovereignty of their own that was wrongfully denied by settler governments. When the existence of locals could no longer be denied, "empty" was reinterpreted as meaning "uncultivated" or inhabited by "barbarous" natives. Communal land allocation without individual property rights was considered an entitlement to occupy or buy off the chiefs to grant title to the settlers, as Rhodes did by securing half of Rhodesia. In Israel one can hear the rationalization that before the Zionist settlement no state "owned" the West Bank and therefore any force that could establish firm control had a legitimate right to do so.

It is often assumed that the settlers feared the numerically superior natives and settler aggressiveness was motivated by survival necessities. This is doubtful in the South Africa case. While Afrikaners were vastly outnumbered by blacks and pondered the "disastrous" consequences of majority rule, particularly in light of declining population ratios, real fear was not a dominant attitude as long as they were in control. Settler colonialists generally viewed "the natives" as a backward people. The "underdeveloped" and "inferior" inhabitants were neither feared nor hated. Dominant attitudes spanned the spectrum from pity to contempt, indifference to denial that natives existed as a political force. Natives were considered part of the natural flora and fauna in early segregated South Africa. If they rebelled, they must have been seduced by communists or "pink liberals," since the good-natured underlings were generally considered loyal to their feudal masters. Only San-speakers ("Bushmen") on the frontier of European settlement were considered habitual cattle thieves and often shot on sight by special raiding parties in the early periods. The few survivors were later used as trackers in special units of the apartheid army.

While condescension characterized dominant white attitudes in apartheid South Africa, denial, ignorance, and mutual demonization prevail in Israel. Once Golda Meir even asserted that "Palestinians do not exist." Likewise, Palestinian schools still do not teach Jewish history or the Holocaust. The Jewish curriculum ignores the 1948 *nakba* (catastrophe), the dispossession and displacement of 700,000 Palestinians from the new Jewish state. Instead of bridging conflicting narratives, the curriculum on both sides reinforces the in-group story. Hebrew University's Nuri Peled-Elhanan (2007) observed, "Today, while the entire civilized world enjoys slandering and smearing the Palestinian education system, there is no schoolbook in Israel that presents a picture of a Palestinian as a modern ordinary person. There is no schoolbook in Israel that presents a map that shows the true borders of the State. There is no schoolbook in Israel in which the word 'occupation' appears."[1]

Despite the legalized segregation in apartheid South Africa, mutual perceptions of black and white differed from this extreme social distance in Israel/Palestine. Apartheid meant institutionalized inequality but did not prevent daily encounters in work situations. The discriminatory laws regulated the occupational and social hierarchy of people in intimate contact with each other. Most whites had their children raised by black nannies, their meals cooked, gardens attended, houses cleaned, or mail delivered by the disenfranchised. In the rural

---

[1] There is a rich polemical and academic literature specifically on settler colonialism from which this chapter draws most of its insights and data. Leo Kuper, "Political Change in White Settler Societies: The Possibility of Peaceful Democratization," in *Pluralism in Africa*, ed. Leo Kuper and M. G. Smith (Berkeley: University of California Press, 1969), 169–209. Kuper's seminal piece remains one of the most insightful early contributions on the topic. Accounts on the comparison of Israel and South Africa as colonial "settler societies" range from Donald Akenson's thoughtful *God's People* (Montreal: McGill University Press, 1991) to the more chronologically oriented overview of Thomas Mitchell, *Native vs. Settler* (Westport, CT: Greenwood, 2000). See also Maxime Rodinson, *Israel: A Colonial-Settler State?* (New York: Monad, 1973); Ibrahim Abu-Lughod and Baha Abu-Laban, *Settler Regimes in Africa and the Arab World* (Wilmette, IL: Medina University Press, 1974); and the most scholarly comparison of British-Irish, French-Algerian, and Israeli-Palestinian relations by Ian Lustick, *Unsettled States, Disputed Lands* (Ithaca, NY: Cornell University Press, 1993). See also the insightful collection of essays on Northern Ireland, Israel, and South Africa by Hermann Giliomee and Jannie Gagiano, eds., *The Elusive Search for Peace* (Cape Town: Oxford University Press, 1990). Fiona Bateman and Lionel Pilkington, eds., 2001. *Studies in Settler Colonialism: Politics, Identity and Culture* (New York: Palgrave) is the latest theoretical collection on the topic. For a more recent comparison of differences and similarities between South Africa and Israel, see H. Adam and K. Moodley, *Seeking Mandela* (2005) from which most of the arguments in this chapter are drawn.

areas, the children of the Afrikaner farmers played with their peers of the African laborers. They learned each other's language early on. In the cities, when legally possible, the black elite had their children educated at the far superior white schools, even if their parents advocated the slogan "Liberation before education." At the height of apartheid, black police personnel outnumbered white cops, and both ticketed for traffic violations, regardless of the race of the driver. This economic interdependence did not allow whites to fear blacks who also knew their masters' habits intimately. In this semifeudal system, whites displayed paternalism toward their underlings but also had to trust and somehow care for them. Paternalism fosters subservience to authority and stunts growth but contradicts dehumanization.

Metropolitan/Settler Relations

Historically, colonizing settlers acted on behalf of a metropolitan power that sponsored them. However, settlers also develop their own interest, independent of and often against their sponsors abroad. The colonial concept leaves unanswered when and how settlers become indigenous. The settler-native dichotomy is not unproblematic for an analysis of contemporary divided societies, because it falsely assumes a continuing colonial relationship with its related moral hierarchy. There are no objective criteria by which it can be decided when a newcomer becomes indigenous in the competition for entitlements, based on ancestral arrival in an area. If arrival time were applied to contemporary immigrant societies for status allocation, latecomers and recent migrants would be permanently disadvantaged compared with earlier migrants. Such skepticism does not deny the historical record of colonial dispossession and the legacy of conquest.

Framing a conflict as "colonial" or labeling it as "nationalist" also affects solutions. Liberation from colonialism means departure of the intruder from "native" territory. In South Africa, only the Pan Africanist Congress (PAC) applied the colonial analogy, while the ANC fudged the issue with the theory of "domestic colonialism," in which Europeans belonged to the land as long as they changed their colonial habits. However, both the PAC and BCM, while emphasizing black nationalism and pride in blackness, also stressed that they were not antiwhite, but anticolonial.

The question of settler colonialism is now most relevant in the Israeli-Palestinian conflict. Most Jewish Israelis view their conflict with their Palestinian neighbors as a nationalist one between two irreconcilable nationalist claims to the same small land, holy places, and scarce water. Most Palestinians, on the other hand, consider the conflict as a colonial conquest by foreign intruders who occupy ancestral territory by superior force and displaced the original inhabitants. Far from mere academic definitions, the opposing nationalist-versus-colonial conceptualizations affect potential solutions. In the ideological warfare, conflicting historical narratives confront each other, and each side claims a monopoly of truth and victimhood. Divergent strategies for intervention and global legitimacy flow from the nationalist versus the colonial definition. If Israel is a colonial "apartheid state," similar anti-apartheid measures of sanctions and boycott can be advocated. Ultimately a South African solution of sharing the common land and resources in one state ought to emerge. However, if the conflict is a nationalist one of two distinct ethnic communities aspiring to self-determination, two viable states with agreed-upon borders could solve the dispute.

As is well known, there are as many different versions of Zionism as there are many different Jewish voices of non-Zionism, anti-Zionism, and post-Zionism. This debate cannot be considered here. Labeling mainstream Zionism a colonial enterprise must identify an exploitative intent and a colonial power from which it emanated and in whose interest it acted. Such a colonial homeland did not exist in the controversial quest for a Jewish state that first arose during the European nationalist upsurge at the turn of the nineteenth century. Although there was some sympathy in the United Kingdom for a Jewish state somewhere in the vast empire and the colonial government may have considered an increased Jewish presence in the Middle East a strategic asset, the 1917 Balfour Declaration promising such a state in British Palestine cannot be equated with economic colonialism. In 1948, the international community, including the Soviet Union, through the UN resolution 181 consented to the creation of Israel in the wake of the Holocaust. This occurred against the will of the native Arab population, which constituted two-thirds of the inhabitants at the time. Whether Zionism is colonialism therefore depends on whether economic exploitation and displacement of natives are considered the decisive criteria.

Always controversial among Jews themselves, early Zionists aimed at a "normal society" where Jews frowned upon employing natives and propagated an egalitarian communal democracy. As is well known, Britain actively opposed and tried to limit Jewish immigration into Palestine. Therefore the question becomes, under what circumstances do refugees become colonialists? The distinguished historian Peter Clarke in his magisterial *The Last Thousand Days of the British Empire* captures the moral dilemma of the newcomers, who had survived the Nazi atrocities but in Poland faced even "more widespread postwar pogroms when they tried to reclaim their ancestral lands." Clarke (2007: 509) points out,

> It was the Polish Jews who were most determined to flee eastern Europe, as it was left after Potsdam, and to make a new life for themselves. Who can possibly blame them? And if they accepted the advice proffered in Zionist propaganda, that immigration to Palestine was their best bet, who would say they were wrong? And if they saw British restrictions on legal immigration as vexatious, who would not in their position? And if they exploited the workings for the arrangements for Displaced Persons to use illegal channels in getting to Palestine, what other options did

they have? Finally, if they saw their arrival as Zionist settlers as a triumph over anti-semitism, British imperialism and American lassitude, little wonder that they established a powerful narrative of their providential deliverance

Does this make the passengers of the "Exodus" colonial settlers? Can refugees nonetheless become colonialists? They displaced natives, regardless of the plight and motives of the newcomers, answer Palestinians. Why should the Huguenots fleeing religious persecution in seventeenth-century France to South Africa be considered colonial settlers and Jews fleeing racial pogroms in Poland not be seen as legitimate immigrant refugees? There are no universal answers to such questions, which largely depend on how the newcomers relate to and behave toward the natives and how they are accepted in turn.

Have persecuted refugees learned compassion toward people escaping similar hardship as they had experienced? Neither in the Huguenot nor in the Israeli case can one answer this question with "yes." Ironically, Israel, a nation founded by illegal immigrants who were restricted in the British-controlled Palestine and held in Cypriot detention camps before 1948, experiences now periodic riots against African asylum seekers, mainly from Sudan and Eritrea. Israel has the lowest refugee recognition rate of all Western countries. The migrants are widely considered "infiltrators" whom, in the words of a Likud MP (Danny Danon), "we must deport immediately before it's too late."

The Israeli sociologist Eliezer Ben-Rafael (2004) distinguishes between "colonialism" and "colonization," which he considers a more accurate, though not morally superior, description of Zionism. Ben-Rafael wants to avoid the negative connotations of a vanishing colonialism, feeding into "Israelophobia," while highlighting the frequency of new nations establishing themselves in the modern era. However, if colonization means "a new population" displacing a local one and building up "a society of its own," as Ben-Rafael defines colonization, the distinction is merely semantic. Permanent conquest may actually be worse for the indigenous people than temporary economic colonial exploitation, the frequency and general acceptance of new settler dominance in the Americas and elsewhere notwithstanding.

Yet the right of settlers to coexist with dispossessed people in the same land has long been conceded by mainstream Palestinian leaders (in the Oslo Accord) and confirmed by the ANC's Freedom Charter of 1955. Disputed issues are the terms of coexistence, the meaning of equal citizenship, and how to redress the legacy of past injustice. The problem in Africa, and particularly in Israel, lies in the understandable distrust of the "settlers" in such assurances of equal coexistence under an agreed-upon rule of law rather than military strength. After all, some members of South African liberation movements once campaigned under the slogan "One settler, one bullet!" The fate of white farmers in the oncepromising Zimbabwean reconciliation also proved not exactly reassuring. The minority Islamist rejection of infidels on sacred Muslim soil justifiably engenders anxieties. In short, when dominant groups perceive their continued existence as based merely on tolerance and on the terms of a former adversary, they are naturally suspicious, particularly when they continue to be labeled illegitimate colonialists.

Doubts about the future have already driven a large percentage of South African whites, Coloureds, and Indians to emigrate. The introspective Zimbabwe-born writer Peter Goodwin (2006: 266) in his moving memoir *When a Crocodile Eats the Sun* has articulated this settler insecurity: "Africa is for me: a place in which I can never truly belong, a dangerous place that will, if I allow it to, reach into my life and hurt my family. A white in Africa is like a Jew everywhere—on sufferance, watching warily, waiting for the next tidal swell of hostility." However, a Jewish person in New York hardly lives on sufferance and does not have to watch warily. Goodwin's noble scruples about colonialism confuse guilt with responsibility: "How many generations will it take before the taste of colonialism has been washed from our mouths? And I have to live my own life in the meantime. I can't bear the guilt, the feeling of responsibility. I can't lug the sins of my forebears on my back wherever I go." Are such reflections mere moral posturing, or does the author express a common settler sentiment in a postcolonial era?

Hardly any South African whites, one could confidently assert, have left the country because of guilt about past colonialism. People emigrate because of uncontrollable crime or better employment prospects. There is no personal guilt for being born into a settler community, but there is always responsibility to acknowledge and make reasonable amends for the sins of ancestors. Realizing the connections between the legacy of the past and the general insecurity of the present distinguishes the politically conscious "settler" from the politically illiterate.

Israeli sovereignty was established in accordance with international law, as was the sovereign independence of South African "settlers" in 1915. The legal foundations of the two settler states, however, did not prevent their illegal policies in terms of international law afterward. There is a clear difference between historical refugees and the 500,000 domestic Jewish settlers who invaded Palestinian territory after the 1967 war. Whether out of religious delusions about the promised land in Judea and Samaria or because of the better life and subsidized housing, the hardliners from Brooklyn and Russia warrant the label "colonial intruders." Transferring its own civilians into an occupied area contravenes Article 49 of the Fourth Geneva Convention. Why have many of the original refugees, including secular Israeli Labour Party governments, promoted and tacitly supported the settlement expansion and illegal occupation? While settlements and land expropriation are rationalized with "security needs," they actually exacerbate Israeli insecurity.

The notion of "settler societies" therefore carries explanatory weight only if their varieties are distinguished. As Canadian historian Donald Akenson (2001: 65) has pointed out, "there is scarcely a society in Europe or North and

South America that is not a settler society." Hence, how useful is the concept "settler colonialism"? This analysis problematizes the usefulness of the label not only for analytical but also for strategic purposes. The underlying assumption that models of decolonization elsewhere readily lend themselves to export ignores distinct circumstances when settlers have become natives. "Settler colonialism" may actually retard imaginative solutions by clinging to visions that may make a bad situation worse. However, the concept is useful for studying history. Only when students acquire a historical and global understanding of migrancy can they understand difference in their midst, shed a parochial nationalist outlook, empathize with refugees, make informed, balanced judgments about immigration policies, and adopt a cosmopolitan mindset, as will be further elaborated in Chapter 8 on political literacy.

6

Xenophobia in Germany

After the experiences of the first half of the 20th century, after the trauma of being crushed and after the "never-again" rhetoric of 1945, and after the decades-long engagement for a united, peaceful, post-national Europe, it was inconceivable that in Germany of to-day so quickly, so efficiently, so fanatically an enemy image is constructed, that unites in nationalist hate almost everyone, from the entrepreneur to the welfare recipient, against the "foreign parasites" to be punished for spunging on the "healthy German body politic."
—ROBERT MENASSE, DER EUROPÄISCHE LANDBOTE: DIE WUT DER BÜRGER UND DER FRIEDE EUROPAS

One could reasonably expect that Germany's unique racist history has shaped attitudes of postfascist generation. Just as South Africa's politicized anti-apartheid history has not succeeded in preventing renewed racialization, so has Germany's past despite great reeducation efforts failed to transform the society entirely into a cosmopolitan model of universal human rights. However, the above indictment by Menasse applies to a minority, despite weekly demonstrations against Muslim immigration by thousands in Dresden and elsewhere under the banner of 'Patriotic Europeans' (Pegida) that were further fuelled by Islamist terror acts. Larger counterdemonstrations exposed the deep rift on multiculturalism in German society. Virtually all German political parties with the exception of the small anti-European *Alternative für Deutschland* (AfD) and sections of the Bavarian CSU support immigration and inveigh against xenophobia. In January 2015, after the Paris attack on a satirical magazine, Chancellor Angela Merkel reiterated a controversial statement by former president Wulff, that "Islam belongs to Germany." Should Germany conceive of itself as an ethnic *Kulturnation* or a *Staatsnation*, a homogeneous volk or a conglomerate of world citizens?

Germans were again jolted out of complacency by the 2013 trial against a neo-Nazi underground group that had killed nine Turks and bombed foreign shops for ten years without the police investigating seriously what they considered internecine conflicts. The episode revealed an astonishing institutional blindness of the German intelligence services toward right-wing extremism that changed only when a German policewoman was also murdered and a bank was robbed by the same group.

In contrast to the complacency about xenophobia, German authorities are more vigilant about anti-Semitism, because such acts have wider foreign repercussions. All Jewish institutions in Berlin are provided with twenty-four-hour police guards, which does not necessarily indicate increased levels of anti-Semitism, although occasional attacks on Jewish individuals or graffiti at Jewish cemeteries are still reported. A thorough investigation by a combined 2012 Commission of Parliament and academic experts concludes, "The surveys of Braehler/Decker as well as those of the Anti-Defamation League [ADL] confirm the Bielefeld insights that the extent of anti-semitism 2009/10 altogether appears somewhat lesser than in 2002" (p. 56). Regular surveys by the Friedrich Ebert Foundation (Decker and Braehler 2012: 27) conclude that 9 percent display a "coherent extreme-right world view" and an equal percentage are classified as "manifest anti-semitic." This places German attitudes in the middle of similar sentiments in other European countries with generally higher anti-Semitic scores in Eastern Europe and lower in the West (for detailed figures see Melzer, 2013). All German surveys trying to discern current anti-Semitisms with items about Jews, regardless of their sophistication, are tainted by what is called *Kommunikationslatenz*. The concept refers to the extreme German conformity pressure to express politically correct opinions as opposed to what the respondent holds as a private, "real" attitude. In short, within the unarticulated "ordinary consciousness," the anti-Semitic sentiments are probably higher than attitude surveys are able to capture.

Nevertheless, conscious of the atrocious past and its negative perception abroad, attitudes toward minorities have shifted over the years. Xenophobia in the twenty-first century no longer singles out only or mainly Jews but has found new targets and rationalizations. An inquiry into the specifics of Germany's inclusion and exclusion provides comparative insights and a better understanding of what new democracies learn and forget in dealing with difference.

Germany has long been a de facto immigration country while de jure rejecting this designation. After World War II approximately twelve million "ethnic Germans" were expelled from Poland, Czechoslovakia, and Russia and absorbed into the bombed-out country without much friction. Labor was imported from Italy since 1955 for help in the reconstruction, followed by a 1961 treaty with Turkey that recruited a larger contingent of Turkish "guest workers" who were later allowed to bring their relatives on the grounds of "family reunification." With the enlargement of the European Union and the free movement of its members for work in other EU states, the influx from East European countries increased markedly in the first decade of 2000, while the number of Turkish residents declined slightly. At the beginning of 2012, the ten leading source countries of the seven million foreigners in Germany, about 9 percent of the total population, were Turkey (1,607,160), Italy (520,159), Poland (468,482), Greece (283,684), Croatia (223,014), Serbia (197,984), Russia (195,310), Austria (175,926), Romania (159,222), and Bosnia-Herzegovina (153,470). To this number must be added the eight million naturalized foreigners, called "persons with immigration backgrounds," including migrants from the Soviet Union and the Balkans, who received their passport upon arrival on the basis of German descent, although many no longer spoke German and were culturally Russians. Jeffrey Alexander (2013: 548n5) reckons that 20 percent of German residents have "foreign backgrounds" if one adds to the nonnationals "immigrants and children of immigrants who have become citizens but may still display marked cultural differences from traditional core groups."

In 2012, 64,500 people applied for asylum in Germany, in 2013 the number rose to 130,000, in 2014 more than 200,000 are expected as a result of the upheavals in the Middle East and Afghanistan, but still below the number of asylum claimants in the 1990s, when in 1992 440,000 refugees from the former Yugoslavia applied for asylum. In the first eight months of 2014 just 1.6 percent were granted asylum status (*Der Spiegel*, 39/2014, 21) and another 26.9 percent were given three year limited refugee recognition or protection from extradition, what is called "Duldungsstatus," merely tolerated for residence, because expulsion to an unstable home country would cause undue hardship or threats to safety; the rest of the applicants saw their requests rejected because they could not prove "asylum-relevant persecution" or fell into the jurisdiction of another EU country where they first arrived. These were mostly people from the former Yugoslavia, particularly from Serbia, Macedonia, and Bosnia-Herzegovina, asserting that they had no option but to leave. While Germany attracted few foreign work seekers in 2008, the booming German economy and the South European debt crisis to the delight of business brought in 300,000 foreign employees, mainly from Poland and other EU Mediterranean areas who can freely choose their country of work. Business spokespersons admonished the public that such an influx of needed skills can be maintained only if Germany develops a "living culture of welcome" ("gelebte Willkommenskultur," *Focus Magazine*, May 21, 2012, p. 24). How you infuse a society that is suspicious of and distant to any foreigners, whether skilled or unskilled, with a spirit of hospitality is left unsaid. All legalized foreigners and asylum claimants are allowed to work and can claim the same social assistance that German citizens are entitled to. Among recognized refugee claimants only family reunification needs special permission.

As long as the number of refugees claiming asylum in Germany is relatively small, the liberal political elite pays tribute to the country's human rights obligations as well as its economic imperatives. In 2013, President Joachim Gauck pronounced, "We need open doors for the persecuted, and not only due to our constitution and our history but also for economic reasons." Gauck encourages a "new welcoming culture." Because immigrants "can help us to keep the living standards" from today for the next generation, "they should be greeted by the people with open hearts or at least be accepted gladly" (www.thelocal.de/society /20130116-47351.html).

Judging by surveys during the past decade, the majority of Germans seem to heed these calls. While many still display social distance to foreigners, a new trend of lesser concern with immigration has emerged. While hearts may not have softened toward gestures of welcome, the previous anxiety about all foreigners as a threat is no longer visible either. Animosity toward foreigners generally has now narrowed to specific groups, particularly against Muslims. So-called incompatible religion has replaced race and ethnicity as the main rallying cry of xenophobes. Race and biology as a rationalization for differential rights and treatment of people has long given way to explanation of progressive and backward cultures as desirable neighbors. Resentment of immigrants is now mainly directed against abuse of hospitality.

However, unlike developing countries with a relatively young population and a high unemployment rate, Germany needs immigrants for demographic reasons. With a birth rate of 1.4 below the replacement level of 2.1 and a declining work force by retirees with longer life spans, social benefits are at risk, like in other rapidly aging industrial states. The Berlin demographer Reiner Klingholz ("Ausländer her," *Spiegel*, August 30, 2010) reckons that the German working population will shrink by 30 percent during the coming years and that the depopulating country needs not only an immigration policy but an actual settlement policy. Either people must work longer or they must be replaced by newcomers from abroad or from the countryside, as in China, India, and Africa, or pensions and social grants have to be cut, or taxes will have to be increased. The least painful response to the demographic dilemma is the admittance of skilled immigrants, provided a country can attract them in a competitive global market. Xenophobia amounts to a disadvantage in this competition. The difficulty of acquiring language fluency and a perception of German society as relatively closed to the newcomer persist as concerns not fully offset by Germany's sterling economic performance with high-quality industrial and professional features.

As is generally the case everywhere else, the higher people rank in the educational and professional hierarchy, the more open they are toward "the other." But even among the low-status senior citizens—the postwar generation in Germany—xenophobic attitudes have softened, asserts one survey (Rippl 2008). Yet another poll by the Friedrich Ebert Foundation (Decker and Braehler 2012) comes to the conclusion that right-wing views are found in "worrisome amounts within mainstream society, be it eastern or western Germany, men or women, young or old, members of democratic parties, or churchgoers" (thelocal.de /national/20101013-30455.html). In this survey a third agreed with the statement that "foreigners come to abuse the welfare state" and "one should send foreigners back home," if Germany is to avoid the danger of being "overrun." Another trend analysis (Diehl and Tucci 2011) concludes, "In 1999, about a third of all German citizens without migration background was strongly concerned about immigration; ten years later this figure has gone down to a quarter. In contrast, the percentage of persons who are not concerned about immigration has increased from 16 to 32 percent between 1999 and 2009." Most experts agree that xenophobia in Germany has declined in recent years. The study just cited calculates that the number of German respondents with ultraxenophobic attitudes has fallen from 9 percent to 4 percent in West Germany with a similar decrease from 15 percent in East Germany. Perceptive outside observers, like the Canadian correspondent Doug Saunders (G&M, June 8, 2013), go further and write about "a seismic change in public attitudes during the past decade, as ordinary Germans and their leaders have come to recognize Slavic and Turkish immigrants and their offspring as authentic Germans." According to our research, this may amount to an exaggeration. It will take some time before the persons with *Immigrationshintergrund* are indeed recognized as authentic Germans. Attitudes have changed opportunistically in Germany toward recruiting skilled immigrants but barring their unskilled family members as a burden on taxpayers.

Forty percent of Germans are also now satisfied with their government's immigration and integration policies. In 2000, the traditional German self-concept of a nation by ancestry was replaced with the birthplace principle. Since then children of migrants in Germany automatically become citizens or can choose between the old and new citizenship at age of maturity, provided some other requirements are met, such as eight years of residency. Allowing dual citizenship instead of choosing one between the ages of 18 and 23 has also been implemented.

In short, while these trends signify a welcome development, it still leaves a group of active and potentially hostile xenophobes. There are still areas in East Germany and East Berlin where foreign-looking persons had better not venture because they risk being attacked by neo-Nazi skinheads. The federal police still receive numerous complaints from dark visitors being singled out for control on trains and in airports, while those with European ancestry are being ignored. Nationality by descent is still anchored in the German self-conception. A foreign-looking person, born in Germany and without an accent, will still be asked, "Where did you come from?" If the answer is Hamburg or Frankfurt, the next question will be, "I mean, where did you *originally* come from?" The German passport and self-professed identity as German still do not make the Turk or Indian a "real" German. This phenomenon of constructing a "we" as the normal and dominant as opposed to the different and problematic other is referred to as *Alltagsrassismus* (everyday racism). The well-entrenched cognitive identity map should caution against the shallow assumption that cultural adaptation, language proficiency, and individual behavior automatically determine acceptance.

The Case of Roma/Sinti

What the origin of most of the Balkan applicants hides is their Roma ethnicity, which subjects them to varied forms of discrimination and prejudice, whether in their home country or in Germany. Even Canada introduced visa restrictions for certain East European countries when it was discovered that most visitors from the area were Romas. The situation of Roma and Sinti (Sinti is the clan name for the one-third of Romani migrants from Northern India who entered German-speaking areas and converted to Christianity in the fifteenth century) can best highlight what has changed and what has remained the same in Germany. The treatment of these migrants also illustrates the dilemmas of a modern immigration policy in a developed welfare state.

In October 2012, the chancellor Angela Merkel in a somber ceremony in the "Tiergarten" near the German parliament finally dedicated an understated, tasteful memorial (a circular pool with a plinth for a fresh flower each day) to the estimated 220,000 to 500,000 "gypsy" victims killed by the Nazis as inferior beings *(Untermenschen)* seven decades ago. At the same time, her interior minister, H. P. Friedrich from the conservative Bavarian Christian Social Union (CSU) sister party, inveighed against "increasing abuse of asylum from countries in the Balkans" and proposed "reduced cash benefits" as well as curtailing the right of appeal for those applicants. An estimated 250,000 Roma and Sinti live in Germany, most with Duldungstatus but without citizenship.

Since a 2009 bilateral agreement, residents from Serbia/Macedonia as prospective EU members can enter the European Union without a visa, but they are not allowed to work. As unemployed visitors, they are not allowed to stay either. Therefore most claim asylum and get deported when the appeal process is exhausted. During this period of several months they receive free housing and €350 a month of living assistance, which is double the €160 a month that a schoolteacher earns in Serbia. For those Roma, Germany constitutes the promised land, similar to South Africa for the African migrants from up north. At home in the slums of Shutka and Skopje or Belgrade, just as in the informal settlements of Luanda, Lagos, or Harare, the hopelessness and poverty are much worse in their makeshift shelters. Moreover, Roma are actively harassed and discriminated in the Balkans, where they form up to 10 percent of the population in Bulgaria and Romania. The interior minister echoes the sentiment of most Germans, who accuse the group of "welfare fraud" at local taxpayers' expense. In 1999, a social-democratic government in North Rhine–Westfalia, shy of deportation, even offered return passages and reintegration assistance of DM400 for each Roma for six months as an incentive for return. In 2010, the interior minister of the city-state Berlin, Ehrhart Koerting, described the "Roma problem" with what could have been lifted from an South African speech: "The current problems arise from more recent arrivals from the European Union member states Romania and Bulgaria. [Roma] are known to work 'under the table' at building sites or in restaurants, clean car windshields at traffic lights, busk on public transport or send their children out to beg" *(Der Spiegel*, September 20, 2010).

Long before the Nazi persecution, Roma and Sinti became one of the most severely discriminated minorities. The initial protection by a regional aristocratic ruler was reversed for the outcasts everywhere, after a Brandenburg count banned them from his land. Any non-Sinti could kill or brand a gypsy in most German provinces during the eighteenth and nineteenth centuries. The outgroup became the most criminalized minority, because of their lifestyle as wandering scrap collectors and traders. Tolerated only in segregated places outside German towns and specially controlled by local authorities, the *Zigeunergeschmeiss* (gypsy scum) morphed into a dehumanized menace in the German collective consciousness. In 1958, a German court stated that the deportation to the concentration camps had been a preemptive criminal measure and not a persecution for racial reasons. (As a child, I remember my mother insisting that all the doors be securely locked whenever gypsies were reported to be in our village). Since 1980 German Roma camp survivors became eligible to receive €3,000 as compensation, but most were too disorganized or illiterate to claim it. In 1997 the government formally recognized Roma as a national minority, but the Central Council of Roma opposed special recognition on the grounds that it would only encourage segregation and discrimination. So the marginalization and exclusion of a small unthreatening minority continues as it has been during the past four hundred years, despite the rhetoric of redemption by political leaders.

Muslims as Enemies

Two differences characterize German immigration, compared with the United States and with other West European countries. In the United States, the majority of Latinos are Christians; they often attend the same Catholic, Baptist, and Pentecostal congregations as other Americans and can even bank on some empathy of their fellow Republican religionists. The majority of immigrants in Germany are Muslims and considered more unassimilable and alien, because of their alleged visible religious and cultural differences. Second, the majority of German Muslim immigrants originate from more secular Turkey, different from North African and other Arab immigrants. Above all, they are not colonial migrants that claim rights in the former colonial empire. Unlike the Muslims from the Maghreb in France or Pakistani or Bangladeshi migrants in Britain, Turkish "guestworkers" entered their new host country not as refugees from postcolonial upheavals, but on the basis of a contract between two governments, where Germany recruited and sought the new labor as replacement for East German workers, cut off by the Berlin wall.

According to a leading German scholar on xenophobic violence, Wilhelm Heitmeyer (2009), more than 60 percent of the population assumes that Muslims are sympathetic toward terrorism. Two thirds in the West and three quarters in East Germany harbor negative sentiments toward all Muslims. The anxiety about *Überfremdung* (cultural alienation) has increased from 33 in 2001 to 44 percent in 2006; the notion that foreigners enrich cultural life has slipped in similar proportions to a minority position. The statement by former German president Christian Wulff that Islam, like Christianity, was "part of Germany" was heavily criticized by other politicians and is now endorsed by only 22 percent (*The Local*, January 7, 2013), although a few provinces proceeded with recognizing Islamic organizations as official religious bodies. There are even some German universities with departments of Islamic Studies. Yet it will take some time before Islam is recognized as a religion, eligible for state collection of taxes, as are the Lutheran, Catholic, and Jewish faith groups. However, half of Germans believe that there are "too many Muslims in the country," and 58.4 percent want to restrict the constitutionally guaranteed freedom of religion for this group (Decker and Braehler 2012: 86).

What was formerly a prerogative of a right-wing fringe has clearly moved into the center. Islamophobia in the guise of defense of secularism or alleged concern for gender equality, has been elevated to a respectable belief. Aggressive acts of terrorism by a small minority of frequently home-bred jihadists are attributed to an entire religion. Historical religious wars about the defense of Christian Europe are invoked. Jeffrey Alexander (2013: 541) concludes, "For increasing members of the European civil sphere, ancient enemies outside were becoming the new immigrants within." Others feel offended by the perceived marginalization of their own traditional religious symbols. A minaret near the dome of Cologne is said to dilute a sacred heritage in a secular country where fewer than 10 percent are active churchgoers. The more a Christian German *Leitkultur* (dominant or guiding culture) resembles a myth, the more it has to be asserted. In contrast, a telling poster hanging from a Stuttgart theater bore the message "46 nations work together to sustain German culture."

Anti-Islamic sentiment has morphed into a permissible bias. In the name of promoting rights of homosexuals, all Muslims are tarred with the stigma of a sharia-obsessed minority. Yet all surveys (Saunders 2012) show that the overwhelming majority of Muslim immigrants condemn forced marriages, honor killings, or the stoning of women for sexual transgressions. Most Muslim immigrants prefer to live under German or French law rather than sharia law.

Generalized antagonism toward Muslims has also replaced traditional German and French anti-Semitism. In the German mindset, Israel is now celebrated as a bastion of democratic civilization against Arab backwardness. While the allied reeducation programs relatively successfully prevented a resurgence of anti-Semitism in the postwar generation, it failed to make the connections with "othering" of other out-groups. The few dissidents on the silent German left, like Günter Grass, are declared "off balance" and violating a "special historical relationship" when questioning Israeli policies on the Palestinians. Criticizing Israel is taboo among German critical intellectuals.

There is no better evidence than the popular reception of Thilo Sarrazin's (2010) book, *Deutschland schafft sich ab* (*Germany Abolishes Itself*) which sold more than a million hard copies. The respectable social democrat, banker, and Berlin finance minister assumes a genetic basis of intelligence and writes about the "German-Jewish origin of intelligence." Among many statistics about the unsustainable welfare payments to nonproductive immigrants, Sarrazin deplores the undermining of German standards by the more fertile Muslim sections with lower intelligence. Even the conservative *Frankfurter Allgemeine Zeitung* called his book an "anti-Muslim dossier based on genetics." The political establishment ostracized Sarrazin, and he lost his position on the board of the central bank, but a large section of the general public agreed with his racist views.

Thilo Sarrazin has joined a string of writers in Europe and North America who warn against the slow subversive infiltration of Europe and North America by jihadists. A "jihad is quietly coming to America" (Pamela Cellar), a "bloodthirsty faith" (Mark Steyn) with "an intense hostility to the West" (Daniel Pipes), with a religious "duty to Islamicise the values of the surrounding culture" (Melanie Philips) which will eventually transform Europe into EURABIA, as a result of a higher birthrate. The Norwegian mass killer Anders Behring Breivik relied on these sources for his 1,518-page dense delusional manifesto. The comprehensive analysis by Doug Saunders (2012), *The Myth of the Muslim Tide: Do Immigrants Threaten the West?* convincingly debunks EURABIA fantasies on the basis of numerous opinion surveys among Muslim immigrants in different countries. They all show that Huntington's "clash of civilizations" does not take place among the overwhelming majority of Muslims in the West; they are well integrated and have adopted the values of their country of residence, particularly in the second generation in North America, as Chapter 7 on Canada further elaborates.

Saunders also shows narrowing fertility rates. Turks in Germany had on average 4.4 children each in 1970. In 2011 this had dropped to 2.2. By 2030 "Muslim and non-Muslim birth rates will be statistically identical in Germany, Greece, Spain and Denmark, and within half a child of one another in Belgium, France, Italy and Sweden." Several Muslim countries experienced their own fertility revolution, and there is no evidence that "Islamic belief leads to higher birthrates." Where Muslim birthrates are high, it is a result of the low status and sequestration of women in the home, not of religion. Saunders mentions Iran, where the fertility rate stood at seven children per family in the mid-1980s but by 2010 had precipitously fallen to 1.7 children, a lower rate than in Britain or France.

However, an integration deficit exists for German Muslims in the areas of employment, education, and naturalization. It has nothing to do with religion. Muslim applicants for jobs have lower success rates, partly as a result of lower educational levels and partly as a result of discrimination. The education shortfall in Europe markedly contrasts with a Muslim advance in the United States. Forty percent of adult Muslims in the United States, according to Saunders, have earned a college or equivalent degree, "making them the second most educated religious group after Jews (61%), and far ahead of average Americans (29%)." While in Canada more than half of foreign-born immigrants have university or college degrees, this figure is less than 20 percent in Germany, which ranks among the lowest six out of thirty Organisation for Economic Co-operation and Development (OECD) countries. The low social mobility of German migrants and Muslims in particular can be explained by two factors: rural parental origin and the German educational system, which "streams" children into different tracks at an early age. Twice as many Turkish children as Germans end up at age 10 at the lowest Hauptschule level, and only 13 percent attend a gymnasium as a prerequisite for university education. Their frequently illiterate parents were recruited from the most backward rural areas (Anatolia), since the German-Turkish labor contract explicitly forbade the export of skilled labor from the cities. The difficult adjustment to a foreign urban working environment by peasants—in contrast to the self-selected educated migrants in North America— explains the differential educational achievements.

The insecure migrants in a bewildering German environment initially tended to isolate themselves in Turkish enclaves offering mutual support. This trapped them into further disadvantage by minimizing contact with the locals and no need to learn German. Children's educational achievements are shaped by the aspirations of parents, which is high among Russian but low among Turkish migrants. Given the generalized hostility toward Islam, such self-exclusion in "parallel societies" is understandable. Now Turks are blamed for making little effort to integrate, without the accusers realizing their own complicity in the process, that their very social distance to the foreigners and lack of an outreach to the newcomers caused the deplored "parallel societies." Nevertheless, there are increasing public role models of soccer stars, leading politicians, and other professionals of Turkish descent who demonstrate the opportunities after exiting the ghetto of communal isolation.

Capitalist versus Communist Xenophobia

German xenophobia since World War II varies substantially according to region. Animosity toward foreigners was always much higher in East Germany than in West Germany, although comparatively far fewer foreigners lived among the seventeen million East Germans than in the western part. Recent representative surveys (Decker et al. 2012) found that hostility toward foreigners declined slightly from 23.7 percent in 2002 to 21.7 percent in 2012 in West Germany but increased from 30.2 percent to 38.7 percent in former East Germany. Attacks by skinheads on different-looking people, spray-painting of xenophobic slogans, and fire bombings of hostels for asylum seekers embarrassed even the Honecker regime that generously hosted some Asian and African political refugees. The authorities in the GDR never allowed those incidents to be publicized. Even twenty years after reunification, this higher intolerance toward foreigners and in particular Muslims in the former GDR has not declined. Fifty-eight percent say that "religious practice for Muslims in Germany should be seriously limited" in West Germany, but 75.7 percent of East German residents endorse this statement (Decker and Braehler 2012). What are the reasons for this disparity, after two decades of convergence? Why would a tightly controlled communist state consistently show higher levels of xenophobia than its capitalist counterpart?

Certainly capitalism could not be blamed for intentionally splitting the working class into insiders and outsiders. Since there was no capitalist system in East Germany, xenophobia cannot be reduced to its contradictions, which furnished developed countries with an industrial reserve army of labor from the colonies, as a classical Marxist theory of xenophobia asserts. A more convincing answer to the first question points to the higher unemployment rate in former East German areas. Many younger people, particularly young women, moved to the West and left behind "losers" without ambition but full of resentment about their dismal prospects of advancement in a depopulating region. They form the reservoir for recruits in the neo-Nazi scene or nostalgically romanticize the communist nanny state that collapsed when it was abandoned by its Soviet protector in 1989. German social scientists have labeled the left-behind underclass the new "precariat." Erosion of regular employment opportunities at the bottom of the social scale in East Germany created widespread "precarity." Different from Marx's *Lumpenproletariat*, precarious workers may include even well-educated persons, unable to cope with marginalization but reacting with intense resentment toward foreigners.

Another answer mentions the lack of exposure to foreigners in the closed communist system, where people could not travel outside the Eastern bloc and at most met only a few Vietnamese or Cuban "guestworkers" at home. They were derogatively called "Fijeans," the equivalent of the *amakwerekwere* in South Africa. Dresden was the only major city in East Germany where popular West German television could not be received that partially explains the concentration of nationalist fervor in this location. The thesis further elaborates that inhabitants of East Germany were more frustrated with their living conditions and felt more powerless in the communist system than their freer Western counterparts. Therefore they selected ready scapegoats in the form of strangers in line with the explanations of xenophobia elsewhere. Yet the high level of hostility toward *Ausländer* continued after reunification when the frustrations from being "locked in" and regimented had disappeared. Another theory blames a confused identity for the higher East German aversion toward foreigners: "After 45 years of living under a separate political and economic system, the East Germans have been undergoing an identity crisis" (Fireside 2002: 474).

A more persuasive theory holds political education responsible for the difference. Such antiracist political education was not practiced in East Germany, which took for granted that it had overcome fascist predilections by definition. A "socialist" state, it was argued, was immune to fascist tendencies, which were seen as a product of capitalism. No soul-searching about the Holocaust or German responsibility for World War II took place in East Germany. The GDR population was forgiven by decree. Anetta Kahane (Haaretz October 3, 2007), the head of a civic organization against right-wing violence, expresses this amnesia well: "As far as the government is concerned, all East German citizens were victims, a working class abducted by a fascist leadership. Overnight they all became anti-fascist, anti-racist and filled with fraternal comradeship. The whole debate about guilt in the West didn't take place in the East. We see the results to-day in the rise of the radical right wing there." Likewise, in the former Yugoslavia, Tito suppressed any debate about the mutual wartime atrocities committed by Serbs and Croats with the slogan "Brotherhood and Unity!" The ethnic hostility and dissolution of the country after Tito's death can be directly traced to this failure to reconcile with history.

In contrast, the massive reeducation programs introduced by the three Western allies in their areas did sensitize the new generation to the racist crimes of the past. Without this successful reeducation and a lively democratic atmosphere of critical discourse, Western xenophobia could be as high as in the East. We maintain that this educational reorientation impacted decisively on the political consciousness of a new generation. In this reeducation process toward liberal individualism and critical thinking, anything that resembled Nazi practices of the past—from communal singing to marching in groups—was frowned upon. Even speech patterns and philosophical concepts that were used by one-time Nazi sympathizers, such as Heidegger, became suspect, as Adorno explained in his 1964 book *Jargon der Eigentlichkeit* (Jargon of Essentialism). An autonomous critique of state dogma was suppressed in the GDR in favor of indoctrination and conformity. In the open society of the West, ideological competition flourished and nobody could claim a monopoly of truth. It instilled a high degree of vigilance toward past totalitarian tendencies. When neo-Nazi xenophobes reared their heads publicly, they could expect an equal militant response from a broad center-left. This collective resistance toward a stifling state power reemerged in the GDR only in the large church-led street demonstrations of 1989 after it had been effectively silenced by the combined Soviet and Stasi might after suppressing the East German workers' uprising of 1953.

The major lesson to be drawn from the divergent xenophobia phenomenon in Germany points to critical political education as an antidote. South Africa at least had its Truth and Reconciliation Commission (TRC). However, the TRC remained a limited onetime affair rather than an ongoing process of interpreting a past that still haunts the present as happened in Germany.

Conclusion

Although most European countries need immigrants for demographic reasons, the notion prevails that "the boat is full." Collective consciousness cultivates the vision of a national home that is diluted by the influx of outsiders. The perception is reinforced by a predominantly Muslim immigration which manifests itself visibly in separate religious practices and dress codes, harking back to a European history of Christian-Muslim conflict, in contrast to South Africa. In traditional immigration countries, such as the United States, Canada, or Australia, all residents are immigrants with the exception of the minority "First Nations." The European idea of exclusive historical entitlement to home and land of a homogeneous kind is weak among the erstwhile immigrants of diverse origin. That allows for easier integration of newcomers in North America. Demonized Catholics and Jews were once considered undermining nation building in the United States, just as Muslims are now in Europe. Catholic Irish immigrants from "Britain's first colony" (Marx) were generally viewed as "Blacks," together with Catholic South Europeans. It remains to be seen whether Muslims in Europe will be integrated as smoothly.

Further Reading. On the wider European situation of migrancy and xenophobia, Roger M. Smith's edited volume *Citizenship, Borders and Human Needs* (Philadelphia: University of Pennsylvania Press, 2011) gives an overview of the discourse in mainly European contexts. The same is true for Laura Morales and Marco Giugni's edited *Social Capital, Political Participation and Migration in Europe: Making Multicultural Democracy Work?* (Palgrave, 2011). The edited book by Catarina Kinnvall and Paul Nesbitt Larking, *The Political Psychology of Globalisation*, focuses on Muslim integration in Western Europe but also in Canada. Klaus Michael Bogdal, *Europa erfindet die Zigeuner*, does the same with Roma/Sinti. Standing out among the more recent books is Thomas Faist, Margaret Fauser, and Eveline Reisenauer of Bielefeld University, *Transnational Migration* (2013); Paul Scheffer's "Immigrant Nations" (2013), which focuses on the effects of mass immigration in both Western Europe and North America; James Hamshire's "The Politics of Immigration" (2013), which reflects on the conflicting paradoxes for immigration policymaking in liberal states; and Massimo Livi Bacci's "A Short History of Migration" (2012), which argues the positive contribution of migration out of Africa for economic development throughout the millennia. We omit the numerous volumes on Latino and Asian immigration to the United States.

7

Multicultural Canada
as an Alternative?

anada is considered an exception to the worldwide reservations and hostility toward culturally different migrants. While many of the reasons for this exceptionalism lie in the specific history and political calculations of past and current power holders, certain aspects of Canada's immigration policy deserve to be probed seriously for consideration in South Africa.

After all, Canada and South Africa share important similarities and differences: both experienced European colonialism; as settler societies they had to transcend racism toward indigenes and unfamiliar newcomers; they both are still ethnically divided societies with fragile state cohesion; and they both rely heavily on mineral resources and face similar problems from extractive industries in a global economic crisis. Furthermore, the substantial exit of skills from South Africa has greatly disadvantaged the new democracy, while Canada massively benefits from the global influx of professionals. Despite double the proportional intake of annual newcomers in Canada (0.8 percent), compared with that of other immigration societies like the United States and Australia (0.4 percent), the country has not encountered a xenophobic backlash, its own racist legacy notwithstanding. While the income levels and wealth inequality in South Africa and Canada differ widely, a prudent South African immigration policy could assist the emerging "developmental state" and decrease the asymmetry between loss and benefit from migration.

There are clear similarities of racism in the history of Canada and South Africa. Canadians have no reason to be smug about their record of racial discrimination. As Van Zyl Slabbert pointed out in a 2008 convocation address in Vancouver, Canadian early settlers are likely to have behaved similarly as their

South African counterparts, had they found themselves confronted with the same conditions.

Just as in apartheid South Africa, Canada adhered to a whites–only immigration policy until 1967. An ingenious regulation did not spell this out but enforced it in practice. Immigrants had to arrive directly from their country of origin without stopping in a third country on the way. "It was an open secret," writes Ali Kazimi in his study on the defining "Komagata Maru" event (*Literary Review of Canada* [LRC], September 2012, p. 31), that "this regulation was aimed specifically at South Asians, and was the most effective exclusionary tool designed by Canada," since no such transportation from Asia existed at the time. In the context of World War II, Japanese Canadian citizens on the West Coast (but not Germans) were deported to the interior and their property confiscated. Migrants of Chinese descent were subjected to a special "head tax" as a deterrent, although they built the trans-Canada railway. Stereotypes about the "yellow peril" have disappeared only during the 1970s.

According to the 2011 voluntary National Household Survey, 20.6 percent of the Canadian population is foreign born. Since 63 percent of all immigrants opt to settle in Toronto, Vancouver, or Montreal, the percentage of "foreigners" is much higher in these metropolitan areas. Of the total Canadian population, 19.1 percent identify themselves as "visible minorities," a unique Canadian term that means "people of color," assuming that "white" is not a color, but the norm. Yet in Toronto and Vancouver more than half of the residents belong to visible minorities, which also includes the 4.3 percent who identify themselves as aboriginal. While before 1971 more than 75 percent of new immigrants originated from Europe, nowadays almost two thirds arrive from Asia, including the Middle East, China, and India. Religious affiliations have also changed accordingly. The percentage of Christians has shrunk to 67 percent; Muslims constitute 3.2 percent, Hindus 1.5 percent, Sikhs 1.4 percent, Buddhists 1.1 percent, and Jews 1.0 percent. In contrast to trends in the United States, the percentage of "No Religion" has increased to 24 percent from 7.4 percent in 1981. In Metro Vancouver, 41 percent of residents indicate that they have no religion. The Canadian secularization rate is probably much higher when one considers the "cultural Catholicism" (Raymond Lemieux) of Quebeckers who no longer practice religion but hold on to their historical identity. This cosmopolitan mix of people from all over the world living side by side with each other has evolved without any major interethnic conflict or sectarian strife during the past five decades. Have a postnational state and multicultural society emerged that could serve as a model elsewhere?

It would be wrong to assume that no ethnic discrimination exists. Despite a higher percentage of working-age immigrants (25 to 64 years old) having a postsecondary education compared with Canadian-born employees (53 versus 61 percent), their job opportunities and earnings lag behind. This is all the more so for immigrant women with comparable credentials. Economists estimate the average wage differential between Canadian-born and immigrant male workers with equal qualifications to be 15 percent during their first five years before they catch up. Skills of professional immigrants are often underutilized, because their foreign credentials are not recognized, which amounts to what has been labeled a "brain waste." For the minority of newcomers who enter without English or French language proficiency, the conclusion of a study about labor market integration applies: "They risk entering a perilous cycle in which poverty, a lack of job opportunities, concentration in low-income neighbourhoods, discrimination and racism lead to long-term exclusion conditions, even for the next generation" (Goupil 2004). This describes the German and South African situation.

Yet even when Canadian job applicants have identical education, skills, and work histories with the same Canadian experience, hiring managers, just as in Paris or Berlin, frequently bypass résumés with foreign-sounding names. This has been proven in an empirical study aptly titled "Why Do Some Employers Prefer to Interview Matthew and Not Samir?" (Philip Oreopoulos and Diane Dechief, Metropolis BC 2011). The researchers had sent out 7,000 hypothetical curricula vitae (CVs) to companies that had advertised openings in several professional fields in Toronto, Vancouver, and Montreal. The study concluded that applicants with English-sounding names were 35 to 40 percent more likely to be interviewed than those with Chinese-, Indian-, or Greek-sounding names. The bias of recruiters against ethnic-sounding names was frequently justified by the assumption that they must be immigrants with lower social skills. The authors recommend video-résumés or masking the applicant's name as the alternative for minimizing discrimination.

Despite this record, we maintain that Canada now manages the integration of newcomers better than other immigration countries, particularly South Africa. We also imply that Canada's much-maligned and equally admired multicultural policy so far can be considered a largely unrecognized success story. This occurred not because of shrewd government intervention to integrate immigrants but because Canadian structural diversity made recognition of divergent identities the most feasible option to avoid conflict.

In South Africa, "culture" was discredited when used as a divide-and-rule policy during apartheid, and the main fault lines of the symbolic order are rooted not in cultural differences but in material inequality. To be sure, the ethnocultural differences between population groups have not vanished and need to be accommodated for those wishing to retain linguistic or cultural heritage. However, this diversity is not only practiced without much friction but also recognized constitutionally with references to cultural councils. What South Africans can learn from Canadian multiculturalism is not recognition of difference, which is a given and lived experience. In South Africa, cultural retention is practiced in the daily use of different home languages, the mutual tolerance of different religions, or even the acceptance of the president's polygamy or a parallel system of customary law. There is no pressure to assimilate into a monocultural regiment of customs and traditions, as exists in Europe or once prevailed in colonial Canada when native children were forced into residential church schools. South Africa could benefit from the symbolic equality that multiculturalism accords to all traditions. In the continuing everyday colonial hierarchy, such equality is still skewed; biases toward "backward groups" are found everywhere, and stereotypes about foreigners abound.

Despite the peaceful coexistence of diverse groups, what our South African research on xenophobia revealed is a deficit in respecting the identity of foreigners, of including them in the horizon of belonging, of valorizing rather than denigrating their potential contributions. Above all, as long as many feel handicapped by an insufficient knowledge of the market language, English, their low self-concept causes resentment and envy of the other. As long as a defunct school system disadvantages the majority, minorities of better-off "outsiders," whether foreigners, local Indians, or Coloureds of a similar discriminated past, are resented and not included in the perception of the in-group.

The Canadian example, on the other hand, places great emphasis on an equally resourced public school system. Schools with a high percentage of immigrant children employ teachers trained in the discipline of teaching English as a second language. It has become a status symbol for aspiring parents to send their children to French immersion schools or Mandarin courses, which are oversubscribed and can be accessed only by lottery. The very mixture of children from many countries in one classroom teaches mutual respect. In addition to schools having a diverse teaching staff, cultural competence is instilled by daily practice through the unspoken culture of respect for difference. In any ethnically divided society, particularly South Africa, at least the teaching staff could be integrated. Yet teachers from other communities, both local and foreign, who could function as models for counterstereotypes hardly exist in township schools. Why this occurs is unclear, since there are hundreds of unemployed highly qualified African foreign teachers who could be enlisted.

During 2011 German, French, and British political leaders declared their experiment with multiculturalism a "failure." Other European countries, such as Holland or Denmark, had abandoned "permissive diversity" long ago under the pressure of ever-more-powerful xenophobic tendencies. Italy deported Roma-speaking travelers, EU citizens entitled to freedom of movement like the rest, in clear violation of statutory requirements. France considered revoking the Shengen treaty of open EU borders when too many refugees from the Arab uprising, equipped with train tickets by Italy, turned up in France (for a general overview, see Lentin and Titley 2011).

In contrast, Canada, and to a limited extent Australia (Moran 2011), is the last Western democracy where multiculturalism remains official policy. This is all the more surprising since Canada is governed by a Conservative Party that celebrates the British monarchy anew and remilitarizes as a proud member of the Western empire instead of pursuing its traditional peacemaking role as a mediating middle-power. Does Canada defy the global trends of the resurgence of ethnic nationalism or merely lag behind European assertions of national identity? Why is there little Canadian concern about dual loyalties, national cohesion, or "parallel societies"? The central thesis of this analysis maintains that the deep historical divisions within Canada itself risk destabilizing conflict by imposing ethnic hegemony but make multiculturalism the most feasible reflection of a social reality, regardless of the ideological preference of power holders.

Save some minor provincial factions in Quebec and rural Alberta, Canada is one of the few countries without a national anti-immigrant party, although the overtly xenophobic segment is estimated to be about 15 percent. Yet Canada is the only country where a slight majority of citizens welcomes immigrants as an asset rather than a liability (Adams 2007). The newcomers are also encouraged to participate in public life. All three federal parties display "visible minority" members prominently in their parliamentary caucus. In TV broadcasts the ruling party ensures that turbaned Sikhs or sari-clad Hindu women always sit behind the prime minister. In 2011, 17 percent of Toronto-area federal MPs belonged to visible minorities, and in the provincial legislature they constituted 26 percent of the same area. Thirteen percent of all MPs were foreign born in 2010, still lower than the percentage in the total population but the highest proportion of all Western democracies. Those foreign-born MPs were generally not elected in ridings with predominant members of their own ethnic group but garnered a fair number of voters from other groups under the Canadian first-past-the-post electoral system. There are few states where a South Asian immigrant of barely 20 years in the country (Uijal Dosanjh) can become the premier of a major province. Even more surprising was the politically astute gesture by the liberal Chrétien government in appointing two visible minority women (Adrienne Clarkson and Michaelle Jean) in succession as governors general, the queen's representatives in Canada. Only at the municipal level on city councils, "visible minority representation is strangely lacking" and "seems to be forever stuck" (Marcus Gee, G&M, November 8, 2011, p. A13) at about 7 percent. Toronto's proud motto "Diversity is our strength" is not evident in its forty-five city councilors, of whom only five are visible minorities. Canadian local politics is not organized along party lines, and without the backing of a major party, candidates are doomed when they rely only on connections in their own microcommunities. On the other hand, there are some remarkable exceptions, such as the popular Calgary mayor Naheed Nenshi, who became the country's first big-city Muslim mayor in 2010, or the Vancouver police chief, who is of Chinese origin. All in all, the Canadian civil service can point to a fair representation of "ethnics" under equity legislation, covering also aboriginals, women, and persons with disabilities.

Currently Canada admits approximately 270,000 immigrants per year, which amounts to 0.8 percent of the total population. This has been a steadily increasing figure during the past decade, regardless of the government in power. Moreover, the newcomers originate from literally all countries of the earth, with more than 70 percent currently arriving from Asia. One scholar (Vertovec 2007) has labeled this mixing "super-diversity." Other British analysts (Stuart Hall 1999: 188) characterized as "multicultural drift" the appearance of visibly different people in all social spheres of city life, where they are no longer perceived as an "alien wedge." Similarly, Paul Gilroy (2005) points to convivial difference as ordinary rather than strange in everyday life, as the earlier classical 1965 study of John Porter had portrayed Canadian society, where ethnic minorities are marginalized in a "vertical mosaic," the title of his seminal book. To all intents and purposes, the phenotype of Canada's population in the major cities has now changed from white to a multicolored checkerboard. This is even more evident at city universities, where the Canadian-born second generation dominates and where white faces constitute a minority at the computer desks. Of thirty OECD countries, Canada leads with more than 50 percent of its immigrants having university or college degrees. In a similar vein, the third-generation offspring of Asian immigrants are visibly overrepresented at music recitals and ballet performances, under the proud observation of highly motivated parents. Once admitted and allocated to a particular province, new immigrants are free to move and generally prefer metro areas. To all intents and purposes, this cultural mix in one of the most heterogeneous countries functions well; friction is minimal and overshadowed by friendly cooperation whether in schools, universities, or workplaces, occasional instances of racism notwithstanding. Frustrated hockey fans, not polarized ethnic groups or alienated ghetto dwellers, riot in Vancouver.

Forced ethnic ghettoes do not exist in Canada. Certain ethnic groups always congregated in certain city areas, but this overconcentration was voluntary, and people oscillate between low cost and upper class areas. The bustling Chinatowns are a far cry from Bradford in the United Kingdom, postal code area 2060 in Antwerp, or Kreuzberg in Berlin. Will Kymlicka (2010: 14) rightly states, "Canada's ethnic neighborhoods have virtually nothing in common with banlieus of Paris." Perhaps the East Hastings district in downtown Vancouver resembles a ghetto, but it is an enclave of addiction and impoverishment in which, sadly, predominantly aboriginals are trapped. A similar situation exists in some of Toronto's housing estates of mainly Caribbean residents. Certainly, Canada does not share the anxiety of Europeans about "parallel societies" in which people live isolated from the mainstream in their own self-sufficient and institutionally complete worlds.

In short, genuine indifference rather than rage about difference characterizes an atomized population in which the visible minorities are often envied, because of their sense of belonging through community cohesion and achievements. One of the clearest indicators of successful integration is the increasing ratio of cross-cultural marriages and cohabitations, although occasionally a source of severe conflict with tradition-oriented parents (for a recent analysis, mainly focused on the United States, see Bystydzienski 2011). Various surveys have found that more than 90 percent of immigrants and Canadian-born inhabitants alike endorse the statement that everybody in the country should embrace "Canadian values," particularly in the equal treatment of women. In 2011, the Supreme Court reaffirmed the ban on polygamy, which had been challenged under the guise of religious freedom. Multiculturalism therefore has not fostered a cultural relativism, as its critics charge, that "anything anyone believes—no matter how ridiculous and outrageous it may be—is okay and acceptable in the name of diversity" (Jeffrey Reitz, quoting Uijal Dosanjh disapprovingly, LRC, July/August 2010). The usual mutual collective stereotypes about ethnic groups are alive and well, but particular ethnicities are not blamed as a whole for drug dealing or gangsterism, nor have particular outrageous terrorist acts, such as the 1984 bombing of an Air India jet by Canadian Sikh separatists which resulted in the loss of 350 lives, led to a backlash against multiculturalism as the killing of a Dutch politician by a resident of Moroccan descent did in Holland. Some may well argue that the outcomes would have been different if most of the victims had been white Canadians.

A Canadian consensus exists that immigrants ought not import the conflicts and violence of their country of origin into their new homeland. While maintaining and recognizing minority cultures is widely supported, equal emphasis is placed on immigrants' blending in and adhering to Canadian habits and rules. When the Conservative government disallowed the wearing of the niqab at citizenship ceremonies, the edict was supported by 80 percent of the population. Some cities, such as Quebec's Gatineau, made headlines by issuing condescending guidelines for newcomers, advising not to engage in bribery and avoiding "strong odors emanating from cooking." More to the point, the federal government's citizenship guide stipulates that Canada's "openness and generosity do not extend to retrogressive cultural practices that tolerate spousal abuse, 'honour killings,' female genital mutilation, forced marriage or other gender-based violence." Whether such paternalistic advice infantilizes immigrants, particularly skilled professionals, remains controversial.

How did an Anglo-Saxon settler society achieve this progressive record of accommodation? Given its earlier history of racism and anti-Semitism; antagonism toward Chinese railway workers, subjected to a "head tax"; attempts to fend off a boatload of Sikh immigrants from landing in British Columbia; its internment and dispossession of Canadian citizens of Japanese descent during World War II; and above all, the shameful treatment of the colonized indigenous population, marginalized by invisible boundaries to this day, the logical outcome might well have been more exclusionary social relations. One answer relates to the factual diversity, what the literature (Sears 2010: 192) labels "structural multiculturalism." Long before the Canadian state articulated an official multicultural policy in 1971, three distinct groups with different identities had to be accommodated, and the later policy merely reflected and acknowledged this factual reality.

Canadian Identities and Cultural Traditions

Three historically distinct Canadian groups make up the country's "mosaic": First, aboriginals, including status and nonstatus Indians, Metis and Inuit, constituting about 5 percent of the population; second, the French-speaking Quebecois, constituting about 25 percent; third, English-speakers as well as the growing number of non-English, non-French immigrants, starting with massive waves of Ukrainians and other Eastern European peasants, recruited to settle the inhospitable Prairies at the beginning of the twentieth century. Anglo-conformity pressure proved unsuitable to unite these different segments. If Canada were to become a nation, then another vision besides that of an outpost of the British Empire was needed.

Aboriginals were the first victims of attempted assimilation. Forced into residential, church-run schools to "purify native savages" and mold them as "civilized" Christians, aboriginals were subjected to cultural genocide. Much of the anomie in current native communities (extraordinarily high suicide rates, alcoholism, homelessness) can be traced to an overall dehumanization implemented through the destruction of indigenous cultural tradition. Missionaries complied in this process, often declaring that they acted in the best interests of the students. Potlatches were outlawed and native languages forbidden in schools, just like the treatment of Afrikaans in English South African schools. Natives were considered "trustees" of the state that exercised benevolent tutelage over conquered people. Thirty-four percent of aboriginal children live in single-parents households as opposed to 17 percent in nonaboriginal homes. Forty-eight percent of all children in foster care are aboriginal. About half of Canadian aboriginals, referred to as status Indians, live on reserves, where 60 percent fail to graduate from dysfunctional schools. Like the South African township situation, poor education is only one aspect of general crisis and disintegration with deeper roots. A Canadian Truth and Reconciliation Commission currently collects testimonies about widespread abuses in the residential school system and promises compensation for practices that lasted until the 1980s. It was only then that native communities were officially recognized as "First Nations" with which federal and provincial governments had to engage in negotiations about broken treaties, land rights, and development projects in native areas. These negotiations dragged on to this day and hardly any progress has been reached, despite high-sounding promises. Neither the dismal situations of non-status people in the cities, nor the life of status Indians in impoverished reserves has much improved.

Canadian courts took native grievances more seriously and assisted healing, sometimes even to the protest of native leaders. Such a situation arose with regard to a Supreme Court judgment concerning preferential treatment. Contrasted with the mechanical application of affirmative action in South Africa, a Canadian case testified to a more sophisticated and mature reaction of victims.

In this instance a prominent leader of a First Nations people demanded fair treatment but rejected unfair advantage of an aboriginal police officer in British Columbia (BC) with a nuanced understanding of affirmative action. The Indian grand chief of BC decried the lenient sentence imposed on the native offender, because the judge had mechanically applied a previous Supreme Court ruling. In March 2012, the Supreme Court of Canada had established differential sentencing principles for aboriginals. Distinct treatment of offenders of native origin arose from the landmark Gladue case, after which judges were mandated to consider alternatives to prison for aboriginal offenders. This caused a stir when a British Columbia judge handed a conditional sentence instead of jail to an aboriginal Royal Canadian Mounted Police (RCMP) officer, Benjamin (Monty) Robinson, who had run over and killed a motorcyclist when drunk, fled the scene and tried to mask his crime by drinking more vodka at home before returning to the accident. The BC Indian chief president, Stewart Phillip, argued that the Gladue principle should not be applied automatically, but only in cases where an aboriginal offender has suffered trauma when growing up. The chief, an outspoken advocate of land claims and native rights, received widespread support among the Canadian public in insisting that aboriginal status should not exempt from custody in all circumstances, particularly for an officer of the RCMP who had a higher duty to uphold the law and safeguard public security. He also argued that the indiscriminate differential sentencing on a racial basis discredited the Gladue principle which he supported. The sophisticated reasoning testified to the right balance between universal principles of justice and simultaneous acknowledgment of mitigating circumstances as a result of historical disadvantage. It is difficult to imagine a similar discourse among the victims of apartheid. In fact, open favoritism is practiced toward high-ranking convicted ANC offenders. Three such persons, Tony Yengeni, Shabir Shaik, and Jackie Selebi, sentenced to multiple years in prison for fraud and corruption in office, were paroled on dubious medical grounds after serving only a fraction of their sentence. Nobody in the ANC hierarchy argued that this differential treatment jeopardizes the impartiality of the South African justice system.

In the Canadian public discourse, Quebec is more of a concern than the powerless First Nations. Recognition of the status of Quebec in the Canadian Federation was preceded by an acrimonious debate. Should the Quebecois merely be recognized as a "distinct people," linked to Canada by "sovereignty-association"? A strong separatist movement forced two referenda about sovereignty in Quebec that almost succeeded in the breakup of Canada in 1995. Only 50,000 votes separated the "Yes" from the "No" vote. Finally in November 2006 the Canadian Parliament passed a motion which states "that this House recognizes that the Quebecois form a nation within a united Canada." The state recognition of a multinational Canada together with co-optation of Quebec demands of greater autonomy and resource allocation ensured that the once-dominant secessionist Bloc Quebecois was reduced to four from previously forty-seven seats in the 2011 federal elections. The overwhelming majority of

Quebeckers voted for the social-democratic, federal New Democratic Party under its charismatic leader, the late Jack Layton.

The Quebec political class always distrusted multiculturalism. Preoccupied with the defense of the French language in a sea of English-speakers, it feared that the policy constituted a further federal intrusion into Quebec's internal affairs, reduced the role of Quebecois as a Canadian charter group to the level of another immigrant group, and thereby downgraded their distinct national status. When the 1995 referendum was lost, the then-separatist leader Jacques Parizeau blamed "the ethnics" for the defeat. Although formally committed to a civic nationalism in which all residents enjoy equal rights, the separatists were at heart ethnic nationalists for whom ancestry matters more than legal equality of all residents.

The World War II postwar immigrants were not interested in intra-Canadian squabbles about who constitutes a "nation," French-language rights, provincial equalization payments, or even "cross-cultural understanding." They were mainly concerned with economic integration and the abolition of barriers to advancement. Theirs was an agenda of not political self-determination, but improvement of economic conditions. During the 1980s and 1990s, therefore, government policy shifted from glorifying diversity to ensuring equal opportunities. Celebrating different lifestyles, the emphasis on song, dance, and exotic food gave way to a focus on equal life chances. Antiracism and antidiscrimination programs were enacted and a government-funded Canadian Race Relations Foundation established. Social justice, civic participation, and the duties and responsibilities of citizens, not cultural heritage maintenance, were emphasized in social studies classes. Left-leaning critics argue that "multicultural education policy in Canada is heavily influenced by neoliberal and neoconservative ideology" and that "diversity is being reframed in ways that stress that those groups identified as diverse are themselves the problem" (R. Joshee 2009: 106).

The more numerous right-of-center academic critics of multiculturalism (Neil Bissoondath, Reginald Bibby, particularly among media columnists such as Robert Fulford, Richard Gwyn, Allan Gregg, Michael Bliss, Margaret Wente, and Jack Granatstein), ignore the success with which potentially conflict-ridden intergroup relations were managed. Neither has the policy weakened identification with the Canadian state, endorsed cultural relativism, or encouraged an isolating communalism, but it has elevated diversity to the core of national identity. At the same time, the notion of "reasonable accommodation" within the framework of shared, mutually respectful and tolerant coexistence has diffused friction and improved the sense of belonging of all groups. Yet not all disagreements about religious symbols are solved with the French myth of state neutrality. When the Quebec city of Saguenau wanted to open council meetings with a short prayer, a court had to override objections, including to the display of a stylized crucifix, with the sensible ruling that the state's neutrality does not require "that society be cleansed of all denominational reality, including that which falls within its cultural history." Yet treating religious symbols as histor-ical artifacts should also apply to non-Christians. This was not followed when the National Assembly barred from hearings four Sikh men wearing kirpans or the previous Liberal government limited the right of Muslim women to wear face veils when dealing with government officials. Tolerance of other religious symbols was not evident when the Quebec soccer federation banned the wear-ing of turbans among young players with the disingenuous argument that this is for safety reasons. Since complete religious neutrality can never be realized in any country steeped in a religious tradition everywhere, wearing religious garb by others cannot be restricted.

Managing its image of equal multicultural diversity leads to other bizarre debates. When ethnicity becomes a contentious subject, even the governor of the Bank of Canada has to address a pseudo-problem and apologize. This happened after the bank printed new $100 notes that portrayed a female scientist before a microscope, to which some focus group participants had objected because they identified the scientist's face as profiling a South Asian person. The head of the central bank, Mark Carney, issued a statement: "In the development of our $100 bank note, efforts by the bank-note designers to avoid depicting a specific indi-vidual resulted in an image that appears to represent only one ethnic group. That was not the bank's intention and I apologize to those who were offended. The bank's handling of the issue did not meet the standards Canadians justifiably expect from us." The statement continues with such obvious innate assertions that "our bank notes belong to all Canadians, and the work we do at the bank is for all Canadians." The bank apologized not for alleged ethnic stereotyping ("Asians excelling in science and technology"), but for not depicting enough ethnic images and thereby acknowledging diversity. Other commentators found the whole debate silly, since the depicted person is a Canadian regardless of ethnicity. The bank implicitly yielded to the racist complaint that a "real Cana-dian" should not look like a South Asian. As Victor Wong, the executive director of the Chinese Canadian National Council, commented, "If Carney needs to apologize for anything, it is for being overly sensitive to political correctness run amok" (NP, August 21, 2012). Ethnic peace was not a foregone conclusion and had to be managed to counter racist populism, particularly in Quebec. As the *Globe and Mail* (December 23, 2008) reported, "For nearly two years, Quebec's balance of ethnic relations teetered on the edge of hysteria. As local media out-lets exposed dozens of supposed outrages of accommodation, Mario Dumont, leader of the Action Démocratique du Québec party, launched a vociferous campaign to protect the cultural identity of francophone Quebeckers." The Quebec Bouchard-Taylor Commission in twenty-two televised public hearings in 2007–2008 successfully calmed an atmosphere of tension through reasoned dialogue about what constitutes "reasonable accommodation."

One other result of multicultural compromise is less antipathy toward Mus-lims on the part of the Canadian population as well as greater Muslim satisfac-tion with the Canadian environment than exists in other countries. The pollster

Michael Adams (2007) has documented that Muslims in Canada are more prone than Muslims in other countries to believe that their fellow citizens are not hostile to them. Will Kymlicka (2010) concludes from this and other surveys that "moreover, Muslims have the same level of pride in Canada as other immigrants, and indeed are more likely than native-born Canadians to state that the country is moving in the right direction: 91% of Muslims said this, compared to 71% of the general population." Those attitudes would support the recommendations of other advocates (Banting, Courchene, and Seidle 2007: 681) of multiculturalism "that there is no justification for a U-turn in multiculturalism policies to that underway in some European countries."

In the 1960s, issues of national identity and the need to address inequalities loomed high on the list, alongside the adoption of the Canadian Bill of Rights in 1960. Very significant were the changed immigration regulations that removed and forbade previous discriminatory provisions, limiting the entry of certain ethnic and racial groups. Subsequent concerns about dilution of Canadian identity gave rise to educational programs to work toward the goal of fostering a pluralist national identity. From the 1970s and well into the 1980s, every province in Canada and every school board formalized some policy to address the needs of a diverse population. It began with multicultural education, or intercultural education in the case of Quebec. What is understood by the term "multicultural education" was indeed varied, in terms of both theory and practice. It was recognized as having the potential for reinforcing or challenging hegemony. The most common cross-cutting themes were education for cultural pluralism, education about cultural difference, education of the culturally different, education for cultural preservation, and education for cultural adaptation. All these approaches emanated from a liberal pluralist view, which assumed that cultural diversity was intrinsically valuable and worthwhile to maintain. Quebec's intercultural option, while lagging the state's responsibility in socializing all citizens to a national culture, prioritized the enhancement of relations between the various groups through increased opportunities for exchange and collaboration. Although the ultimate aim of such programs was the accommodation and maintenance of diversity, there was always the potential danger that they could be exclusionary in their group-specific nature, emphasizing boundaries at the expense of interconnections.

In the literature on multicultural education, however, aboriginal groups were mentioned only in a peripheral manner. The reasons for this lay in the construction of aboriginal people as an integrated part of the indigenous Canadian culture, almost like the flora and fauna and portrayed as natural fixtures, to be hauled out for highly formalized symbolic recognition and then stored away.

What distinguished cultural accommodation from cultural preservation was the relative openness or permeability of the very boundaries necessary to nurture identity. At one end of the spectrum it may be seen as a loosely organized cultural pluralism, while at the other it may constitute segregation. The role of economic barriers and inequalities in recognition spearheaded much of the groundswell of critique against multicultural education as overfocused on lifestyles at the expense of life chances (for more detailed discussion of these issues, see Moodley 1995, from which these arguments are drawn). This gave rise to a flurry of programs against racism beginning in the late 1970s and gaining momentum in the 1980s. Neo-Marxist-inspired antiracism became the radical alternative to multiculturalism. In contrast to the consensus-based multicultural education, antiracism education sought to understand individual and group experiences within institutional and power structures. Through a knowledge and understanding of the history of racism, the process of conquest, and the different forms of domination, antiracism education promoted political education. Federal departments such as the then–Ministry of Multiculturalism responded to this trend by the inclusion of antiracism as an integral part of their own priorities, alongside multiculturalism. These changes occurred in the context of debates around race relations that climaxed in the 1984 report of an all-party parliamentary national investigation of the experiences of visible minorities, titled *Equality Now* (House of Commons 1984). This report heralded subsequent programs of affirmative action and employment equity that were federally mandated through the Employment Equity Act of 1986. However, the relationship between policy and implementation is never totally linear and consequent. Barriers and boundaries persist alongside changes. In the 1990s a combination of the politics of neoliberalism and economic pressures to reduce expenditure resulted in the demise of diversity-related initiatives. With reduced funding and newer priorities, many provinces simply abandoned earlier policies or let them lay dormant. This was to be followed in the next decade with the era of conservative politics, which considered these trends even less important and subsumed them under the goal of citizenship.

One example of language parochialism may suffice to show the current reality of rhetorical or nominal multiculturalism. While Canada houses a cross-section of all the people of the world, it does not mean that they everywhere can read, listen to the state radio or watch TV in their own languages. Even the most numerous immigrant groups draw a blank. There are pockets of astonishing linguistic parochialism in the most unlikely places. In the many newsstands scattered throughout Vancouver International Airport, the esthetically appealing busy gateway to Asia and Europe, one can choose from hundreds of U.S. girlie, sports, and men's health magazines, but not one French, let alone Mandarin or German, publication is on sale. Even the public libraries in Vancouver stick to their English-only lending in an officially bilingual country. The staff of the public library in one of the most multicultural sections of Vancouver, Point Grey adjoining the campus of UBC where we live, was baffled when we once inquired why they did not subscribe to *Le Monde*, *Liberation*, or *Der Spiegel*, but to dozens of U.S. publications. The myopia of English-speakers toward multilingualism is also evident in keeping French a voluntary rather than a compulsory subject in British Columbia schools, despite high demands from parents. The few French immersion programs in British Columbia are oversubscribed, and places are allotted by lottery. (Neither our two children nor recently our two grandchildren could get a spot in the immersion school nearby.) English-speakers assume as normal that their mother tongue is spoken or understood everywhere. In short, linguistic curiosity as the key to understanding other cultures is neither perceived as necessary nor facilitated in parts of Canada. As has been pointed out by others, symbolic multiculturalism exists without its corollary of multilingualism. It is even worse with First Nations languages, where only 17 percent indicate that they still can speak or understand their mother tongue. The Quebec obsession with language maintenance, including Quebec's own language police and problematic right to determine the language of instruction of non-English immigrants (allophones), is understandable in light of these trends. Just as in South Africa certain ethnicities, particularly Afrikaners, do not want to become extinct or diluted by losing their language as a public medium in a sea of English-speakers, so multilingual Quebec separatists want foremost to preserve cultural values rather than economic "nationhood."

How to Select Immigrants

There are several identity options for immigrants in a new society. Identity does not depend on citizenship alone. It is a chosen self-concept; subidentities can coexist with a national one; the nation as "a community of character, destiny, and purpose" may be an outdated concept in a global economy, and as one commentator (Jacobson 1997: viii, cited in Abraham 2010: 976) has observed, we now "live in a patchwork of communal identities which can occupy the same geographic space and in which the public realm may bring together people who have no common felt identities." Canada, where diversity itself constitutes the national identity, comes close to this description. South Africa approaches this situation to a certain degree as well, although inclusive "nation building" is still official policy.

For the sake of simplicity, three choices for immigrants can be distinguished: assimilation, where minorities adopt the identity of their new country and give up their old one; separation, where immigrants retain their old identity and reject the new national one; and integration, where both identities are embraced, which is the multicultural model. For a variety of reasons Canada resisted the current overseas trends of assimilation, though it may well be described as a melting pot on the slow boil. It avoided developing isolated enclaves of immigrants in a hostile environment. However, it should not be ruled out that U.S. and European anti-immigrant sentiments also find resonance in Canada: "Contemporary Canada is vulnerable to the potential rise of ethnic hatreds, and it is naïve, not to mention ahistorical, to assume that our mythologized consensus over tolerance cannot easily be eroded" (Erna Paris, G&M, October 28, 2011, p. A15). Therefore, a closer analysis of what causes the divergent developments is called for. Kymlicka (2010: 30) stressed that "it is important to research the specificity of the Canadian experience in relation to other countries, and to try to identify when the experience of other countries does or does not provide important lessons for our future." Likewise, such a comparison can also reveal whether Canadian multiculturalism can be exported to Europe or South Africa. As Jeffrey Simpson (G&M, October 29, 2011) has pointed out, "No country in the world has been more successful with its multicultural experiment, testimony to which is the number of delegations from other countries arriving here to study how it works."

There are several reasons why the Canadian multicultural model is difficult to emulate in Europe. The obstacles blocking Canadian multiculturalism in Europe are structural, historical, and political. To list these impediments does not ascribe priority to one over the other, because they are intertwined. The example of Germany can best illustrate the difference to Canada. As elaborated in Chapter 6, in Germany most of the persons "with an immigration background" (as the "non-Germans" are officially referred to, even if they have acquired German citizenship) are of Turkish peasant origin with low educational levels. In contrast, immigrants in Canada are found in all social strata and are highly represented among professionals. Asian schoolchildren generally outperform their Canadian-born peers, even if English is not their mother tongue and is either their second or their third language. A careful selection of immigrants contributes to acceptance. Requiring proficiency in one of the two official languages facilitates integration. Changing labor market needs figure prominently in the Canadian selection criteria. However, only a minority of newcomers were selected according to the point system in the past. The majority entered Canada under the category of sponsored family reunification or were selected for humanitarian reasons under the UN refugee program or as independent asylum seekers, with yet a smaller group applying as entrepreneurial investors. Subsequently the conservative government has heeded the advice of its internal critics, such as the economist Herbert Grubel and the Fraser Institute, to prioritize specific immigrants, according to labor market shortages. Sponsorships of applications from parents and grandparents were suspended for two years in the fall of 2011. In 2013 this was lifted but limited to 5,000 applicants per year. The policy was changed without parliamentary approval or public debate. One of the leading Canadian academic immigration experts, Jeffrey Reitz (2011), summarized the new shifts: "We are opening the doors to more and more temporary workers (it used to be only nannies and tightly controlled seasonal workers); we are pinpointing 29 specific occupations for exclusive eligibility under the skilled worker program; and we are developing the selection of immigrants from Ottawa to the provinces at a very rapid rate." New immigration rules are geared in favor of younger applicants in order to ease the demographic changes of a fast-shifting ratio between working-age and retired persons. The new rules also privilege newcomers with existing language proficiency in English and/or French, since younger immigrants with language skills have proven to be more easily adaptable and higher earners in a changing labor market. The emphasis on language, critics argued, may temporarily at least disadvantage applicants from China and South Asia, where English and French are less established than in former British or French colonies. Overall, the new rules facilitate the recruitment of desired workers by employers. In addition to a changed "Federal Skilled Worker Class," a new "Federal Skilled Trades Class" was created and the "Canadian Experience Class" was updated. Foreign graduates of Canadian universities, the bulk in this group, do not have to return to their home countries and are now courted and fast-tracked to stay as "landed immigrants." South Africa could benefit from an equally generous policy on scarce skills.

Under the revised point system in effect since 2013, 67 out of 100 possible points are required to pass. Points are awarded in five categories as follows: (1) Language proficiency is awarded a maximum of 28 points, up from a previous 24. (2) Age is awarded a maximum of 12 points, up from 10. Workers over 47 years will receive no points for age, while applicants between 20 and 29 years obtain the 12 maximal points, which decrease by one for each year above age 30. (3) Work experience outside of Canada was reduced from 21 to 15 points. (4) Adaptibility remained the same with 10 maximal points. (5) Education with 25 points remained unchanged. Under a new parallel "Express Entry system," in effect since January 1, 2015, the weight given to prearranged, confirmed employment was greatly increased to 50 percent of points needed and "having a close relative in Canada" abolished in the calculation of eligibility for permanent residence. Critics spoke of a "privatization of immigration policy" and turning the department into a "giant manpower agency." According to *The Economist* (January 10, 2015), visa officers fear "that an employer-led system will be 'fraught with fraud.' They worry that non-existent employers will offer fictitious jobs to residents' friends and families." More important seems that mere economic calculations now dominate at the expense of the previous principles of family reunification and giving shelter to needy refugees.

If South Africa were to adopt a similar rational immigration policy, it could harness the skills of potential immigrants from around the world, particularly Africa, rather than letting millions of work seekers fend for themselves in a state of legal limbo. Such policies, as in Canada, could still ensure that employers give preference to equally qualified citizens before turning to immigrants. At the same time, South Africa could benefit from job creation by migrants entitled and encouraged to establish small businesses.

All over the world, immigrants are overrepresented among small-business owners, defined as those employing fewer than 100 people. Common wisdom explains why people with ambition and energy to uproot themselves and establish a new existence in a foreign country should also be successful entrepreneurs. In addition, prejudices in private-sector employment and even more in the civil service force immigrants initially into small-scale independent enterprises, such as leisure and hospitality, taxi operations, restaurants, and grocery corner shops, as well as various professional services. A *New York Times*

(June 30, 2012) editorial reported a study of the Fiscal Policy Institute, based on census data: "The study found that there were 900,000 immigrants among small-business owners in the United States, about 18 percent of the total. This percentage is higher than the immigrant share of the overall population, which is 13 percent, and the immigrant share of the labor force, at 16 percent. Small businesses in which half or more of the owners were immigrants employed 4.7 million people . . . generating $776 billion in receipts." It is also known that among a majority of patents registered, immigrants played a substantial part. Despite the shift from university professionals to less educated skilled workers, it would still be correct to say that Canada creams off the better-qualified and more desirable persons keen to emigrate around the globe. However, Canada has never discussed reimbursing developing countries for their training of doctors or IT professionals from which the country now benefits without having incurred costs. Why should immigrant-receiving countries not be required to compensate the foreign universities that trained their doctors and engineers at great costs?

In a study called "Immigrants as Innovators" (Michelle Downie 2012), the Conference Board of Canada established empirically another overlooked advantage of immigration. A direct correlation exists between the presence of expatriates and international trade. An increased number of immigrants from a particular country also translates into higher imports and exports to that country, regardless of wealth, language, or geographical distance. The established networks and social capital of immigrants facilitated trade relations with countries of origin. This also applied to an increase in foreign direct investment (FDI) from the countries of newcomers. A similar correlation was shown for Spain in which the percentage of foreigners increased from 1 percent in 1995 to 10 percent in 2008. In the same period, international trade went up from 35 percent to 44 percent of GDP.

In the U.S. immigration debate, the economic advantages of immigration and trade and investment hardly figure, because immigration is framed as an illegal activity to be stopped. The Obama administration has proposed "mandatory electronic employment verification" as part of a new immigration policy. An unprecedented 409,849 were deported from the United States in 2012. The stricter controls paradoxically increased the number of "illegals" by reducing out-migration. The Princeton sociologist Douglas Massey ("Isolated, Vulnerable and Broke," NYT op-ed, August 4, 2011) explained: "This disrupted a significant but largely circular flow of illegal migrants: according to estimates from the Mexican Migration Project, between 1965 and 1985, for every 100 undocumented entries there were 85 undocumented departures, yielding only a small net increase in the undocumented population each year." Anticipating the difficulties of return, most illegals stayed and the number of undocumented migrants increased from three million in 1990 to twelve million in 2012. It is estimated that in the United States more than half of Mexicans and an even higher percentage of Guatemalan and Honduran migrants fall into the category of "illegals," or better referred to as "irregulars." The shorthand "illegals" is inaccurate, because only acts can be illegal, never human beings.

Given the strong political resistance to genuine immigration reform in the United States, or even the legalization of undocumented children ("Dream Act") born in the United States, the Obama administration adopted a halfhearted compromise that resembles the laissez-faire policy in South Africa. The compromise aims at protecting ambitious youngsters from indiscriminate deportation, although it affects only an estimated 1.7 million of the country's 12 million irregular immigrants. A *New York Times* editorial (August 12, 2012) celebrated the small administrative step and summarized that under the program, applicants must have been brought to the United States before turning 16, be under 31, have clean records, and have lived in the United States for at least the last five years. Those who are accepted will still not be legalized, even if they are given permission to work. They will instead be granted two-year deferrals of deportation, which are renewable. In addition each applicant must pay a fee of $465. With the rest still being subject to arrest at any time, the majority of irregular immigrants will be further cowed into accepting low wages and rightless treatment without protest. As long as they accept these conditions and make themselves invisible, they will be tolerated.

The moral panic about migrant invasion, particularly during election time in the United States or Europe, incited by conservative party populists, is best countered by a clear, regulated immigration policy, geared to a country's needs. Renewed electrified fences, as established in apartheid South Africa and demanded again now, satisfy delusional anxieties, whether in Arizona or in Mpumalanga. As has been astutely pointed out in another context, "Walls, then, are built not for security, but for a sense of security. The distinction is important, as those who commission them know very well. What a wall satisfies is not so much a material need as a mental one. Walls protect people not from barbarians, but from anxieties and fears, which can often be more terrible than the worst vandals. In this way, they are built not for those who live outside them, threatening as they may be, but for those who dwell within. In a certain sense, then, what is built is not a wall, but a state of mind" (Costa Bradatan, "Scaling the Wall in the Head," NYT op-ed, November 27, 2011).

Canada has avoided the *laager* mentality of isolation and grasped the need for internationalism in attracting scarce human capital. South Africa too could substantially improve its progressive admission policy, which would benefit both the state and the migrants. It could (a) regulate its inflow with clear criteria, (b) gear those to labor market needs in addition to humanitarian assistance, (c) process applications speedily and transparently, (d) establish acknowledged "best practices" to integrate newcomers socially, (e) enable early acquisition of SA citizenship, along the Canadian model, (f) allow dual or multiple citizenship in order to attract global skills, (g) recognize foreign professional credentials without compromising SA standards, and (h) immunize against xenophobia by educating the public about the advantages of immigration, as discussed in

Chapter 8 on political literacy. Any fears of recolonization by too many skilled non-African applicants could be alleviated by allocating additional points to Africans with the requisite skills. South Africa would surely be criticized for draining skills from the rest of the continent. In response, it could reimburse the emerging sending countries for their training costs, which Canada fails to do. In any case, free movement of individuals cannot be prevented, and South Africa, with so many other attractive features, would join the competition for the best on the international migration market.

Opportunistic Multiculturalism

Unlike in Europe, in Canada active integration efforts are reinforced by political calculations. Canadian multiculturalism is embraced by all three federal parties, because they all need to vie for the immigrant vote. The Westminster system of first past the post dampens political extremism, because parties cannot afford to alienate 20 percent of foreign-born constituents nationally, or more than 50 percent in certain city ridings of Toronto and Vancouver. In contrast the mixed and proportional voting system in Europe (with the exception of the United Kingdom) allows and rewards right-wing, anti-immigrant populism. Historically, Canada's Liberal Party was associated with the immigrant vote and considered the champion and inventor of multiculturalism. However, since 2006, the Liberal Party was replaced by the Conservatives, in no small measure because of a substantial share of the "ethnic vote." New Canadians, themselves often predisposed to traditional values and steeped in the authoritarianism of their upbringing, were attracted to the Conservatives' "Law and Order" agenda, respect for tradition, and doubts about many manifestations of modernity, such as same-sex marriages.

Since all Canadians with the exception of First Nations people are immigrants, the European idea of historical entitlement to home and land of a homogeneous kind is weak in Canada. So is Canadian nationalism, which could never portray itself as a monolithic entity, because of Quebec. The presence of a French nation together with First Nations has multiculturalism built into the fabric of Canadian society, regardless of government policy.

From this multinational reality, in contrast to the European uninational nation, inevitably flows tolerance toward difference. There is no Canadian *Leitkultur* (dominant or guiding culture) toward which conformity could be demanded. Therefore *Überfremdung* (cultural alienation) remains an abstract concept in Canada, while it is real in a more monocultural environment. Canadian tolerance may amount to indifference, rather than welcoming recognition. Some analysts go as far as denying the existence of any Canadian nationalism or even Canadian culture. Ger Mennens ("Multiculturalism and Postmodernity," *Open Democracy*, August 5, 2011) writes, "In Canada, nationalism and national identity are not the same, because there is no official ethnic or national majority group. This does not mean that there are no majority identity groups within

Canada, but that Canadian politics has explicitly opted for not choosing one ethnic group as dominant. Multiculturalism in Canada articulates the ideology of a non-nation." The Globe&Mail (November 15, 2014) columnist Margaret Wente has illustrated the Canadian "non-nation" in contrast to Europe in simpler terms: "Our identity is not defined by blood, or by our sense of destiny. We have no concept of *Volk*. We're just folks. We don't care who you are or where you come from or who or what you worship, as long as you share our good bourgeois Canadian values. Don't litter, send your kids to school. Wear a poppy." Wente could have added: apologize, even if it is not your fault; be always politically correct and inoffensive; never jump the queue; never fight, unless it is a hockey game.

Finally, the relative short period of three years after which immigrants can acquire citizenship contrasts with the longer time frame and greater obstacles for political enfranchisement of newcomers in Europe. Immigrants in Europe are put into a political quarantine while they are courted in Canada. Moreover, Canada allows multiple citizenship, which makes the Canadian passport a document of convenience rather than a testimony of a single identity. However, the past relatively easy acquisition of citizenship has also encountered criticism and led to a decline of applications. Only 37 percent of newly eligible permanent residents acquired citizenship in 2011, compared with 48 percent in 2006 (*Vancouver Sun*, May 9, 2013, p. B5). Waiting times of twenty-nine months of fully eligible applicants are common. Stringent new language requirements and new citizenship tests, introduced in 2010, are blamed for the higher failure rate. Previously, obtaining citizenship after only three years of uninterrupted residence and no criminal record was considered a sure way of incorporating newcomers, who now face much greater scrutiny. One of the reasons for the Canadian shift lies in the alleged misuse of the previous liberal system by some claimants who did not intend to reside in Canada but only aimed at a Canadian passport. Particularly, Hong Kong residents sought the Canadian document as a safety valve in case of a crackdown by an authoritarian Chinese government. In 2006 Canada had already been alerted to an invisible diaspora when Lebanon became embroiled in a war with Israel. Apparently 50,000 Canadian passport holders in Lebanon became eligible for Canadian support services and evacuation from the war zone, only to return to Lebanon three months later when the war had ended. The number of Hong Kong–born Canadian residents has steadily declined since 1997, and it is estimated that Hong Kong now harbors 350,000 Canadian passport holders (Douglas Todd, *Vancouver Sun*, May 18, 2013, p. D7). While many reasons motivate the return of immigrants to their original homeland (such as taxes, better employment opportunities, and family ties), the successful acquisition of an "insurance passport" ranks top among current Chinese and other East Asian Canadian residents. We know parents who have secured three and more passports for their children as insurance against future emergencies.

The relative welcome of immigrants has led to a glorification of multiculturalism by Canadian immigrants that no party can ignore. In survey responses to the question "What makes you most proud about Canada?" multiculturalism consistently ranks second (Adams 2007). To be sure, multiculturalism is more of a symbolic feel-good reward than tangible assistance for newcomers, but it is psychologically important for the self-concept as equals nonetheless. The inferiority that immigrants in Europe sense, begging to be admitted into a closed hierarchy of habits, accents, dress codes, and unspoken status symbols, Canadian newcomers can avoid in the cosmopolitan Babylon that labels itself multicultural.

Should the unique Canadian experiment fail, it will set a globalizing world back into parochial nationalism. Should it continue to succeed, as is likely, it is a cause for celebration of cosmopolitan, postnational modernity, despite its flaws.

III

Political Literacy

8

Xenophobia and Political Literacy

G iven the impossibility of effectively controlling borders in Africa and elsewhere, one has to assume that only political education can reduce xenophobia. The core of such an attempt lies in making people understand *why* they hate. It implies not more information about the other, but basic knowledge about nation, patriotism, ethnicity, race, identity, ethnocentrism, tribalism, communalism, sectarianism, and other concepts with which we explain our world and construct meaning. This chapter clarifies some relevant aspects of such an exercise.[1]

During the December 2012 ANC conference in Mangaung, political education figured prominently in several resolutions, and the outgoing Deputy President Kgalema Motlanthe was put in charge of this new ANC initiative. However, it is questionable whether the ANC's notion of political literacy coincides with what is outlined here. Increased political literacy may well counteract support for the ANC. In the past, South African political education, if at all pursued seriously, has focused mainly on voter education around electoral procedures and processes. It has regurgitated the history of the liberation movement and celebrated heroes of the struggle. It has neglected critical analysis and moral education in enabling citizens to arrive at mature and

---

[1] Some ideas in this chapter were first presented at a Diversity and Citizenship Education in Multicultural Nation States conference hosted by the Center for Multicultural Education at the University of Washington, at the Rockefeller Conference Center in Bellagio, Italy, on June 17–21, 2002. The topic was later expanded and published in different versions in various journals as our approach to teacher education on antiracism and xenophobia evolved (Moodley 2010; Moodley 2012). This chapter summarizes our current understanding of political education drawing on this literature. It covers not only the situation in South Africa but also comparable situations in other regions.

informed judgments in ethical predicaments. How education for active, participatory citizenship can transform a historical reality of inequality into a new better life for liberated people has defied solutions thus far. Increasing evidence suggests that new nonracial injustices are even harder to combat than the more overt, morally discredited, previous racial system.

International comparative research has shown that civic education impacts on nationalistic and xenophobic sentiment in different ways. Some authors argue that education as an antidote to xenophobia is overrated. In some cases education may even reinforce divisions between "us" and "them," because education operates within the boundaries of society and all the myths and symbols of national images. However, a consensus has emerged that the right type of political literacy combats xenophobia effectively. Michael Hjerm (2001: 37), who surveyed eight European countries plus Australia and Canada, concludes, "Levels of nationalist sentiment as well as of xenophobia decrease with increasing levels of education in all the countries examined, despite substantial differences between the educational systems in the countries."

What has been the story of political education in South Africa, both pre- and postapartheid? The emphasis in political education under the apartheid system had been diametrically opposed to that of the liberated postapartheid order. The former was ethnically based authoritarian indoctrination for compliance with imposed group identities, while the latter promotes constitutional values of nation building in an inclusive democracy. However, the visions of a progressive curriculum notwithstanding, citizenship education in South Africa is undermined by a public discourse on corruption, crime, and morality that contradicts the values taught in schools. Well-intentioned educational initiatives are overshadowed by contrary government practices that frequently defy the very ideals that the constitution espouses. This "public curriculum" impacts more deeply the political consciousness of students than formal civics lessons. The public curriculum contrasts with the school syllabus and triggers cynicism and alienation from politics instead of active engagement. Political interest and participation in civil society have declined. In one of the most unequal societies, issues of democratic governance are relegated to the luxury of a privileged elite but hardly concern most of the impoverished and marginalized majority. Their identification with democracy depends on delivery of employment, safety, housing, and other preconditions of a normal life, which is taken for granted in established Western democracies.

Comparing Political Education in Multiethnic Societies

Most of the global literature on "Educating Citizens in a Multicultural Society" concerns itself exclusively with the problem of integrating minorities and immigrants into the mainstream. Particularly in the North American context, powerless minorities of color battle prejudice from the outside and struggle to maintain self-esteem within marginalized communities. Antiracist citizenship education aims at "cultural, economic and political equity" (Banks 1997: 123) and making "full Americans" out of variously excluded residents. In Europe, sensitizing the majority to accept difference, eschew xenophobia, and embrace multiculturalism poses a particularly onerous task.

In postapartheid South Africa, the challenge of citizenship education is different. A formerly disenfranchised majority of color has acquired political power, although economic leverage (capital and skills) remains largely in white hands. Many minority members feel excluded and estranged from the new political order or eye it skeptically. This group needs to be reconciled with the new state, so that the vision of a truly nonracial society of more equal citizens may emerge.

The ruling black elite moved from a culture of resistance into positions of political power. Traditions and habits acquired in a difficult struggle do not always coincide with the democratic virtues expected in normal politics. A liberation movement differs from a political party, and the transition is not yet completed. The commitment to democratic values of liberation leaders has been questioned. Unlike the powerless minorities in North America or Europe, majority governments in Africa can inflict harm on minority citizens. Therefore, antiracist education in South Africa has to be broadened to include other kind of racisms as well as possibilities of despotism against fellow citizens. Civic education for a dominant group needs to focus on protecting democratic safeguards and constitutionalism, rather than merely making space for neglected cultures in the curriculum. A vibrant and self-confident South African black culture with an established rich linguistic base survived internal colonialism because of its critical mass. It was also not territorially displaced and subject to assimilationist pressures, as were immigrants and indigenous minorities in the Americas.

Western democracies display many deficiencies, not the least of which is that they conceive of themselves as procedural rather than participatory democracies. However, at least internalized adherence to entrenched procedures may be taken for granted, regardless of political differences. Transitional societies do not necessarily comply with their constitution in the same way. When the ANC caucus in Parliament unanimously declares a rigged election in Zimbabwe as "legitimate," it implies that a similar future situation in South Africa could also be endorsed. When in 2013 the ANC inveighed against the advertisement of a bank in which unscripted schoolchildren criticize government shortcomings, free speech was intimidated.

In such a context where the survival of the rule of law itself may be at stake, it would seem vital that citizenship education not only foster a deep understanding of constitutionalism and ensure that democratic habits are internalized but also cultivate a willingness to defend citizens' rights should they be at risk. Above all, South African students have to recognize undemocratic practices at all levels of government, detect a potential erosion of their constitutionally guaranteed rights, and feel an obligation to actively resist. This presupposes an enduring political interest and active participation in public affairs and civil society that may not be necessary to the same degree in consolidated democracies.

Citizenship equalizes inhabitants of a state by bestowing them with identical rights and obligations, regardless of their other differences. At the same time, citizenship excludes "foreigners" from access to such entitlements, including voting rights and welfare benefits. Living and working in wealthy states and gradually participating in welfare benefits by joining the social contract of citizens represent a much-sought-after privilege by persons from impoverished areas. Economic globalization and growing transnational migrancy have made immigration regulations one of the most contested political issues, particularly in European nation-states.

Colonialism everywhere operated on the distinction between citizens and subjects (Mamdani 1996). Just as women in Europe were variously disenfranchised until the first half of the twentieth century, so indigenous subject populations in Africa or North America were treated as "trustees" of the state, unworthy or incapable of participating in public affairs as equal citizens. British colonialism in particular aimed at solving the "native problem" through erasure of difference. Anglicization and assimilation of an elite and class-based segregation for the general population in India or Africa were envisaged.

Afrikaner nationalism, in exclusive control of the South African state since 1948, institutionalized the Anglo informal segregation policy into formal, legalized apartheid. This grand experiment of race-based social engineering eschewed any assimilation in favor of fostering ethnic difference and group pride among the black population. "Separate development," as the ideology of divide and rule was euphemistically labeled, attempted to ethnicize the black majority and racialize the white minority of different cultural origins, as Mamdani has pointed out. Thereby it tried to unify "Europeans" (particularly the 60 percent Afrikaans and 40 percent English speakers of the white minority) into a "white nation" but fragment Africans into nine "tribal" ethnic groups, alongside Coloureds and Indians.

Segregated education with different curricula and differential allocation of resources was one of the main tools with which this policy was to be achieved. Bantu education was shaped by essentialized notions of what the black mind was capable of and what kind of lower skills were needed in an industrializing economy. This also led to an expansion of basic education, as Hermann Giliomee (2012) has argued. During this early apartheid period, at most, citizenship education was confined to tribal history with a special twist. Depoliticized compliance, acquiescence, and acceptance of the status quo as the natural order of things were the expected attitudes of the products. More open missionary schools were brought under state control. The few African, Coloured, and Indian students who attended the liberal white universities were channeled into new own-group tribal colleges, all located in remote rural areas with the exception of the Coloured University of the Western Cape and the Indian University of Durban-Westville. Most "faculty" at these institutions were initially conservative Afrikaner civil servants. Little did the apartheid planners envisage that these colleges would gradually evolve into hotbeds of black nationalism and anti-apartheid resistance (Moodley 1971). Ethnically based apartheid education, although imposed and resented, nevertheless built on entrenched traditions and linguistic backgrounds that are alive and relevant among the African rural population. Even in the cities, virtually every black South African speaks an African language and more often is polyglot, although the medium of the public discourse is almost exclusively English, despite eleven official languages. Yet English, poorly taught as a second language, severely disadvantages many African learners in the competition for good grades and jobs (Moodley 2000).

Those living in the rural areas under the authority of traditional chiefs are further handicapped by customary law. Officially recognized as a concession to powerful traditional leaders, customary law does not sit well with liberal notions of equality and individual freedom. An unresolved contradiction exists between individualistic notions of citizenship and community-based rights and customs. The authority of chiefs does not rest on democratic legitimacy. Traditional leaders insist on inherited, dynastic rights. Women in particular suffer under communal obligations and status inequalities. Mamphela Ramphele (2001: 7) speaks of a "dual citizenship that creates tensions between loyalty to the nation and to one's own group, however defined." The tensions remain unresolved, and glaring discrepancies exist between the constitution and customary law. For example, the constitution insists on gender equality, but under customary law women cannot inherit property. Precolonial African society tends to be romanticized as communal decision making by consensus, but the monopoly of power in the hands of male elders and chiefs can hardly be called democratic.

Unlike the Soviet Union or the former Yugoslavia, which formally recognized subnational membership in the passports of all citizens, postapartheid South Africa is not an ethnically based federation. Civic nationalism of a common state for all its citizens infuses the new order. Ethnoracial identities persist as informal, unrecognized categories, except in equity legislation, with the aim to overcome such differential citizenship by equalizing past disadvantage. With constitutional patriotism as the binding glue of the common state, political literacy would seem the crucial precondition for realizing the utopian ideal.

Political Literacy as Strategy
to Combat Xenophobia

Drawing on the pioneering work of the British philosopher Bernard Crick and subsequently that of Anna Douglas, "political literacy" refers to the skills of inquiry needed to understand the ways in which power operates in democratic and autocratic social contexts. The aim is to acquire basic knowledge gained through a critical reading of the way institutions function and an understanding of how democracy works in practice at the local, national, and global levels. At the same time, political literacy is more than political knowledge and more than citizenship education. Within the framework of human dignity, equality, and social justice, political literacy also focuses on the process of deconstructing the causes of social conflict, the way in which diversity works, and the nature of dissent in society. Through acquiring habits of staying critically informed on current events, the underlying goal is to engage in transformative action by shaping democracy through the use of well-formulated, reasoned argument. Although Crick in his later work has been criticized for failing to respect the "politics of difference" and for encouraging a consensualist view of society, his earlier conception of political literacy does not support this critique.

In most of the scholarly educational literature, political literacy is viewed as a tool and precondition for young people to become active and engaged citizens. Political awareness flows from knowledge about public issues and motivates political participation. Henry Milner defines "civic literacy" as "knowledge required for effective political choice" (Milner 2002: 59). Left-leaning critics argue, however, that assuming effective choice among center parties that increasingly resemble each other—as in the case of the U.S. Republican and Democratic parties—already borders on political "illiteracy." This is held to be even more so, if the "choice" mainly boils down to a selection between personalities rather than one based on issues.

Any issue in the public domain can be considered political. Some feminists have argued that even the personal is political and that the distinction between public and private affairs is illusionary. Therefore, the skill to read all issues and events politically constitutes the highest form of political literacy. Comparative research indicates that civic education, as William A. Galston's study (2004) shows, is most effective in the late high school years and in early adulthood. Comparison between Europe and the United States also reveals a higher political literacy in countries with a high level of newspaper reading such as in Europe and lower in societies with what Milner calls private "television dependency" (Milner 2002: 55). The quality of most U.S. and SA media—with their focus on parochial local issues combined with overreporting of crime, disasters, celebrities, and sports, compared with the deeper exposure to international issues in public television and print media in Europe, Canada, and Australia—also accounts for surprising differences in voter participation and civic knowledge levels. However, the use of new technologies—especially social networking interfaces like Facebook and Twitter—by young voters can also overcome political apathy and mobilize large youth sectors, as Barack Obama's U.S. presidential campaigns have demonstrated. The youth uprisings in the Arab world in societies without freedom of speech and independent media in 2010 and 2011 reconfirmed the power of informa_ communication and political discourse under repressive conditions.

Above all, political literacy not only informs about contested ideas but enables a person to distinguish and make sense of competing values. Bernard Crick has rightly described po_tics as "a lively contest between differing ideals and interests, not a conventional set of stuffed rules" (Citizenship Foundation 2012: n.p.). Teaching political _teracy as merely lawmaking, or constitutional prescriptions of how conflicts between government agencies are settled, or how scarce goods are distribu_ed, or what constitutes good and bad governance misses the moral and _thical issues that always underlie political debates. Such a focus on political institutions is likely to stifle political interest among students.

Students are motivated when they are invited to solve political problems rather than being lectured on how a political system functions. Exposing young learners to moral controversies encourages autonomous, critical thinking. If such disputes are derived from current affairs and country-specific debates, they will stimulate active participation rather than reduce learners to passive recipients.

A salient challenge for educators, then, is how these concepts can be translated in the classroom. What would be some of the moral predicaments in which students could become engagec? U.S. educators have mentioned examples in light of recent U.S. history that could also be used in South Africa: Is torture illegitimate under any circumstances? Or is it to be tolerated if lives can be saved? Should all politicians be forced to resign if they intentionally lied to their constituents, and how can this be enforced? How can whistleblowers—workers who report rampant corruption _n their employer's company—be encouraged and protected? Or should they be ostracized for betraying colleagues? Does the international community have a responsibility to protect citizens of tyrannical states? Or does such intervention constitute illegitimate imperialism? Should a wealthy country like the United States welcome refugees and asylum seekers? Or restrict poor migrants and send them back to their countries of origin? Should prejudices and extremist views of other groups be tolerated in accordance with freedom-of-speech values? Or should they be prohibited and criminalized as hate speech?

A useful lesson about the pitfalls and merits of political education can be gleaned from antiracism education. In the spirit of the literature so far discussed, a more detailed examination of the noble intentions and shortcomings of antiracism teaching highlights the essential necessity of political literacy for teachers and curriculum designers. In the quest for social justice, attempts to counteract racism often unravel the hidden privilege of dominant groups, expose their complicity, and reinforce the dichotomy of the privileged and the oppressed in color-coded terms. Developing sensitivity and empathy for "the other" constitutes a strong component of such moral exercises. What is frequently neglected in such approaches is the political literacy that emanates from a deeper sociological understanding of racism, its functions, and its ever-changing forms. Racism is neither eradicated by preaching tolerance nor reduced by providing information that contradicts the stereotypes of the other. Unless the predisposing conditions for denigration are addressed, the racist mind finds rationalizations for inferiorizing ever-changing targets. The behavior or appearance of the minority hardly influences the authoritarian character that is conditioned to prejudge, regardless of the behavior of the "other." The victims are always interchangeable. Just as psychoanalytic therapy aims at making conscious the unconscious—transforming id into ego, in Freudian terms—so the most lasting cure is to make the prejudiced individual understand why she or he cherishes such deep resentments. As all people are prejudiced to varying degrees, this political education in the most genuine sense should be geared to everyone, not just individuals singled out for special consciousness-raising.

Political literacy, to some extent, immunizes against racist temptations. Political literacy differs from political education usually considered central to the participation of citizens in government. Instead, the aim is to nurture the ability to read critically and deconstruct issues, events, and debates. It is a way of making sense of how inequality works, to understand institutional racism, to comprehend how racial binaries become entrenched as well as to challenge them. Specific counteracting policies flow from such understanding, which is a precondition for successful practice.

Policies, procedures, consequences, and accountability for racist incidents need to be in place in all schools. So, too, should compulsory education in the skills to deal with a multiethnic clientele for teachers, police personnel, social workers, or hospital staff. With few exceptions, these do not prevail, despite supposed commitments to cross-cultural communication. Deterrence and communication skills, as necessary as they are, are no substitute for political literacy. It is this wider context of understanding racist behavior that is missing in most present attempts to fight an obvious evil. Instead of demonizing racism or espousing the moral superiority of the "unprejudiced," the need to adopt a racist mentality has to be understood. The need arises within unfulfilled individuals who are unable to establish a secure identity, except by debasing others. Social conditions increasingly deprive people of the security and self-confidence that ward off the impulse to stigmatize others. With the decline of self-realization in a political economy where more and more people are declared superfluous, scapegoating and other artificial forms of self-realization increase.

Racism may manifest itself in individual psychology, but it also needs to be understood in relation to the social structure at large in which character development is always embedded. In this deeper sense, successful antiracism is predicated upon societal transformation. An apolitical consumerism that prioritizes the private realm while denigrating the public sphere, however, cannot grasp the political significance of racism, let alone envisage the alternative that would eliminate the need for racial stigmatization. In short, the best job educators can do to combat racism is to ensure a global political literacy.

Such a global political literacy would be based on a sound education to provide a *historical* understanding of the nature of prejudice, discrimination, and racism. This historical knowledge would draw upon a *comparative* and *international* perspective, cosmopolitan in nature. The underlying questions would be, How do local specifics differ from discrimination elsewhere? Why do particular manifestations of inequality and exclusion develop the way they do? What role did the state, public compliance, and specific group interests play in allowing unique characteristics to unfold? Critical analytical skills constitute the motivating force to decode mythologies and demystify popular ideologies. Students are encouraged to question conventional wisdom and to develop interrogative skills in distinguishing, for instance, apartheid from fascism, old from new forms of racism, and racial, cultural, and gender-based essentialisms. Racism and xenophobia as explanatory concepts themselves become the focus of critical inquiry.

What this means can be summarized best by clarifying seven different manifestations of racism:

- *Legal racism*, epitomized in apartheid South Africa and the Jim Crow laws of the U.S. South, which have now been abolished. As in the case of slavery previously, public opinion and effective forms of resistance such as the civil rights movement, strikes, and economic boycotts turned against such obvious systems of inequality.
- *Scientific racism*, which was biologically rationalized and which once justified colonial rule with its assertions of the superior intellectual and genetic qualities of European conquerors and its converse of inferior innate qualities of those whom it subjugated. It has also gone out of fashion and has become discredited.
- Subtle *social racism*, which is experienced subliminally through a cultural hierarchy of arrogance and may be even more debilitating in its effects than legalized collective discrimination. It has frequently replaced the previous cruder forms of discrimination and exclusion. Social racism often justifies the avoidance of social interaction with other groups on the basis of different "tastes," preferences, and comfort levels in contact with others.
- *Cultural racism*, which has become a modernized form of "race-talk." Utilizing the more acceptable terms "culture" and "ethnicity" for "race," difference could be reconciled with the goal of equality without disturbing the power hierarchy. Yet through their implicit essentialized content, it served the same purpose that "race" did previously. What constitutes valuable and worthwhile knowledge neglects non-European sources. Students learn to question the assumption of

universal applicability of Western values and are introduced to an understanding of cultural relativism.

- *Economic racism*, which survives as the most significant indicator of an unaddressed past. Unequal educational and opportunity structures and barriers in hiring practices serve to reinforce unequal life chances. Ethnic groups are locked into positions without chances of mobility.
- The *religious racism* of the Hindu caste system, which likewise stigmatizes and degrades groups, placing them firmly in an unequal division of labor. Social contact between castes is shunned at all levels. Students learn that racism not only is a black–white phenomenon but occurs wherever segments are discriminated on the basis of ancestry or inherited group membership into which they are born and from which they cannot escape.
- *Psychological implications* of denigration and exclusion based on racism, which focus on how denigrated groups often internalize the dominant view of themselves. Being disempowered and stigmatized from above predisposes them to ostracize others below them or to identify with their own oppressors.

The insights gained from these broader understandings of discrimination; the similarities and differences from one context to the next; the relationships between class-, race-, and gender-based inequality; and the human costs involved all serve to educate rather than indoctrinate. They provide the intellectual scaffolding to deal with the tension between the ideal of colorblindness and "color-consciousness" to recognize just how "race" and racialization work. Students exposed to this kind of broad historical and comparative reasoning are thereby enabled to acquire the necessary skills to critically evaluate solutions and policies that are locally appropriate. These could range from what kind of affirmative action can best address historical disadvantage to personal involvement as active citizens in a democratic culture.

Nation, Nationalism, Ethnicity, Ethnocentrism, and Critical Patriotism

Students in all societies need an understanding of nationalism, patriotism, ethnocentrism, and cosmopolitanism. South Africans in particular confuse these concepts in the discourse about nation building, "rainbowism," and ethnoracialism.

We follow Anthony Smith's (1986: 22) widely accepted use of ethnicity as designating a historical community of cultural similarities with a shared sense of solidarity and belonging and memories, symbols, or myth of descent. When such distinct people aim at either greater political autonomy or their own state, they form a nation. Nationalism can be described as politicized ethnicity.

Analysts of nationalism frequently refer to its "Janus face." The good side of nationalism consists of communal solidarity, the sense of belonging, affirmed identity, caring, and security among like-minded people with the same cultural heritage. Yet these laudable features are often overshadowed by negative attitudes of parochialism, ethnocentrism, discrimination, and racism, not to speak of aggressive expansionism in nationalistic mobilization against perceived adversaries. Too many lives have been sacrificed on the altar of nationalist wars for the glory of an imagined community.

Colonial expansion was fueled by nationalism. Nationalism aided colonialism by providing the emotional motivation to serve as cannon fodder for the colonial army. Generations of young men willingly and enthusiastically risked their lives so that the nation could live, expand, or be reborn. A particularly aggressive brand of nationalism thrives on historical grievances, which it promises to redress through unity. In its quest for redress, nationalism aims at an all-class alliance. Rich and poor, educated and uneducated, men and women merge in the fantasy of advancement in one strong whole. Being part of a triumphant nation makes for the all-class appeal of nationalist mobilization against alleged threats. Both settlers and natives have embraced nationalism. Settler nationalism defends privilege and native nationalism mobilizes for liberation from foreign domination.

In the great European nineteenth- and twentieth-century wars, ancestry is elevated to the criterion of belonging. Where ancestry is not visible, religion, language, and accent serve as markers of boundaries for the in-group. "Biblical origin" served as the main cohesive bond for diverse Jewish groups. Those features define ethnic citizenship, in contrast to the citizenship of civic rights for all legal residents in a given territory, regardless of religion or origin.

Ethnocentrism is the glorification of one's own group. It rests on stereotypes that are positive about the in-group, in contrast to mostly negative stereotypes about out-groups. Most enlightened people consider themselves free of stereotypes. Yet stereotypes are signposts in a complex world, and everybody is oriented by these prejudgments, prior knowledge, or prejudices, because nobody can investigate each new encounter. Ethnocentrism facilitates this difficult task, because it provides yardsticks by which the unknown can be measured. "Aliens" are categorized according to one's own cultural practices and mores. However, even identical behavior and appearance of the out-group does not preclude animosity and in fact can increase it, as the Freudian concept of "narcissism of small difference" asserts.

Whenever nationalist movements compete with liberal and/or left mobilization in divided societies, the nationalist calls are usually heeded, because they do not attack culture. Marxist theorists generally consider cultural identity as retrogressive and parochial, to be eventually swept aside by an all-leveling, all-embracing capitalism. In contrast, both Zionism and Islam enjoy this connectedness with cultural conditioning in early socialization. The working class has no nationality, argued Marx. However, nationalist and colonial wars were also supported by left parties on both sides in Europe. Early Zionism was embraced by many socialists. Marxist theorists frequently underestimate this nationalist appeal. Given the deep-rooted ethnoreligious "false consciousness" in the Middle East, it amounts to wishful thinking that "opens for them (the oppressed) the hope of self-determination, and violence will wither away of itself," as Joel Kovel asserts.

Equal civic rights for citizens with different origins, some argue, lacks the emotional glue of appeals to common descent. Constitutional patriotism, the pride in a genuinely inclusive democracy, represents an ideal that few states have managed to generate. Much more common is the official or inofficial recognition of ethnicity. An "ethnocracy" only privileges in-group members. Ethnic citizenship thrives on the dichotomy between indigenous and nonindigenous, between those who belong to the nation and those who are strangers, newcomers or migrants from somewhere else. With the mythology of returning home after two thousand years of absence, Zionism has reversed the indigenous–alien distinction: Jews have instantly become natives and Palestinians foreigners in the eyes of the new settlers.

Generally speaking, and as Germany past and present proves, even if "strangers" are "naturalized" or "nationalized" and in the sense that they acquire all the habits and attributes of natives and identify with the "homeland," they remain nonnatives from the vantage point of ethnic nationalism. For example, most German Jews had totally assimilated to German virtues and vices, and even fought in World War I with the same fervor. Yet abandoning traditional identity did not save them from Nazi paranoia. Second- and third-generation Turkish migrants, born and educated in Germany without any Turkish cultural traits, are still not "real Germans," despite their German passports. Likewise, fifth-generation South African whites or third-generation Indians, regardless of their political identification, are still not considered "Africans" in the social and customary sense.

With globalization and increased migration, the cleavages between ethnic insiders and perceived outsiders are likely to sharpen rather than transform into a global citizenship. Resource competition has made "nativeness" an important criterion of entitlement. Passports and migration laws have become the last bastion of a "hollowed-out sovereignty" of the nation-state.

Patriotism manifests itself in the collective rituals that express pride in one's country. The singing of the national anthem or the display of the flag signals loyalty. Compared with Europe, Canada, or South Africa, the United States is widely considered a particularly patriotic nation, despite that or because the state is historically made up of immigrants from all parts of the world. Newcomers from different traditions are politically assimilated through unifying patriotic symbols.

As far as patriotism engenders collective solidarity with fellow citizens and loyalty to the laws and democratic constitution, it is a positive and useful attitude. True patriotism fosters social responsibility and civic courage to defend the rights and freedoms that a democratic political culture bestows. The German philosopher Juergen Habermas speaks of "constitutional patriotism," a pride in the rule of law and constitutional guarantees, not ethnic affinity, as the emotional glue that should hold a multiethnic society together. Problems arise when one group of residents claim themselves to be the "true patriots" and aim at discriminating against or dominating others as untrustworthy "traitors" or "intruders." Then immigrants and newcomers are relegated to the bottom of a "hierarchy of belonging."

In this situation patriotism becomes a double-edged sword that comprises both positive and dangerously negative attitudes. In the name of true patriotism, intolerance toward dissent is frequently propagated, freedom of speech is restricted, and an arbitrary consensus is imposed. The very accusation of "unpatriotic behavior" intimidates teachers and students into self-censorship. They bow to conformity pressure that emanates from powerful media and authority prescriptions of what is legitimate and what is out of bounds and "politically incorrect." Nobody likes to be ostracized and marginalized as an outsider to the national consensus. In the United States, particularly after the national trauma of 9/11 and the ill-named Patriot Act, many members of certain religious and ethnic minorities suddenly found themselves labeled suspects, regardless of their individual loyalties. During the 1950s, Senator Joseph McCarthy went on a similar indiscriminate witch hunt against suspected traitors in the ensuing Cold War.

To guard against such abuse of patriotism, teachers need not shy away from fostering national identity, let alone embrace Samuel Johnson's dictum that love of country is "the last refuge of a scoundrel." Teachers need to emphasize *critical patriotism*. This approach eschews the fashionable "My country, right or wrong!" Critical patriotism encourages pride in the "right" but engages equally forcefully with the "wrong." The very foundation of an open society is based on critical discourse in which nobody can claim a monopoly of truth and patriotism. Teachers therefore require not only knowledge in social studies or even tolerance toward unpopular opinions but an attitude that nurtures autonomy and questioning of conventional wisdom among their subjects. As Henry Giroux (1983: 181) has persuasively argued, "The real crisis in schools and youth culture may not be about censorship, freedom of speech, or other alleged evils of political correctness, but whether students are learning how to think critically, engage larger social issues, take risks, and develop a sense of social responsibility and civic courage."

Cosmopolitan Consciousness

Cosmopolitanism refers to a mindset curious about the world everywhere, an orientation of openness and broad-mindedness that transcends the narrow confines of one's own group, be it locality, religion, ethnicity, or nationality. Cosmopolitans perceive of themselves as citizens of the world. Martha Nussbaum defines their primary allegiance "to the community of human beings in the entire world" rather than their own national citizens. Cosmopolitans are ready to immerse themselves in other cultures, engage with difference, and acquire diverse "cultural capital."

Nussbaum contrasts cosmopolitan universalism and internationalism with parochial ethnocentrism and inward-looking patriotism. She extends "an invitation to be an exile from the comfort of patriotism and its easy sentiments." In opposition to Richard Rorty's emphasis on shared American traditions, these cosmopolitans do not "rejoice in our American identity," but celebrate a "politics of difference."

Advocates of cosmopolitanism rightly inveigh against an educational system that leaves students at best indifferent toward others beyond national borders and at worst ignorant about the outside world. Eighty percent of adult Americans do not own a passport and obviously have little desire to explore other countries. However, cosmopolitanism need not be opposed to a critical patriotism. Pride in one's own heritage can be reconciled with appreciating other traditions. A reflective national or ethnic identity does not preclude a cosmopolitan outlook, and may even be a prerequisite for a broader perspective. Politically, the slogan "Think globally, act locally" best expresses a useful strategic synthesis.

The case for cosmopolitanism can be argued on moral as well as on pragmatic utilitarian grounds in an intertwined world. In the Kantian tradition cosmopolitans universalize moral obligations and advocate international solidarity. In Nussbaum's words, "If we really believe that all human beings are created equal and endowed with certain inalienable rights, we are morally required to think about what that conception requires us to do with and for the rest of the world." The treatment of noncitizens as neighbors puts this imperative to the test.

Cosmopolitanism in practice, as opposed to this noble, idealistic theory, however, faces two major obstacles. (1) Despite economic globalization, the world is still organized into nation-states. As has been elaborated previously, none of the 200 sovereign states have open borders that would allow people from everywhere to live anywhere without passports and permissions. The rich societies refuse to share their wealth with their poorer neighbors out of sheer greed. Our entire institutions militate against international solidarity and shape mindsets that are focused on the national good, the locality, ethnicity, or family. (2) If sociobiologists are correct, this selfishness of our species rests on evolutionary conditioning. According to this controversial view, people always prefer kin over nonkin, because such nepotism provided an evolutionary advantage in the competition for scarce resources. Survival depended on looking after your own first. Sociobiologists like Pierre van den Berghe posit that ethnocentrism is universal, while racism is not. Van den Berghe (email, January 15, 2013) clarifies that xenophobia is not a necessary concomitant to ethnocentrism, but much stronger with the additional element of competition. However, "the biological predisposition is to favor kin over non-kin, not to hate non-kin. Barring adverse experiences, cautious indifference and curiosity are more the norm toward strangers than hatred or fear, leaving open the possibility of a mutually profitable relationship of reciprocity." If this view is correct, then local–immigrant relations can also be improved by mutually beneficial reciprocity.

It is doubtful, however, whether nationalist and ethnocentrist attitudes serve the same useful purposes in an integrated world, where events in the remotest parts affect the rest of the globe. When the tropical forests are denuded, the climate everywhere changes. New diseases, like severe acute respiratory syndrome (SARS), rapidly spread. Pollution of the air, terrorism, and migration out of poverty and civil wars do not stop at artificial borders. Global institutions like the World Bank and the International Monetary Fund have to bail out failing economies in Europe or Africa. Isolationism is an option no longer.

This interconnectedness of the modern world requires international cooperation and global planning. People with a cosmopolitan mindset are better equipped for these complex tasks than parochial persons, who speak only one language, are comfortable only in their own culture, and are oblivious to other people's thinking. We are all inexorably entangled with the rest of the world. Based on sheer self-interest, it behooves us all to master the cosmopolitan cultural and political competencies to deal with this role with moral responsibility and strategic savvy.

How does one infuse minds socialized in narrow communalism, parochialism, or sectarianism with a necessary cosmopolitan outlook, particularly in the South African context? An effective approach is critical introspection about tradition in each SA ethnic group. Once problematic aspects of celebrated traditions are questioned, students are no longer captives of their socialization. They change into autonomous reasoning citizens.

In the African tradition, the questioning could start with *ukuthwala*, the rural practice of abducting young women. Originally it aimed at inducing the two families to negotiate the terms of a consensual marriage, but it has deteriorated into powerful older men raping the abducted females and thereby branding them as property. The whole patriarchal tradition of gender inequality could find resonance among a susceptible African learner's audience and applies to all other groups as well. It should include the still-prevalent North and East African tradition of clitorectomy, fortunately not practiced in South Africa, as well as the circumcision of young men in initiation camps. Are there alternatives that would minimize death and injuries? The role of traditional healers and untested muti as medicine could come up for critical discussion.

In the Indian tradition, the Hindu caste system in India could be the ideal subject for scrutiny. Although the caste order has been abandoned by the indentured laborers imported into Natal by the British colonial authorities, the 140 million dalit outcasts still suffer from a customary tradition despite its being outlawed in India. Other topics for critical analysis of tradition could focus on attitudes to gender, the merits and disadvantages of nonconsensual arranged marriages, the dowry system, and the role of family honor and endogamy in general.

Afrikaans-speaking students could be exposed to their parents' complicity of overwhelmingly supporting apartheid uncritically. For white Afrikaners, introspection about the ways in which the desire to preserve a distinct culture and language—worthy ideals in themselves—lead to social distance and exclusion of others could be examined. Why was language maintenance not defined as a common good, so that all Afrikaans-speakers as well as non-Afrikaans-speakers wishing to learn another language could have been included? Why did Afrikaner nationalism acquire such a hold over a group's collective mind for so long? Answers to these questions provoke an examination of racialization for a variety of reasons.

South Africa provides a case study of whether and when political struggles become ethnicized, or vice versa, when various cultural traditions become racialized and mobilized for political ends. At the same time, the tenacity of racial ideologies are tested when racism becomes dysfunctional in an interdependent economy. The legal deracialization in the face of increasing costs (such as sanctions, industrial action, and illegitimacy) suggests a surprising rational choice in favor of a redefinition of a former racial identity. Ethnic identity was not abandoned, but pragmatically readjusted to fit changing circumstances. In its self-perception, the National Party negotiated itself *into* power, not *out of* power. Both sides claimed victory in the negotiations: the ANC for having achieved power through the ballot box, and the National Party for having locked the ANC into a Western liberal democracy and secured the survival of the capitalist order.

Political literacy could culminate in the question, "What was liberation supposed to mean beyond equal rights?" The ANC has not solved the tension between altering the economic structure radically or merely populating a colonial economy with black faces. Built on comparatively cheap labor and the migratory labor system, the colonial economy has endured, regardless of who sits in corporate boardrooms. What has changed is that the unrest, xenophobia, and gross inequality flowing from this condition are policed by a new regime—an ingenious "solution" for the old, illegitimate ruling class. However, given the constraints of a global economic order and South Africa's dependency on this system, was there any realistic alternative? When students grasp these intricate connections between the local and the global, they have achieved a truly cosmopolitan consciousness.

9

Theorizing Xenophobia

Various theoretical conceptualizations from the social science literature shed further light on South African xenophobia. For reasons discussed in the literature review, we omit the reductionist economic precipitants and focus instead on psychosocial theories. Four perspectives will be briefly sketched: first, the notion of "moral panic," used by critical criminologists, such as Stanley Cohen (1972); second, the reflections of Fanon on the postcolonial condition; third, the Freudian theory of the "narcissism of small differences," which provides in our view a more convincing explanation; fourth, our own theory of "identity assertion" in line with Horowitz's notion of "reversal of dishonor."

"Moral panic," used since the 1970s and 1980s, describes reactions to various imagined and real dangers to society, ranging from communism during the Cold War to drug trafficking or Islamic terrorism later. The behavior of a designated group is viewed as harmful and threatening to the well-being of a community. As "moral panic" spreads and hostility increases, the accused group is demonized as "folk devils." A clear division between "us" and "them" emerges. Moral panic is characterized by disproportionate action taken against the constructed threat and its actual danger. It becomes a moral duty of every rightful citizen to join the campaign to counter the threat. Moral panics are viewed as highly volatile. They often disappear as quickly as they are embraced, which testifies to their manipulative and constructed nature. The mass media play a major role in turning incitements to moral panic on and off.

However, the notion of moral panic is largely descriptive. It sheds light on a process of how attitudes spread through contagion and how targets are perceived but does not address the "why." Blaming media manipulation is insufficient in explaining why xenophobia suddenly declines or succeeds with a push of a button.

Among classical authors, Franz Fanon stands out with his insights derived from the anticolonial struggle in Algeria. On the violence after political liberation, he observed, "The colonized man will first manifest his aggressiveness which has been deposited in his bones against his own people. . . . The colonized man is an envious man." Since decolonization mainly benefited an indigenous political elite and in the absence of material decolonization without changing the life chances of the decolonized masses, Fanon predicted that the envy in the postliberation period turns on outsiders: "From nationalism, we have passed to chauvinism, and finally to racism. These foreigners are called on to leave, their shops are burned, their street stalls wrecked. . . . We observe a permanent seesaw between African unity, which fades quicker and quicker into the mist of oblivion" (cited in Suren Pillay, Chimurenga, 2008: 12). The real culprits of impoverishment—the indigenous political elite in cahoots with the old ruling class in a neocolonial arrangement—cannot be targeted, since they still wallow in the glory of liberation, pretend to have the interest of the masses at heart, and effectively silence dissent. This describes also the South African situation. Fanon emphasizes envy of ascribed foreign traits that are missing in the self-image of poor locals. As two South African social scientists have written and our research in Khayelitsha has revealed, "Perpetrators single out target groups for their apparently superior abilities, which are feared, resented, loathed and detested. Violence becomes a desperate but decisive method of last resort with which perpetrators compensate for their own shortcomings" (du Toit and Kotze 2011: 162). Alan Whitehorn (2007: 16), in outlining the stages of genocide, refers to some preliminary steps, which resemble the perpetration of xenophobia. One step is the classification of other people into simplified dichotomous opposites, a prerequisite to stereotyping, which ignores the existing differences within each category as well as the areas of shared attributes: "People often employ verbal and visual shortcuts in classifying, ignoring diversity and labeling groups with a simplified name or symbol." In this case, labels such as *amakwerekwere* seize upon the way the language of "others" sounds. It expands to attributes such as the clothing they wear, their behavior, and physiological features. Labeling and dualistic thinking of the unfamiliar readily lead to stigmatization and slip from "describing to judging" despite the inaccuracies involved. Dehumanization follows from these precedents. It is manifest in the everyday humor of the locals which as Whitehorn describes "can easily turn from childish play to adult hate speech, cruel jokes and vengeful caricatures." These tendencies are reinforced by significant others, among them parents, teachers, and a range of leaders. That makes it easy to blame the newcomers as a group for society's ills.

"Narcissism of small difference" refers to a concept coined by Freud in 1917 and further elaborated in *Civilization and Its Discontents* (Freud [1930] 1961). As is well known, Freud, controversially, assumed an "inclination to aggression" in everybody and considered the Christian commandment "to love one's neighbors as oneself" an idealistic illusion. "Nothing else runs counter to the original nature of man," he wrote, adding that "instinctual passions are stronger than reasonable interests." However, while passions may override interests, those emotions are let loose, triggered, restrained, or repressed by different circumstances. Aggression does not express itself uniformly among human collectivities.

Freud maintained that our uniqueness is threatened not by others with whom we share little in common, but by groups that resemble us most. We exaggerate our difference and invent artificial distinctions to assert our identity the more an out-group shares the same features with us. In the absence of visible differences, imagined pseudodifferences are magnified to reinforce an uncertain identity, to reaffirm self-worth, and to prove unique selfhood. In short, the narcissist is injured by the "nearly-we," who imperil our self-concept. A psychologist in the Freudian tradition, Sam Vaknin (2011: 36), writes, "The narcissist feels humiliated, shamed, and embarrassed not to be special after all—and he reacts with envy and aggression towards this source of frustration." Vaknin applies these insights specifically to immigrants: "The ugliest manifestations of racism (up to genocide) are reserved to immigrants who look, act, and talk like us. The more they try to emulate and imitate us, the harder they attempt to belong, the more ferocious our rejection of them." A historical example is European Jews, who were most viciously prosecuted and decimated in the one country into which they had long ago fully assimilated by adopting all German virtues and vices. Shedding of an original identity did not save them, but only exacerbated the fury of the perpetrators.

The late Christopher Hitchens (NP, July 3, 2010) has added further examples to Freud's insight that "it is precisely the minor differences in people who are otherwise alike that form the basis of feelings of hostility between them." Hitchens highlights a long list of contemporary long-standing conflicts between similar ethnic entities: In Cyprus, it is hard to tell a Greek from a Turk, but they do not intermarry; Serbs and Croats inflicted mutual atrocities on each other, even though both used the same language in the same state and subsequently reinvented language differences to reinforce the divide; French- and Flemish-speaking Belgians cannot agree on basic rules; Muslim Pakistanis fought a vicious war of separation with Muslim Bangladeshis; the number of victims in the earlier partition of India after independence is rivaled only by the 1990 genocide in Rwanda, where Hutus wiped out Tutsi neighbors of the same religion and language. Hitchens concludes with a reaffirmation of the common evolutionary sameness of humans that spurred rather than prevented the hostility: "One of the great advantages possessed by *Homo sapiens* is the amazing lack of variation between its different 'branches.' Since we left Africa, we have hardly diverged as a species. If we were dogs, we would all be the same breed. We do not suffer from the enormous differences that separate other primates, let alone other mammals.

As if to spite this huge natural gift, and to disfigure what could be our over-whelming solidarity, we manage to find excuses for chauvinism and racism on the most minor of occasions and then to make the most of them."

The question of why minimal difference triggers hostility still needs to be answered. Here psychoanalytic reasoning provides further plausible answers. It also reveals the limits of legal efforts to contain ethnic antagonisms. The psychoanalytic explanation, first explicated in the seminal research on bigotry and anti-Semitism in "The Authoritarian Personality" (Adorno et al. 1950), established empirically that an individual who is prejudiced toward one group usually also holds negative attitudes toward other minorities, sometimes even fictitious groups. Bigotry as a syndrome comprises racism, homophobia, xenophobia, anti-Semitism, parochial ethnocentrism, misogyny, and other forms of denigration of out-groups. Analysts of ethnic strife in this tradition like Michael Ignatieff (1993) or the Cypriot psychiatrist Vamik Volkan (2006) have emphasized the crucial correlation between early socialization, ego-development, and later attitudes toward collective attachments. In this tradition, all socialized behavior we learn amounts to repression of instinctual id drives. If this necessary repression by societal rules, typified by the superego (conscience), is not mediated by a strong ego of a self-assured, autonomous person, then group conformity guides behavior.

The Indian psychoanalyst Sudhir Kakar accounts for Hindu-Muslim riots with the images emboldened in early childhood. Kakar, following Freud and Erikson, reminds us that the community in which we are socialized is always part of our personal identity. Its myths, history, rituals, and symbols are idealized by the young child "in the enhancement of self-esteem for belonging to such an exalted and blessed entity" (Kakar 1996: 189). However, the internalization of necessary social rules (culture) also clashes with a person's natural drives. This conflict is solved through projection of "bad" representations onto others. "First projected to inanimate objects and animals and later to people and other groups—the latter often available to the child as a preselection by the group—the disavowed bad representations need such 'reservoirs' as Vamik Volkan calls them. These reservoirs—Muslims for Hindus, Arabs for Jews, Tibetans for Chinese, and vice versa—are also convenient repositories for subsequent rages and hateful feelings for which no clear-cut addressee is available. Since most of the bad representations arise from a social disapproval of the child's animality, as expressed in its dirtiness, and unruly sexuality, it is preeminently this animality which a civilized moral self must disavow and place in the reservoir group" (Kakar 1996: 189). This psychoanalytic account explains why in every ethnic hostility the other group is ascribed sexual licentiousness, drunkenness, and other forbidden behavior. In short, we tend to project onto others what we have to suppress in ourselves.

Strong ethnic attachment presupposes boundaries of who belongs and who does not. Those defined as "outsiders" are often victimized. Bigotry is attractive to people in search of an identity. They can borrow strength from the glory of the group. Some people realize their identity and self-esteem in religion and the hope for afterlife, others in work and professionalism, others in sport or consumerism or even from the type of car they drive. Uncritical communalism and ethnonationalism are on offer among many bases of identity. The less fulfillment and sublimation are guaranteed in an uncertain work sphere, the more attractive the ethnic in-group becomes. Because of the common socialization experience, associated with early security and comfort, individuals fall in easily with "my people" at the expense of solidarity with others in a crisis. However, in South Africa we do not deal with the problem of dogmatic conflicting identities clashing with each other, as in India, but with the very opposite: insecure, fragile identities searching to assert themselves, develop self-esteem, escape humiliation, and reverse denigration.

"Identity assertion," our fourth closely linked dimension, is a concept that emerged in varying guises during our group discussions and open surveys when respondents tried to define who they are in relation to foreigners. It is best illustrated by a story told by an astute South African novelist. Jonny Steinberg (ST, January 2, 2011) reports an assessment by a Somali township trader:

> Most of our customers are unemployed or on welfare. They are the laughing stock of South Africa. But when they come to our shops, they are king. They can come with R2. There are only a few things you can buy with that: single cigarettes, one or two chewing gum sticks, sweets. The customer can come with his coins and say, "Give me a cigarette." I get one. He says, "No, I've changed my mind; I want chewing gum." I say, "Yes, Bra," and get it. By the time I am back at the counter, he has changed his mind again. "No, Kwerekwere. I want sweets." A South African shopkeeper will not tolerate that. He will say: "You are wasting my time. F*** off.' A Somali cannot afford to say f*** off. He can only say, "Yes, Sissie. Yes, Bra." And so the laughing stock of South Africa come to us because our shops are the one place in their own country where they can say, "I want this!" and someone will respond.

Both sides hold each other in utter contempt, but the powerless customer empowers himself by ordering the foreigner around, who has to react with superior discipline not to enrage fury. This interchange encapsulates the relationship between insider and outsider, who each transcends his victim status for a few moments and feels good about it.

The shopkeeper has unwittingly articulated the key to understanding South African xenophobia, in line also with the academic explanations of some sociologists. Xenophobic violence represents the reversal of daily humiliation. For fleeting moments it establishes recognition and a satisfying identity that daily life denies. Donald Horowitz (2001: 536), on the basis of a comparative study of ethnic violence, has pointed out that "the violence that aims at thwarting domination, particularly the violence of so-called backward groups, is suffused with affect born of humiliation. Much of the pleasure that violence brings, springs from the mastery that reverses dishonor." In a similar vein, the South African sociologist Simon Bekker (2010: 137) has drawn attention to the joy of perpetrators when they attack foreigners: "The body language appears to be devoid of guilt, of remorse and of fear of retribution. The young men shown carrying weapons or loot emerge as disinhibited and often as revelling in, as deriving pleasure from their actions." Bekker is correct in asserting that economistic theories of relative deprivation and resource mobilization that dominate most social science explanations are too rational. They fail to account for the emotional element of xenophobia that symbolically frees from real deprivation: "Young men in this urban underclass seek to develop and sustain strategies of coping and of survival in an otherwise hostile and exclusionary environment. They seek personal dignity in this humiliating environment. Given few choices to survive in their society moreover, many opt for activities defined by the state as criminal and often find themselves involved in violent behaviour in pursuit both of resources as well as of tangible triumph over dishonour and humiliation" (Bekker 2010: 147).

The reemergence of necklacing in Khayelitsha can be explained in similar terms as a reversal of humiliation, and not only because of lacking police response. The vigilante killers frequently also come from a category not normally expected to brutalize victims. As the media (CT, February 6, 2014) reported one such case, "Kose screamed for mercy and begged for forgiveness while being attacked by a crowd of about 20 people, mostly young women, who used planks, rocks, sjamboks and makeshift weapons" before dragging the alleged thief of appliances into a fire with a tire around his neck. Necklacing amounts to democratic brutality. The powerless community takes power by deciding over life and death in a gruesome ritual. Even children participate as onlookers in the horrendous spectacle. In January 2013, after dozens of similar attacks on alleged criminals the year before, an Angolan shebeen (beer parlor) owner, Joseph Hipandulwa, was first assaulted and then set alight after twenty men had detained and fetched him from a nearby informal settlement. Residents said his cries for forgiveness could be heard from blocks away: "He cried like a baby, but people wanted to make sure he is dead." His corpse was partially eaten by dogs until the police collected the remains four hours later. Assuming there were no foreigners in the townships inhabited by the same materially and psychologically impoverished people, they would certainly invent other vulnerable targets for rehabilitating their insecure identity. The real culprits for the misery of perpetrators—government and business—are immune to the rage, because they have the power to retaliate. They have the "spatialized racism" (Samara 2011) guarded "robustly," as South African real estate agents advertise the security of their apartments on the market. In the absence of retribution, powerless foreigners become the easy victims of the even more powerless and frustrated perpetrators. If it had not become such a cliché, "scapegoating" people for the failure of others would be the right concept. Social psychologists interpret scapegoating as exonerating wrongdoing: "Scapegoating is both a means of exorcising guilt and of defining social, religious and national identity through the construction of a moral order against the dangerous, disruptive, defiling other" (Igglesden 2002: 8).

If our concept of identity assertion is accurate, why then do we find xenophobic attitudes as strong among South African elites, black and white, as among lower classes? Elites normally possess a secure identity. Stellenbosch political scientists Pierre du Toit and Hennie Kotze (2011: 164) use the World Value Survey for a breakdown of xenophobia according to class and race and find "this dislike [of foreigners] is found even in the ranks of the upper class, those most able to compete effectively with foreigners and to insulate themselves socially from their presence." The authors also detect "no significant changes of opinion among the basis of race differences," except that Indians seem to be more tolerant, compared with blacks and whites. One in ten Indians, but one among three blacks and one among four whites agree with a total prohibition of "people coming here from other countries." This sentiment of closure in all racial groups has steadily increased since 1995. Higher-class members too have bought into the widespread belief that foreign migrants are the main source of crime in the country, although they are the preferred employees in skills.

However, "elites are more willing to put up with them as neighbors than are the general South African public" (du Toit and Koetze 2011: 167). Neighbors of a different nationality in upper-class areas can usually afford the place and are of similar class or educational background. They are not resented, but even admired, in Horowitz's (2001: 197) definition, because of their "excess of enterprise, ambition, energy, arrogance, and achievement," rationalizations with which the urban poor attack foreigners. Besides, upper-class higher tolerance of foreigners does not include "liking," but merely coexisting with them, because they are not competing with them for status or scarce resources. These elite members, despite their reservations about too many foreigners, have no reason to go on a rampage; on the contrary, they reinforce their superior status by inveighing against xenophobic violence of the poor or even contribute to charity for victims.

In line with this reasoning, the Danish academic Christian Lund (2011) has added an intriguing theoretical twist by conceptually connecting property and citizenship, especially land rights and belonging in Africa. It is worth quoting Lund at some length: "Few things are more fundamental in social life or politics than what we have and who we are. Property and citizenship, in the broadest sense, are perhaps the most overt and familiar manifestations of these core dimensions. The core element of both is recognition. The process of recognition of political identity as belonging and of claims to land and other resources as property simultaneously work to imbue the institution that provides such recognition with the legitimation and recognition of its authority to do so. These are the 'contracts,' so to speak, that link citizenship and property to political authority in society" (Lund 2011: 72). Lund asserts that the dynamic connection between claims to land and social identity defined through property rights "is valid for post-colonial societies in general—and is a rewarding entry point to the analysis of power in any society" (72).

This assertion is problematic. As important as land claims are for belonging when there is communal ownership, as in most of Africa, belonging of South Africa's urban poor does not rest on land. In fact, most own nothing, neither land nor any other property. The urban poor own only one thing symbolically: the state as citizens with an ID card. In their understanding, that should give them access to the wealth of the state as rightful owners. Since state resources are seen as fixed, foreigners as noncitizens have no claim to these limited assets. Yet foreigners are experienced as better off and more advanced in everything, and therefore must have acquired this status unrightfully. The anger of the locals about their own deficiencies is directed against those clever "thieves." They have outmaneuvered the rightful owners of the property in an uneven playing field.

If it is true that "the urban poor occupy a different universe of meaning to us" (Hassim 2008: 53), then only political education can unify the vision of South African citizens. As long as a substantial number of the population have to exaggerate their insecure identity, combined with the resentment that they not truly belong; as long as they are not recognized tangibly but only rhetorically by the managers of the state, the need for identity assertion persists and therefore the potential for xenophobic rampages continues.

Conclusion: Alternatives and Global Trends

P olitical education about xenophobia provides a window of opportunity to broaden the South African mindset about the rights of others. South Africans have glided smoothly from an authoritarian era to a democratic one without grasping fully the lessons from their own previous exclusion for human rights and citizenship in the new order. Apart from public education, what else can South Africa realistically do to minimize xenophobia? What migration policy serves South Africa best, given the high number of refugee claimants and scarce resources? These are the most difficult questions, to which there are no simple answers. However, there are three practical alternatives that can be implemented: first, legitimating migrants; second, improving conditions in source countries of refugees; third, integration of qualifying newcomers through a new immigration policy.

Xenophobia is strongly tied to "authority values." The political culture of a country frames the debate about the legitimacy of migrants. Utterances of politicians, legislation, and immigration policy shape perceptions of belonging. In Europe otherness is constructed by charging immigrants of abusing public resources and contaminating national traditions. Not so in South Africa, where refugees are mainly held responsible for the high crime rate. One has yet to see any figure that shows the ratio comparing convictions of nationals to convictions of foreigners. Politicians have a duty to address such myths, refuse to criminalize foreigners, and publicize the positive contributions of refugees. An ongoing media debate over issues of belonging, identity, and justice can deepen understanding of xenophobia. Such a "communicative democracy" (Young) also acknowledges legitimate concerns about migrants straining wage levels of locals. The condescending concept of "tolerance" should be dropped. Instead, an appreciation of diversity as enrichment can be fostered. While some differences are irreconcilable and some foreign habits may irritate others, interacting across cultural and ideological borders also provides a rewarding experience.

Zimbabweans constitute the overwhelming majority of migrants. If Pretoria were to instill a genuine human rights culture in Zimbabwe, by ridding the state of its tyrannical leadership through effective economic sanctions and political pressure, millions of Zimbabweans would not want to leave and hundreds of thousands would want to return. Such a policy lies within the capacity of the dominant Southern African power, but lacks the political will. As an incentive, South Africa could even provide repatriation and integration assistance, as the European Union does in some Balkan countries. While Pretoria's influence over other African source countries is far weaker, the same principle could apply there.

Skilled economic migrants who wish to settle in South Africa constitute an asset. This needs to be recognized by a sophisticated immigration policy along the Canadian model of a point system. Many foreigners in South Africa fall into this category of desirable immigrants. Most "irregular" migrants already in the country need to be regularized, integrated, and offered recognition. Their self-selection as ambitious risk-takers with the initiative to leave hopeless conditions is already proof of their capacity and potential to become future good citizens. The new U.S. immigration policy toward eleven million undocumented foreigners suggests criteria as to who should be accepted or excluded on the basis of criminal convictions. If all newcomers are issued with IDs that employers have to register, such a regularized and transparent immigration system can be managed to the mutual benefit of citizens and noncitizens alike. For example, if the South African Teachers Union (SADTU) were to recognize foreign teaching credentials and actively welcome those professional in its ranks, local learners and teachers' horizons would be expanded.

The fundamental questions to be answered are: Why does a society that liberated itself in the name of human rights turn against fellow Africans who escaped human rights violations at home? Why do victims become victimizers? Why has a highly politicized anti- apartheid movement failed in its expected solidarity with suffering in other parts of Africa?

One answer points to the depoliticization of the "born free" generation, the consumerist colonialism, and the culture of corruption that have undermined the vision of liberation. A progressive constitution, designed by a Westernized elite, does not resonate with substantial sections of the electorate. The government itself shows little interest in resurrecting the spirit of liberation, because the liberated would likely turn it against their self-proclaimed liberators.

In South Africa, xenophobia embodies both rational elements in exposing locals to unwelcome competition with foreigners in the labor market and retail trade as well as irrational elements that resemble conspiracy theories. The Norwegian mass murderer Anders Breinik located "cultural Marxists of the Frankfurt School" as the conspirators behind multiculturalism. That outsiders are being brought in to undermine, pollute, and harm a national body is a common fantasy of xenophobes. It is not to be dismantled with more accurate knowledge. The more false information is debunked, the more a "backfire effect" (Nyham) kicks in that motivates a search for more arguments to bolster a misguided world-view. Knowing "the hidden truth" while the rest believes in the official pro-paganda restores agency to the powerless conspiracy theorist. The paranoid believer can wallow in the elitist feeling of being wiser and more knowledge-able than the manipulated masses. Therefore, the conventional wisdom of scapegoating in a competition for scarce resources and entitlement needs to be supplemented with psychosocial explanations. Xenophobia cannot be reduced to labor market exigencies alone. Abandoned powerless slum dwellers empower themselves by constructing a superior identity. "Identity assertion" provides meaning to a meaningless life for fleeting moments.

In a political culture of cynicism, distrust, and crime, violent xenophobia thrives. Steven Pinter (Interview, G&M, May 11, 2013) has perceptively asserted that "the violence of anarchy is on the whole worse than the violence of tyranny." The latter is predictable and foreseeable, and one can guard against it to a certain extent. Anarchic violence, in contrast, occurs randomly and indis-criminately without a state authority protecting victims. South African town-ship life exemplifies constant anarchic violence. Victims do not expect instant police protection or trust state assurances. While South Africa cannot be called a "failed state," neglected communities in informal settlements cannot rely on government assistance. Instead, the frustrated poor engage in preemptive aggression against anyone defined as an enemy, whether foreigner or criminal.

Yet responses of students surveyed in township schools also point to a res-ervoir of goodwill that can be utilized to shape a progressive, collective mindset. A more sophisticated moral intelligence is on the rise in the modern world almost everywhere. The treatment of women and children has become a public issue. Sexual relations without mutual consent and bullying at schoolyards, con-sidered as normal or inevitable in previous generations, are now treated as seri-ous crimes in most societies. Racism, while still not eradicated, has itself become widely stigmatized. Health and environmental consciousness has dramatically improved. Even in developing countries, high smoking rates are on the decline. The rise of the average IQ score in North America from 72 in 1900 to 100 today has not altered the brain potential at birth, but produced new cognitive skills in a one world connected by ever-more-complex communication and stimula-tion. Why should "othering" in xenophobia be exempt from such global trends of moral reasoning, quite apart from pragmatic reasons? A renewed political literacy and other interventions beyond charity can also improve the situation of migrants in South Africa if teachers and national leaders recognize the problem and show the resolve to tackle it.

Our study has largely ignored another category of migrants: internally displaced persons (IDP), because legally they are citizens, although frequently treated as outsiders in city slums. This group is likely to grow dramatically with climate change. "Environmental refugees" escape from unlivable conditions, as a result of predictable water shortages or other natural disasters. Increasing droughts, drying up wells, and sinking water levels with permanently parched land have already extended the Sahara desert and pushed traditional cattle-grazing people onto the land of other people, which lies at the heart of the ongoing conflict in the Sudan and neighboring states. In the Southern African region, frequent flooding in Mozambique had similar effects. Some low-lying island states in the Pacific and Indian Ocean are threatened to disappear altogether, because of rising sea levels. Most of these environmentally displaced people move into already overcrowded city slums in the same state and face internal xenophobia, despite being citizens. Many of the climate refugees also cross borders, confined to UN-administered displacement camps, never to return to an unlivable homeland.

Yet those environmental migrants are refused the status of refugees, which is legally defined in the 1951 United Nations Convention. In this document a "refugee" is restricted to "a person who owing to a well-founded fear of being persecuted for reasons of race, religion, nationality, membership of a particular social group, or political opinion, is outside the country of their nationality, and is unable to or, owing to such fear, is unwilling to avail him/herself to the protection of that country." This outdated definition excludes "environmental persecution" and needs to be expanded to climate refugees. However, the UN High Commissioner for Refugees (UNHCR) has repeatedly rejected this change on the grounds that lumping both groups together would water down the issues and assist neither type of displaced group. Since forced environmental migrancy is permanent in most cases while political migrancy is open to correction in the source country, the environmentally displaced should surely be entitled at least to the same, if not higher, level of assistance and protection as temporarily displaced political migrants.

Another increase of migrancy originates from the global economic crisis, particularly in the southern European states. They register half of their youth as unemployed. Given the EU integrated labor market and the wage discrepancies, the more ambitious job seekers from southern and eastern Europe move to northern European states and carve out niches of employment, similar to millions of Central and Latin American irregulars as gardeners, food industry employees, office cleaners, and construction workers in the United States. Polish women, for example, have established themselves as the preferred caregivers in Germany in similar ways as Philippine household helpers and child minders have in Canada. As long as they are employed in "undesirable," low-paying occupations, they are tolerated but largely live as marginalized outsiders. This cultural division of labor has reinforced essentialist stereotypes about what certain nationalities are "good at," and thereby shaped perceptions of collectivities, including identities among their own members.

To its credit, South Africa at least allows foreign passport holders into the country and allows them to register as asylum seekers, albeit without any financial assistance as in Europe. In contrast, wealthy Europe has closed itself totally off. Neither economic opportunism nor monthly pictures of young men climbing tall fences around the two Spanish enclaves in Morocco or rickety boats cramped with frightened women and children in high waves can move European populations toward human solidarity. It is estimated that about three thousand people drowned in the Mediterranean during 2013 while attempting to reach Lampedusa or Malta. In October 2014 an overcrowded boat with mainly Palestinian refugees from devastated Gaza capsized when it was rammed by another boat in an apparent quarrel among smugglers. Close to five hundred people died in this incident alone. (See Jim Yardley, "Shipwreck Was Simple Murder, Migrants Recall," NYT, October 21, 2014). Unscrupulous smugglers are often the only way refugees have to escape their war-ravaged countries. The drowning tragedies are utterly preventable and implicate the European bystanders. If the EU member states were to set up immigration offices at their diplomatic missions in North Africa and the Middle East, at least some of those desperate refugees could enter Europe legally and would not have ended up as casualties. An orderly application process would also establish procedures to accord priority to genuine refugees and distinguish economic migrants from hardship cases. The EU governments could also select from a large pool of skilled migrants those most needed in their respective economies. For EU citizens themselves, the great progress was, as Sylvia Kaufmann (NYT, February 23, 2014) observed, "a continent where 70 years ago people were still slaughtering one another; today 500 million citizens can live wherever they wish in 28 countries." If the anti-EU and anti-immigrant parties succeed in destroying that fragile construct, the return to parochial nationalism, perhaps even slaughtering, will not be far off, as the Ukraine and Bosnia already demonstrated. If neither empathy with the poor of the world nor legal obligations within the European Union will succeed in dampening nationalist mindsets, then economic rationality remains as the last hope. Chrystia Freeland (NYT, op-ed, December 26, 2014), a member of the Canadian Parliament, is correct when she writes: "The world's rich countries are falling into two camps: those who are able to attract and welcome immigrants and those that are not. Western industrial societies and parts of Europe that are unwilling to accept newcomers, and to allow themselves to be transformed by those immigrants, are destined to demographic and economic decline." Unfortunately, when liberal political leaders are faced with a nationalistic electorate, most will be ready to choose reelections rather than to take the risk of voter rejection. Among European leaders, the conservative Angela Merkel stands out as a commendable exception by advocating long term prosperity through more immigration. In contrast to her British or Danish counterparts, in her New Year 2015 message she forcefully rebuked a new right-wing German protest movement *Pegida* (Patriotic Europeans Against the Islamization of the West), appealing to Germans to shun anti-immigrant calls for both economic and humanitarian reasons (NYT, "Merkel Targets anti-Muslim Rallies," December 31, 2014).

The Pew Research Center (March 8, 2012) reports that as of 2010 about 3 percent of the world's population, or about 214 million people, have migrated across international borders, that is, have resided for more than a year in a country other than the one they were born in. In light of the above indicators, this percentage of migration is likely to increase significantly in the future. However, not all of these exiles are poor or refugees, but an increasing number are academic high-flyers or "millionaire migrants," roaming the globe for business opportunities. What is also often overlooked are the remittances with which migrants contribute to the development and poverty alleviation in their home countries: "According to the World Bank, migrants sent $401 billion to their families in developing countries. That's eight times the United States' budget for foreign aid, including military and economic assistance. It's roughly equivalent to the gross domestic product of Austria or South Africa. By 2015, the number could rise to $515 billion" (Marie Arana, op-ed, NYT, May 15, 2013). How have and will governments and populations react to the increased presence of foreigners in their midst? Three trends stand out.

First, borders have been militarized. While some trading blocs, like the European Union, have abolished internal borders for economic migrants, even legally crossing external borders has become more difficult. To receive a tourist Shengen, British, Canadian, or U.S. visa in South Africa requires personal visits to the embassy, long waiting periods, and higher fees. Past arrangements to encourage reciprocal tourism have been discarded. "Asylum shopping" for the most hospitable country has been outlawed by returning refugees to the first free country they entered. "Securitization" of borders, not their abolition as analysts predicted, has accompanied the spread of migrancy. Drones now patrol the U.S.-Mexican border, the Caribbean as well as the Mediterranean Sea. Since the inofficial war on terror has been declared, every foreigner is a potential terrorist unless thoroughly vetted. Arrests and punishments for "illegal" border crossings have multiplied. The *New York Times* (May 28, 2013) reports that U.S. detentions for such acts rose from 11,000 in 2002 to 85,000 in 2012. Annually more than 400,000 persons are deported from the United States.

Second, in many migrant-receiving states, the acquisition of citizenship has been made more difficult. Preconditions for citizenship have stiffened, residence requirements have lengthened, language tests have hardened, history examinations have become more complicated, background checks for felonies have become more thorough, and application fees have increased. As a consequence, successful citizenship applications declined or are not even attempted, as long as residence permits do not entail material disadvantages, except voting rights and exclusion from public service. The controversial U.S. immigration reform of the eleven million undocumented migrants envisages a mandatory waiting time of thirteen years before the irregulars can fully regularize their status as citizens.

Instead of using citizenship as a normal path of integration, citizenship exclusion prevents political engagements and feelings of belonging. Many

migrants are relegated to the position of permanent outsiders. This applies particularly to the increased importation of unskilled or semiskilled labor on
temporary work visas in many countries. In Canada these "permanent tem-
poraries" currently number 350,000, advocated by oil patch executives, mining
houses, and construction firms. These employers are allowed to pay lower wages
to the mainly male laborers under the pretense that no domestic workers are
available to fill the jobs. When the outsourcing of middle-class IT jobs was also
attempted by Canadian banks in 2013, public opposition forced the government
to scale down and tighten the policy of temporary work permits. The negative
example of Germany's permanent Turkish "guest workers" was frequently
invoked.

Third, a countertrend has emerged in what has been called "the transnation-
alization of higher learning" (Ong 1999: 49). Elite U.S., Canadian, and European
universities now compete for high-performing students from developing states
and also incentivize their own students to study abroad. Private universities
position themselves with satellite campuses in foreign locations as global knowledge centers. Many American and European institutions want to retain their
foreign graduates as permanent knowledge producers, particularly in science,
technology, and business administration. More than half of U.S. Ph.D.'s awarded
in these fields go to foreign recipients; a high percentage of successful start-ups
in California's Silicon Valley are by Indian and Chinese graduates. This inter-
sects, as Ong has shown, with Asian elite interests to secure multiple passports
and residencies for operating as international venture capitalists, for having
retirement choices, or simply as risk insurance. In Vancouver on the campus of
the University of British Columbia, a whole new suburb with dozens of high-
rises has been built where the sales agents openly declare in publicity materials,
"Intended market: Chinese." Well known is the talk about the business traveler
as an "astronaut" who "is continually in the air while his wife and children are
located in Australia, Canada, or the United States, earning rights of residence"
(Ong 1999: 127). In several countries this mobility of the wealthy is aided by
fast-tracking residence status through investment in a government trust for job
creation or real estate purchases. For example, Portugal has granted instantly
almost 2,000 Shengen permits to Chinese investors, while the poor refugees
simultaneously drown nearby.

Ong's perceptive book about the political results of this collective elite
behavior and state collaboration is titled *Flexible Citizenship* (Ong 1999). A more
accurate title would have been "Opportunistic Citizenship" or "Citizenship of
Convenience." In short, with ease of travel and communication citizenship and
national identity no longer coincide. For skilled migrants, "home" is increasingly
multilocational. "Belonging" is fluid, dependent on opportunistic calculations
of advantage and risks. Allegiance to the state of residence, as citizenship was
defined previously, is doubtful, if not wholly absent. Governments can no longer
bank on the loyalty of citizens, whether in tax collection or security behavior.
Emotional identification with home and state has weakened for a growing group

of postnational migrants. It was said of true intellectuals and artists that they are "at home everywhere and nowhere." This cosmopolitan mobility now includes a variety of globally sought-after talents.

With its xenophobic skepticism and parochial naval gazing, South Africa is in danger of missing out and lagging behind these global trends. South Africa has already lost a large number of talented citizens who emigrated because of crime, corruption, or perceived injustices of affirmative action. They thrive abroad, but not at home, where they are needed most. Many self-exiled South African professionals nostalgically yearn to be useful to their country of birth beyond their annual holiday in the Cape. Yet unlike China with its "Thousand Talents" scheme to attract expatriates back, South Africa has no such incentives in place. The Chinese venture capitalist or European entrepreneur searching for a safe retirement haven encounters the same bureaucratic indifference as the Nigerian or Ghanaian professional, not to speak of the resentment of the Somali or Pakistani shopkeeper.

Yet apart from its unresolved widening inequality and sociopolitical problems of an imagined liberation gone sour for half its population, South Africa has most of the ingredients of successful postcolonial countries. Its economic assets aside, its pleasant climate, its English-language medium, rule of law, first-class universities, vibrant civil society, robust public discourse, and occasionally threatened but still functioning democracy should make the country attractive for innovative cosmopolitan minds. Like Canada, South Africa lacks a core group that could force assimilative homogeneity on its diverse population. Unlike Europe, which has abandoned multiculturalism for reassertion of primordialism, South Africa is not gripped with Islamophobia. It also does not practice the sectarian violence of the Middle East. The legalized racial groups do not hate each other, but the system that once imposed their identity and unequal separation. If the enduring legacy of this past can finally be overcome, the Mandela state at the periphery could again morph into the center of global admiration.

Responses to South African Xenophobia: Ten Arguments

1. The responses to the January 2015 looting of hundreds of foreign shops in Soweto and elsewhere reveal more about the South African national consciousness than the events themselves. The empty condemnations, the denial of xenophobia in preference to labeling it criminality, the blame of victims, and the convoluted excuses of the perpetrators are almost worse than the official silence and long-standing passivity about well-known xenophobic attitudes. Serious media and academic explanations of these hate crimes are far too rational to grasp underlying psychological causes.

2. The very presence of thriving Somali shops insults unsuccessful, impoverished township dwellers. They endure daily exposure as failures. Envy breeds resentment. Perceived humiliation fuels extreme nationalism. Low self-esteem searches for enhanced identity. Powerless people empower themselves by attacking those below them. While the ruling elite enriches itself by looting the state, the forgotten slum dwellers claim their share by collecting the crumbs from the vulnerable *amakwerekwere*. The derogatory label this time included not only other Africans, mainly Somalis, but also Pakistani and Bangladeshi informal traders.

3. In 2014, the former South African ambassador to the United States, Ebrahim Rasool, at the U.S.-Africa Leaders Summit declared South Africa "a moral superpower," able to teach the world the way Nelson Mandela managed conflict resolution. In this view, liberated citizens cannot be xenophobic if the image of a glorified rainbow nation is to be salvaged. Admitting racism toward fellow Africans would deprive the ruling party of its moral high ground. How will the horrific attacks, together with all the other maladies, affect the standing of the country? In a 2013 BBC poll of twenty-two countries tracked, the "moral superpower" ranked in the lower half, with a 35 percent rating of "mainly positive" and 30 percent "mainly negative." One can safely bet that in the next poll, the negative perceptions will outweigh what little is left of South Africa's past reputation.

4. Hunger and poverty do not drive frenzied youngsters to rob stores. Drug addiction does. Most looters own cell phones, and stealing vouchers for airtime was a priority. The breakdown of family cohesion in mostly fatherless households has eliminated shame and neutralized moral inhibitions. Township teachers have utterly failed to instill political literacy to comprehend global migration. South Africans of all hues cultivate an exceptionalism of being in Africa but not of Africa. Visitors from the alien, dark continent are not to be trusted. Well-qualified foreign science and mathematics teachers could function as role models, besides raising standards. However, the self-declared Marxist-Leninist teachers' union (SADTU) does not welcome cosmopolitan non-nationals in its ranks, let alone being lectured on political education.

5. Competition for jobs by unemployed youth amounts to a cliché. Looting schoolchildren are not yet in the job market. Neither does alleged inequality between foreigners and locals explain the antagonism. Somali tenants mostly start from scratch with loans from relatives; they frequently employ locals; they extend credit to customers and pay rent on time. But they work longer and harder and sell cheaper because they have a small profit margin and "collective entrepreneurship."

6. Why can't locals emulate the foreigners and learn from them? Why can't they also buy wholesale? "We don't trust each other," answered many local respondents in our research. In an atomized space of marginalized people, mutual trust of responsible citizens amounts to a delusion. The very notion of community is problematic. At the most, an exclusionary solidarity exempts local shops from being looted but not equally poor blacks from outside being attacked.

7. Some pundits have criticized Home Affairs for extending work permits to Zimbabweans while so many locals are unemployed. Not only are the foreigners preferred by employers because they go the extra mile, but how else could the foreigners survive when they have to fend for themselves? Pretoria should be criticized for supporting a tyrannical regime in Harare, not for easing the burden of its escapees. In contrast to the migrants in Europe, most Zimbabwean refugees would return home if conditions were to improve.

8. A sad indictment in the xenophobic drama must be reserved for the police management. The commentator Justice Malala cites incontrovertible evidence: "The police, in large numbers, are aiding, abetting and even partaking in the looting," but mostly looking away. *City Press* quotes a story of police ordering people to queue up to "loot in an orderly manner" by entering a shop four at a time. However, police merely reflect the attitudes of the population at large. Their training has not incorporated any lessons from the 2008 xenophobic outbreaks.

9. Victim blame abounds. Ignoring the attacks against foreigners, Home Affairs announces that their legal status would be investigated. Adding to the moral panic around outsiders, a ruling party leader blames weak immigration laws and their potential to give rise to terror organizations such as Boko Haram. The most asinine statement by a cabinet member insists on foreigners "revealing their trade secrets" as a precondition for being allowed to operate. Barring groups from certain activities on the basis of their ethnic origin violates the South African constitution. The humiliating treatment of refugees by Home Affairs officials in the renewal of permits reinforces for an already suspicious population the need to guard against outsiders. Taxi drivers tell you a widely held belief that most crimes are committed by foreigners. Yet the government has never published statistics about the number of nationals and nonnationals convicted.

10. Compared with the dramatic rise of xenophobia in Western Europe, South Africa originally differed in two respects. First, in Europe antagonism against foreigners is mobilized from above by populist demagogues; in South Africa the resentment originated from below and was condemned by all political leaders as shameful. No Marie Le Pen has yet emerged in South Africa. However, the schizophrenia of feeling embarrassed by the xenophobic label and simultaneously playing to

the xenophobic gallery, particularly at the local level, does not rule out a gradual nationalist shift. The apartheid government restricted Indians from settling in the Orange Free State; Idi Amin expelled their counterparts from Uganda, and the African Union elected Mugabe as their chair in 2015. Who can guarantee that the South African rainbow does not dissolve similarly?

Second, Islamophobia and anxiety about an incompatible religion play no role in South Africa. Whatever motivates the animosity toward Muslim Somalis, religion has never featured. Unlike in Europe, Muslims in South Africa are not attacked for undermining an entrenched homogeneous culture. This second difference from Europe allows more optimism. The divided South African society has long learned to coexist with diversity. That is the main hope to overcome xenophobia.

Appendices

Autobiography I

Navigating "Difference": Insiders, Outsiders, and Contending Identities

KOGILA MOODLEY

This is the story of how marginalized people, considered "aliens" in a discriminatory political system, advanced against all odds, how they gave meaning to their lives, adapted, and redefined their identities in different settings, illustrated by my own personal trajectory as a South African of Indian ancestry.

I reconstruct the fragments of my memory from a peripatetic life. I was Durban born and ejected, Cape Town adopted, Frankfurt and Berlin—as halfway stations—received and accepted; and Vancouver became "home" to me alongside immigrants from all over the world. Comings, stayings, and goings have their advantage. One rediscovers parts of the deeply etched past. Some monochromatic snapshots are favored over others, and then there are the sepia-tinted, gilt-edged memories; the backgrounds in which they are embedded fade in and out. From time to time, a comment, a conversation evokes a refocusing and brings in forgotten details more sharply. Comparisons of the then and now ensue. They all tug at chords of the heart in different ways and at different times and phases of one's life, and yet sustained through all of this is the constancy of South African roots. Only there are we understood as we are, as Indian South Africans. Only there are we hybrids of a particular kind, for the most part using English as home language, neither Indian nor fully African. Yet paradoxically even in post-apartheid South Africa, our authenticity as South Africans depends on laundering the remnants of the third and fourth generations' Indianness. This version of Indianness is hauled out for ceremonial purposes, put away on demand to flaunt our national identity and refashion our sense of belonging. Persisting phenotype continues to exoticize, distinguish, and differentiate. In the past we were "Westernizing"; now we are "Africanizing," which means downplaying the "Indianness" rather like the superego keeping the lid on the sewer-like id.

Where do we sit, or better yet, fit in the national portrait? As a third-generation South African of Indian origin, I do feel strange to belong to a group about whom so little is known by non- Indians within Natal and even less by those outside of Natal. Narratives about Indians in South Africa span different depictions. Initially they were welcomed in the 1860s as a source of "reliable" labor, but subsequently resented. The

Wragg Commission in 1887 reported "the majority of white colonists were strongly opposed to the presence of the free Indian as a rival and competitor, either in agriculture or in commercial pursuits." Attempts to encourage "voluntary repatriation" having failed, discrete Natal English formulae to segregate were based on "gentlemen's agreements" encouraging Indian collusion and compliance in keeping a good distance. This translated into "Do not make offers on houses for sale in white areas."

Early Afrikaner Nationalists referred to us as "coolies," the "unassimilable minority," "those who do not identify totally with South Africa and have one foot in Africa and one in India." So initially the only preferred solution for such "permanent aliens" was "repatriation." Later, when repatriation was abandoned, our presence gradually became "useful" for legitimating ideologies of "separate development" and "community development." Likewise, in African everyday parlance, "amakula" and "amaindia" (African terms for Indians) reiterated these views about the eternal foreigners with a pejorative slant. History textbooks in my schooldays routinely featured sections on "The Indian Problem." It was not difficult to "read" the undesirability of one's group. As a returning graduate from an American university in the mid-1960s, I was interviewed for a position as a lecturer in sociology at the then–University College for Indians on Salisbury Island. One of the questions I was asked by my Afrikaner colleagues is, "Are you familiar with the birthrate of Indians? How would you reduce it?" I reflected, while answering about fertility rates at a theoretical sociological level, why do "we" (i.e., you) incentivize some groups financially to produce more children and seek ways of curbing the reproductive rates of others?

Echoes of Bob Dylan's lyric, "How many years . . . ," play on in my mind. Despite 150 years of South African citizenship, the theme recurs. In 2011 at a rally in Thembelihle, south of Johannesburg, near the predominantly Indian suburb of Lenasia, Julius Malema, speaking in Sesotho, incited a crowd at a meeting on "economic freedom" with "Your children must be allowed to go to school with coolie [sic] children!" Those defending Malema say the translation in Sesotho is not meant to offend. Yet I still recall the taunts of "Shaya Makula!" (Attack the Coolies!) during the 1949 riots in Durban, when I was an 8-year-old child and we fled for our lives and hid in the darkened upper story of our apartment building from rioting mobs who were out to get at any Indian in sight. I remember vividly being traumatized that my father had not come home from work and my grandmother, who had just gone for a walk shortly before the attacks began, had not returned. Our poorest relatives, living in wood-and-iron shanties in the outlying areas of Durban, were the worst hit, and many were hospitalized from injuries sustained. The nearby schools were transformed into refugee-holding institutions for poor people escaping from the riots. I can still smell the disinfectant used to keep the place clean when we took relief supplies to the school. In a strange way I remember thinking what fun it must be to sleep in rooms together with kids of the same age. I also recall family discussions afterward, trying to make sense of it all. They commented that not all Africans were involved in the riots, that there were Africans who helped to get my father and uncles safely home from work, after it became dark, that day. Self-searching discussions in my extended family, after the riots, instilled in us the need to learn to speak "proper Zulu." We were not allowed to use the Tamil word Kaapri, a derivative from the Arabic term for nonbeliever, to refer to Africans, but from then on we used the word Sudesi, which means the indigenous people of this land. This raises the question, why so little introspection by others in using offensive labeling? Around the same time as Malema's incitement, Judge Isaac Madondo, commenting on the three candidates for the contested position of Kwa Zulu Natal judge president, in which Justice Chiman Patel was a leading contender, said "the job should not go to an Indian, because . . . we still have things to address: imbalances, all kinds of things which need more insight, which a person who is not a black African cannot be privy to. . . . We were oppressed but not in the same way."

Both black Africans and Indians were victimized by white racism. Yet during the 1949 violence as now, Africans single out those closer to themselves in the social hierarchy rather than the beneficiaries and perpetrators of political and economic domination. How similar is this to the current outbreaks of xenophobia in the townships?

Hidden behind all these stereotypes and images of each other are shared experiences of exclusion where class and color intersect across the board. Undoubtedly, Africans faced more discrimination under apartheid, which is why politically conscious Indians continue to experience some guilt for their relative privilege and intermediate status in the old order. Forgotten in this self-imaging are their starting points as indentured laborers, in the wake of the abolition of slavery. At least slaves as the property of their masters were cared for. Indentured laborers signed an agreement to accept minimal monthly remuneration, to labor long hours on their own. Men, women, and children, with very minimal shelter and no educational provisions, were expected to live on monthly rations of *dhall* and rice. Many who chose to stay on and not repatriate to India sought employment in municipal maintenance work, sometimes as street cleaners, living in barracks provided by the local municipality. Others chose to grow vegetables and subsisted on their sales. From these poor beginnings, some developed small-scale commercial projects.

For subsequent generations, community self-help was furthered by the traditional extended family structure. The children of all the brothers and sisters were considered as one family. My maternal uncle prepared sandwiches for all fifteen children in the extended family delivered daily by a helper with a bicycle. St. Anthony's School, an all-Indian missionary institution but heavily subsidized by the community, allowed us to leave class five minutes before lunch so that we could gather near the school fence ready for the delivered lunch, each day. I can still remember the tablecloth that was spread out under the trees, and all of us, complete with cloth serviettes, were given our sandwiches and something to drink—even ice cream for dessert, occasionally.

When my uncle and his wife traveled to India, a rare occasion in those days, they brought back masses of clothing, musical instruments, glass bangles, and sandals of all sizes, so that every child in the extended family received something. The mind boggles at the organizational aspects behind this communal responsibility, not to speak of the public-spirited generosity.

We are speaking here not of enormously wealthy tycoons, but of ordinary middle-class individuals who could only do this because of pooled family resources, economies of scale, and a concept that we all belonged together and needed to take care of each other. Pooling labor of five brothers in my maternal extended family, with very frugal remittances, enabled the purchase of small businesses, one by one, and then an apartment block in which all the brothers and sisters and their spouses could each have their own spaces. Often, in order to be there early to open the store, the unmarried brothers would roll out mattresses and sleep in the store on the floor overnight. As a man without secondary school education but with incredible drive, my mother's elder brother learned all he could about how to make ice cream and opened an ice cream factory in Durban, called Crystal Ice Cream, that became a frequent feature in our daily school lunches.

Listening to my mother's stories about the role of men in the domestic economy gave me new insights into the inaccurate depiction of Indian men as only chauvinistic and paternalistic. In the case of all the men in my grandparents' generation, on both sides of the family, the widowed single fathers were able to prepare meals, use the sewing machine to make alterations to children's clothing, and launder and iron their clothes. One maternal uncle took lessons in floral arrangement and even learned how to make a few nice salads from a hotel chef, which were served with pride when the clan gathered. In this sense they were androgynous people crossing over traditionally male and female domains and extending their culinary tastes.

The home of my adolescence, pre–Group Areas Act, was in Heswall Road, Durban, not far from the Botanic Gardens and Mansfield Boys High School. In this neighborhood lived a true mélange of people: two Coloured families, an Afrikaans-speaking couple, an African lawyer who lived in the back garden suite of an Indian-owned home, five Indian families, and one English couple whose wife was a secretary at the University of Natal. Reggie Ngobo, the lawyer, had the smartest four cars parked on the street. On the weekends he was always dressed in white flannels for tennis. Despite being the best educated and probably the wealthiest on the street, he was not allowed to purchase property in the city, which is why he lived in the backyard quarters of someone's home. Mr. Mistry, the owner of the duplex next door, was a boxing trainer and discreetly ran a boxing school frequented by a few young Africans. On the upper floor lived the Mistry family. Mrs. Mistry never left the house. All the shopping for food and clothing was taken care of by the husband. She was expected to conform to his dietary preferences as a "pure" vegetarian and prepared the most delicious dishes. On occasion, the grapevine had it that her relatives smuggled some cooked meat under a pile of rice and vegetables, to provide a change. Despite this confined existence, she had the most vivid imagination, constructing the most amazing stories about the goings on outside. Whether they were based in fact or not, their value for us lay in the humor they brought us. The lower floor of this duplex was rented to a well-known Indian photographer, Dennis Bughwan, and his talented attractive wife, Devi, who was a teacher at the time and went on to become a professor of speech and drama. She was a pioneer in hosting the Sunday morning SABC "Indian program," which she did in the most impeccable English, even anglicizing Indian names! This was a very congenial neighborhood, though there was little social interaction among the residents apart from exchanging ritualized pleasantries.

We lived here until our modest home was confiscated under the Group Areas Act designating our quarter for the exclusive use of the white racial group. To add insult to injury, we were given six months to vacate the house, which had to be fumigated at our expense and sold below market price to a newly arrived British immigrant in 1966. The trauma of displacement we all felt is hard to describe. It was not as if one could look at other available real estate and find a new home easily. Because of the scarcity of property designated for Indian occupancy, in the few enclaves near the city, prices were highly inflated for dwellings not even closely resembling what we were forced to leave behind. Land available for Indians was located miles out of town. We were urban people who had lived in the city, not far from amenities. Jewish friends, incensed by this legislation, offered to purchase the house to allow us to continue living in it, but it would have been illegal to live there, even after it had been sold. Recognizing that it was time to move on, my father declined gratefully and put his energies into seeking an alternative place to live. We, the younger generation, were irritated by what seemed to us a passive response to this legislation, and engaged in protests to express this opposition. Only decades later, as my father lay on his deathbed, did these issues surface in his hallucinations. He seemed to be panicking about "not having a place to stay. We are six people; we can't stay in such a small place. . . . The government took my home; they forced me to close my business . . . and no one ever apologized to me!" A few hours later that day, he insisted that we call the manager of the beachfront apartment to which they had moved in 1994. When she arrived he asked her, in his weakened state, "Can we stay on here? Are we allowed to stay on here?" This rather gentle English woman had tears in her eyes. "But Mr. Moodley, you can stay here as long as you like. You own this apartment!" And then he seemed at peace: "Thank you! Thank you!" He was 86 years of age, and remnants of the trauma of displacement still surfaced. Yet he stubbornly refused to apply for compensation for land confiscation, provided under postapartheid legislation, as his children had urged him. There were poorer people who needed that money more, he replied. At one level, he had moved on.

What puzzles me is, how did our parents cope? How did our parents, without high school education and much wealth, manage to protect us from the scars of apartheid, the loss of self-esteem, and the lack of normal opportunities for advancement? People of our parents' generation were badgered in the workplace, psychologically devalued in their circumscribed curtailed movements, forced to sell and relocate from homes they had labored long to buy, disallowed basic rights, and tolerated at best. My father was sneered at by white colleagues and superiors for "wasting your money educating your daughters, when they are going to end up with the pots in the kitchen!" Yet these emasculated adults returned each day to families and a community with higher ideals, which repaired them and restored their own self-esteem. In the eyes of their wives and children, the men were still kings, and they had to live up to this image. Working women faced workplace indignities too, but even more than the men, they endured and often took their double disadvantages with the express purpose of giving their children a better life. They held on to a belief that they were "morally superior" people with good values which would triumph in the end. What must it have taken to educate children not to be reverse racist, to believe in their capabilities, to pretend that they had the capacity to become whatever they chose, to be citizens of the world when they themselves were only disenfranchised, second-class citizens in the land of their birth? From what I learned in sociology, we were being raised with a "false consciousness." Eugene Genovese's work on the world the slaves made for themselves applied to some extent to our lives as well. So too did Gramsci's admonition that to conquer domination, a grasp of social capital would provide the necessary tools to sustain resistance.

The late Percy and still strong 99-year-old Amartham Moodley, my parents, were two such remarkable individuals for the family they raised: three daughters with Ph.D.'s and a creative son who left South Africa at a young age to complete his education in the United Kingdom and then moved on to become a successful entrepreneur in the United States. My father was a bright, very articulate man who came top of his class at school in Clairwood. He was forced to go to work at the age of 15 to contribute to the family income. This meant a denial of secondary schooling years, and of course there was not even a hope of postsecondary education. He found employment in office work. As soon as he was on a firm footing, he decided to take part-time education after work and obtained a diploma in bookkeeping and accounting, which enabled him to teach bookkeeping part time. This led to his employment as a sales manager and subsequent promotion to a more senior financial management position in a wholesale motor parts company. He had a good writing style and sometimes published critical think pieces on customary Indian cultural practices such as lavish weddings for people who could ill afford them.

These parents were ahead of their time. They were progressive and radical without even knowing it. For what little they had in educational backgrounds they gave generously, without a thought about what they were doing. We had wonderful childhoods. Each evening my father looked forward to coming home and bathing us. Often after dinner, he read to us. On warm summer evenings, my parents would take us to the beach to play until we were exhausted and then fell asleep. We often went to the amusement park on the beachfront, and I recall a time when my father would no longer even drive by the place. Only later did I learn that we were no longer allowed to have rides there or use the paddling pools that were now reserved for whites. Rather than fill us with resentment about the pernicious practices that excluded us, he chose, for a time, avoidance as a coping strategy, so that we would not think of ourselves as "excluded" people. To keep us busy, other positive approaches were taken. My father coached me, the eldest daughter, in tennis. As a professional tennis player himself, he taught me good technique. Each day when I came back from school I would practice against the garage wall. It was not surprising that I played for the school tennis team, though I was not the strongest player. I loved the game but not the competitiveness that went with it. My father also included us in all the household repairs he was doing. I learned some basics about electrical work, car mechanics, carpentry, and putting things together, experiences from which my girlfriends were all too often excluded. As soon as I was of driving age, he bought me a secondhand Volkswagen Beetle so that I could independently get myself to and from the university. At that time, I was probably the first girl in my age cohort to have my own car.

Our education was quite well-rounded, as we went to political rallies some evenings at "Red Square" where our family friend affectionately known as "Uncle Monty" (Naicker) and others would address the crowd at protest meetings. We were politicized simply from discussions around the dinner table. At high school I engaged in fundraising to support the treason trialists. My eighteenth birthday almost ended badly when the conversation moved to a discussion about whether South Africa was a fascist state, a position challenged from a sociological perspective by my friends Margo and Martin Russell but viewed as soft on apartheid by the others. While my father strongly sympathized with ANC political visions and supported those on the run by providing them with all sorts of goods, he never became a frontline activist. Perhaps he considered the risks of government reprisals on all those dependent on him as too severe. He saw his role as providing both his nuclear and his extended family with basic security and stability.

Public speaking came easily to all four of us, as we were given opportunities to address small social gatherings in the community and were totally comfortable on stage in public. It helped too that we were given "speech lessons" from a very English teacher once a week, who made us speak as if we had the Elgin marbles in our mouths! I must admit that I found this all a bit fake and imitative as a child, but one learned when to use it and when not! Each day after school we went to Tamil School, where I remember falling asleep during the singing of Thevaram songs. The teacher sent an older child to sprinkle water on my face to wake me up. Being cosmopolitan in his orientation, my father tried to get me to learn Hindi as well, but this was all too much and did not last long.

For a while, a teacher from India, Mr. Kannabiran Pillay, was hired to teach Tamil to all the children in the extended family, after school hours. We gave the poor teacher a hard time, teased him mercilessly, and nicknamed him "Johnny Walker!" I cannot say he did a lot for our Tamil-language education. We simply did not give the poor man a chance! Already at this stage, we had learned, as many minority children do, the differential status of languages, that English was "more important" than the vernacular. So we did the minimum we had to do to learn it and even less to speak it, answering in monosyllables when spoken to in Tamil. Nevertheless, the backdrop of the language in use by the older generation did leave a certain knowledge base about the classics. The same was true for exposure to Indian classical music used as a background at family gatherings. My mother, who was a romantic in many ways, pointed out the meanings of the beautiful images being used in the language, which remain with me to this day. I often reflected on why it was that I could respond with the same stirring emotion to the singing of Subbuluxmi as I could to similar genres of music from the haunting ring of Om Kulsum's voice in Cairo coffee houses, Edith Piaf in Paris cafés, and German romantic lieder. There was for me a commonality that they evoked which I have been unable to dissect exactly, other than to feel a resonance.

Confidence was the greatest gift our parents gave us. We were encouraged to take on responsibility for others who had less than we had. So, after school, we participated in teaching in our back yard the domestic workers employed in the neighborhood who could neither read nor write. Once they learned enough basics, they could move on to higher-paying jobs, which was not very popular with many neighbors. A dramatic move was when one of our domestic helpers first became an attendant at my uncle's gas station and then moved up to become the head of the Breakdown Service! Also, at the instigation of my parents, we organized literacy groups twice a week, with Indian mothers who wanted to improve their spoken and written English.

Ours was a busy social home. People were frequently "dropping in," and there would always be food to offer members of the extended family and friends from other communities. We, in turn, visited many relatives from all income groups and friends who were Muslim, Christian, Jewish, and Zoroastrian. We celebrated Eid, Christmas, Passover, Bar Mitzvahs, and the Parsee holidays with them, never viewing these as diminishing our own roots. This was our parents' way of exposing us to a wider world and an embracing of Gandhi's influence in South Africa.

In the later years of high school, we were given the task of renovating the three-bedroom home in which we lived. We were given a budget, contacts with painting specialists, and a contractor who did tiling. We had to come up with a plan with color charts, curtain fabrics, shelving materials, ideas for light fixtures, and other accessories. The outcome was not conventional, but we all loved it, and to this day I think it was a brilliant exercise in children's empowerment. The outcome was not bad even by today's standards. We decided against tiling and instead had the old wooden floors sanded and refinished. We replaced the lace curtains with nice hessian fabric, wallpapered the walls in a nice off-white textured wallpaper, removed old carpeting and put in a very large circular swazi mat, and installed a very large, white Chinese paper lantern off to one side of the room, which gave beautiful light to the room. The room was lined with bookshelves on two sides up to the windows, which added a lovely warmth from the colors of the books.

When I was in my final year of high school, my father had the foresight to arrange for me to meet with the student advisor at the University of Natal. It was a very bold step for him to have undertaken, since the university seemed a highly elitist, "white" domain. I am sure it must have taken much courage for him, as one denied entry to these portals. I recall his deferential demeanor as we entered the office. The advisor in question was kind and welcoming, and I could tell from his behavior that he was quite moved at the aspirations of an Indian parent for his daughter's education.

The University of Natal found an "elegant" solution to admitting students of different colors. A separate non-European section was set up in a warehouse building on Warwick Avenue in Durban. Although we paid full-time student fees, we were not allowed any of the sports and other extra facilities offered to white students at the Howard college campus up on the hill. It was there that I was exposed to scholars like Leo Kuper, who defied university rules by insisting that he would only teach sociology to integrated classes which would be held on the white campus. It was individuals like Leo Kuper and a visiting scholar, Pierre van den Berghe, who left lasting impressions on me for the way in which they theorized race and ethnicity. For the most part, other professors taught in a way that paid scant attention to the political context in which we lived separate lives. Most students fell silent when discussion was expected of them, since there seemed no common ground for talking. Worst of all was Speech and Drama, which for some reason was highly popular among many students of color but which reduced us all to what Fanon called "mimicry." It was this experience of "falling silent" in the presence of arrogant, ill- exposed white instructors that made me write the piece I did, "The Dialectic of Higher Education for the Colonised," in response to the legislation's calling for separate ethnically based universities for each group. Steve Biko invited me to talk to the groups he was working with, since it focused on the unintended consequences of what was aimed at limiting educational opportunity and isolating black groups from one another. Unfortunately I had already left for the United States and was unable to participate.

After I had completed my degree and took a teaching position at the Durban Indian Girls High School, I applied for an American scholarship to do postgraduate work in sociology. The day the news of success arrived, my father had tears in his eyes—tears of joy. In the early 1960s this was an unusual happening, all the more for a bright man who had never had the opportunity for even a regular secondary education. It was the realization of a dream, a chance to fly beyond the mundane and the local. All our lives he had been educating us, unknowingly, for this chance to sail wider. He taught us how to use cutlery properly, so that when one went to a restaurant one could be familiar with correct practices. Of course, the irony of it all was that there were no restaurants for Indians. We were introduced to different tastes—a barrel of olives from Greece sat in our pantry, and special cheeses from Holland were sent by business associates as gifts. My father had an uncanny ability to reach out to people and establish a wide network of friends in an age without Twitter and Facebook. Unwittingly all these attempts at socializing us were to serve me well when I studied abroad.

About a hundred members of the extended family and friends showed up at the airport to bid me farewell when I left to take up a scholarship in the United States. Prior to that, I had been advised by a friend of my parents who had studied medicine in the United Kingdom. He told me to familiarize myself with the basic tenets of Hinduism to explain them to Americans, who were certain to be very interested in learning about other religions. He suggested too that I arm myself with some good titles of books on the subject to which I could refer people, should I not know the answers to all the questions. I was strongly advised to wear a sari and to take warm clothing, since it would be chilly in America. So armed with sari, warm coat, umbrella, and a cosmetic case someone gave me, I must have made a hilarious appearance in New York in midsummer! In New York, friends introduced me to Krishna Shah, an India-born off-Broadway producer who had visited South Africa and produced two well-publicized plays, Tagore's *King of the Dark Chamber* and Alan Paton's *Sponono*. His advice to me was, "Whatever you do, while you're in America, avoid getting cloistered with other Indians!" "Avoid the Sarala's of the world and broaden out!"

The "signals" I put out when I first arrived must have been very confusing to my American hosts, who wondered how quickly I had become "assimilated" when they found me switching to Western clothes with such ease. In fact, my anthropology professor, Ruth Useem, whose area of study was India, was quite concerned that I had assimilated too quickly to Western clothing after only a week in the United States. With no knowledge of how our lives in South Africa had hybridized us and how we were comfortable in both lifestyles, she found it difficult to comprehend this rapid fusion.

One can never underestimate the value of an opportunity to study outside one's own society. As a recipient of an American scholarship, which took me first to Yale University and then to Michigan State University, I faced expectations to be knowledgeable about my country of origin. The politicizing lived experience of inequality under apartheid made one critical of inequality everywhere else. I was horrified to find how much racism still prevailed in the United States. During one field trip, as part of a course on "community development," my classmates and I spent a few days in a little Michigan town called Cold-water, around Christmas time in 1963. I, along with other foreign students, as we were then called, attended a community event. A month prior, the community had turned down the request to locate a factory in the area because it would employ some black employees as well. When my turn came to speak about South Africa, I referred to its inequalities, differential rights for different groups, segregation, and their effects. A poignant moment arose, which I have never forgotten. Someone raised a hand to ask a question: "If things are as bad as you tell us they are in South Africa, how did you turn out to be as well-educated and articulate as you have demonstrated today?"

The answer to this compliment lies in the confidence instilled and the value of a broad education to break out of the imposed barriers, stressed by farsighted parents. Despite a pernicious system, my parents carved out niches, on a very limited income, where we could lead normal lives in an abnormal society. Objectively we were victims, but psychologically we were saved from the self-pitying of internalized victimhood.

One does not leave the country of one's birth easily. In 1966, upon my return from the United States, the only place where I could teach because of my "race" was University College, Durban, as it was then called. It was the tribal college for Indians, and despite our earlier boycotting of these segregated institutions, there was no alternative for students who could not afford to go abroad for postsecondary education. A small number of Indian faculty members worked alongside mostly Afrikaner academics. There was no social contact between faculty across the color line, and "knowing one's place" was the unspoken norm. Washrooms for staff and faculty were racially segregated, and no one protested. A young Afrikaans-speaking colleague, for whom the junior lectureship was a promotion from the civil service, had difficulties communicating in English, and students complained that he read his lectures from the University of South Africa (UNISA) correspondence course materials. When he and I had to share the marking of a batch of student papers and I knocked on his office door to fetch these, he jumped up in fright and made sure to push the door wide open, clearly to avoid any charge of violating racial barriers. When I did try to forge friendships across the color line with a female colleague with whom I played tennis on campus, we received a notice reminding us that tennis courts were reserved for the exclusive use of white faculty members on x and y days and for Indian faculty members on g and h days. Such was the atmosphere of the institution, which was located on Salisbury Island, once a military barracks, tenuously connected to the mainland by a narrow causeway. Because of my somewhat suspect training in the United States, I had been hired by the rector for a one-year term only. With some reservations, after a very interrogative interview, my contract was renewed, but again for a one-year period only.

University College was a strange place in some respects. Ironically the students who were involved in the early phases of the BCM would perform quite publically satirical cabaret about aspects of Indian life. There would be dialogues between Indians which went as follows: "What, you sending your son to University College? Is he training to become a policeman or what?" And then the students carousing and singing, "We are marching to Pretoria!" What I recall quite vividly was the rector laughing and enjoying these performances, naively thinking that these were just Indians, acting like Indians, speaking just like Indians speak, making fun of themselves. He obviously did not get the political critique.

During that year, 1966, I was introduced to a visiting German sociologist, Heribert Adam, from the Frankfurt School of Critical Theory, by the head of my department. I was "told" to let the visitor address my sociology class. At the time I had been teaching a course in introductory sociological theory and had developed an interest in the work of Max Weber, so it seemed the appropriate spot. The department head, Professor Engelbrecht, was very pleased to demonstrate his limited knowledge of German when he introduced the visitor. So taken up was he with his own introduction of the speaker that he overlooked the content of the visitor's lecture, in which he referred to sources such as Baran and Sweezy, Andre Gunter Frank, and other left-leaning authors. This immediately caught my interest and dispelled any fears I had about the political leanings of the visitor, who encouraged me to apply for a German exchange fellowship to the Deutsche Akademischer Austauschdienst (DAAD), which I subsequently did. He was fascinated with South Africa and wanted to learn as much as he could about how, what he thought were the "Nazis of Africa," maintained control. I was fascinated with the questions he raised and how he was analyzing this from the perspective of studies on German anti-Semitism. I had only read his doctoral supervisor's classic work on the Authoritarian Personality, and now this opened up a range of new vistas for me. The mutual attraction grew, and after returning to Germany briefly, he came back to South Africa to spend a year teaching at the University of Natal but mainly to convince my family that they should let their beloved daughter abscond with him. Being attracted to one another and living separately with the risk of being arrested under the Immorality Act made it incredibly difficult to have any kind of normal contact. We could not go to the same movie theaters, or the same beach, or any restaurant, and always had to meet in the company of friends and family. The American consul in Durban at the time, John Savage, became quite friendly with us, and his home was a frequented venue for social gatherings. When we were ready to drive home from a party together, a colleague of Heribert's took on an avuncular role and insisted on driving us separately for fear of arrest. And so it was ironical that in the heart of educational apartheid an illegitimate union flowered.

Some months later, I was pleased to hear from the DAAD, to whom I had applied for a German exchange fellowship, that they were favorably disposed to my application and now all that remained was for them to get SA government clearance for me. Within a month of this, two things coincided. I received a letter from the DAAD, with great regret, that they were unable to honor their initial acceptance, since they failed to get the necessary government approval for me. Around the same time, the rector, S. P. Olivier, called me into his office for a very early morning meeting which seemed urgent. I was then told, "Miss Moodley, due to circumstances beyond my control, I have to terminate your contract with the university." This came from the deadpan face of a Moral Rearmament adherent. My questions about why or how went nowhere, with some murmurings about "security concerns" and "needing to identify with one's community" until I said in exasperation, "I have a question for you: As head of an academic institution, how do you feel about making a decision like this on nonacademic grounds?" The evasive answer was unforgettable: "Miss Moodley, the Lord opens new paths when old ones close."

With this decision came a moment of great recognition for the German foundation about what their "government clearance" requirement entailed. They informed me that they would honor their decision and I should plan on arriving in Germany. So I was soon on my way to Frankfurt and then Berlin. In Frankfurt, I was warmly welcomed by Heribert's extended family. To my eternal chagrin, when Heribert was still in South Africa, he had sent a touristic postcard with the picture of four bare-breasted African women to his shocked Catholic mother, with the inscription,"Guess who of these will be your daughter-in-law?" His mother looked relieved to meet a fully clothed heathen in a sari. My very limited German at this stage seemed to break the ice. Whenever I did not understand anything, Heribert's mother simply raised her voice, and we got through with a lot of humor! After four months of intensive German-language training in Berlin and two months visiting different German universities, Heribert and I married in mid-1968. My family arrived for the occasion. Since Heribert was a lapsed Catholic, one uncle, a priest and then rector of the University of Mainz, refused to conduct any traditional ceremony between a nonobservant Catholic and a non-Christian like me. My family was keen on some kind of ceremony to mark the event. Since the closest Hindu priest was in London, my mother went to a family friend, the head of Religious Studies, Professor Varadarajulu at University College, Durban, and asked him if he would tape record the service and she would perform the ceremony. He was fearful for his job, since I was by then persona non grata and this was under South African law an illegal union. But his wife prevailed upon him, reminding him that the former Indian ambassador to South Africa, whom they admired greatly, had a daughter who had married an American. So it came to pass that we were married by a tape recorder in the garden of a nice suburban home in Stierstadt im Taunus near Frankfurt. The *Haven kund*, or pot in which the ceremonial fire was lit, was a Roman artifact that had been unearthed on the property. The wedding feast, according to Hindu tradition, had to be vegetarian and alcohol free. For the otherwise carnivorous German guests, it was an event remembered to this day. So began a rich life of shared interests, mutual curiosity about experiencing other worlds, welding together a new identity, and implicit unspoken promises to respect each other's family traditions, guided by our common goals of secularism and cosmopolitanism. Heribert was thrown into an extended family of four siblings and numerous relatives and my cultural baggage of responsibility toward my aging parents and younger siblings when they needed support, which he continues to honor admirably to this day. Remarkable in the seamless welding of our relationship has been the absence of any conflict about "cultural differences," based on the underlying similarities of openness and generosity in both our traditional multigenerational families. Even more important were our shared intellectual goals and commitments.

Mixed marriages were also a taboo in the Indian community at this time. When the Durban extended family heard the news, they came to see my parents. Some rural relatives came to sympathize and express condolences for the loss of a daughter to an outsider. Others said, "What can we do? It was just fate that she should marry out like this!" Another "uncle," a teacher, said, "You really must not worry. What she has done, everyone else will be doing in twenty years' time. It will be a common trend!" Two more liberal, consoling aunts came. One said to my mother, "Don't worry—at least he's not English!" and the other aunt said in support, "Even Indira Gandhi's son is marrying an Italian girl!" My cosmopolitan parents took things in their stride when the newspapers hounded them and the *Sunday Times* published a report on the wedding on its front page. Our two lovely daughters, Kanya and Maya, must have "inherited" a similar predisposition for cultural hybridity when they both married two stellar Capetonians in modified versions of Hindu-Jewish ceremonies on wine farms in Stellenbosch. The German political scene from my location in Frankfurt and Berlin was intense. Very different from the antiapartheid struggles were the student challenges to authority and the traditional academic hierarchy on university campuses. Heribert's mentors in Frankfurt, T.W. Adorno and others, were also being attacked for the discrepancy between their radical theorizing and their own "bourgeois" lifestyles, their political passivity, and their patriarchal attitudes. We participated in some anti–Vietnam war demonstrations and marches for disarmament amid the heckling of opponents.

Later that year we decided to emigrate to Canada to begin a new life. Canada, unlike the United States at the time, was not involved in a war, and it held out better prospects. Heribert was offered a position in Vancouver at Simon Fraser University by Tom Bottomore, who had set up the equivalent of *the London School of Economics* (LSE) there and was on the lookout for young radical scholars. For me, it was the chance to complete a doctorate, which I could do much better in the English-speaking world than in Germany. We have never regretted this decision to move to a strange but beautiful city where we initially did not know anybody.

Canada of the late 1960s had for the first time extended its immigrant intake to include countries previously excluded on the basis of "race." Under Pierre Elliott Trudeau, the Liberal government chose "multiculturalism" as a way of integrating its newcomers from all corners of the world, not just from Europe. From being an Indian South African, I now became an "East Indian" and later a "visible minority."

Much of my academic work reflects comparative explorations of these issues, and my insights into intergroup relations grew. I discovered the racist past of Canada and in daily life learned how people of color had been marginalized. When multiculturalism was promoted, I was an active critic. I argued for equality of life chances rather than equality of lifestyles. Racism continued to surface in differential employment opportunities, and institutional policies, and barriers to access needed to be addressed. Despite my critical interrogation of multiculturalism, or perhaps because of it, the University of British Columbia (UBC) appointed me to an advisory position on institutional transformation in the office of the president, and subsequently awarded me the first David Lam Chair. Surprising was the willingness of government policy makers to consult widely, take critiques into account, and make attempts to modify and broaden the scope. It was not long before Heribert and I were included in several such think tanks and conferences at the federal level, and on the first Race Relations Committee of Vancouver. Over time, what became clear was the fundamental difference between South African–style multiculturalism, known as separate development, and its Canadian variant. Unlike the divide-and-rule ethnicization during apartheid, in Canada, difference was at least theoretically "validated" on an equal footing. The multiplicity of origins of new and old citizens was equalized and officially recognized as worthy of preservation. No longer were the pressures to assimilate so strong that they forced new citizens to abandon their languages of origin. Instead of replacing home languages with English or French, the "additive" versus "subtractive" principle operated in language education. Gradually school districts with larger numbers of Panjabi or Mandarin speakers, for instance, began to offer those languages for all students who chose to take them, not just native speakers. With such an emphasis, "difference" became incorporated as a "common good," not simply for "cultural maintenance" purposes. With immigrant integration as a prime goal, one might well say that in fact Canadian multiculturalism is a form of "melting pot on the slow boil," as we elaborate further in Chapter 6 of this book.

Autobiography II

Controversies: Peacemaking
in Divided Societies

HERIBERT ADAM

*This autoethnography consists of three parts: personal memories of my childhood and stu-
dent days in Germany, and an account of academic controversies I was involved in after
leaving Germany in 1965.*

My most vivid memory as a child growing up in a small village of two thousand
inhabitants twenty kilometers east of Frankfurt was the fear of bombs during the last
years of World War II. Almost every day when the siren sounded in the middle of the
night, my mother dragged me and my younger brother from the first floor into a fortified
small basement room. My grandparents, who lived on the ground floor, were already
there, and we all put metal pots over our heads to protect ourselves. We cowered there on
two sofas, half asleep and half awake, until another siren tone signaled "Sky clear."

Many afternoons, squadrons of dozens of what looked like gray birds high in the sky
flew past our village. Yet one day the antiaircraft guns had managed to shoot one plane
down, and a parachute drifted into a nearby field. With great excitement I joined other
villagers with a hammer in my hand ready to attack the intruder. Fortunately, the police
were already on the spot and had taken the airman into custody and protected him from
the enraged crowd. How far off could the British bomber General Harris have been when
he argued that bombing civilians would demoralize the German population and encourage them to rise up against Hitler?

Sometimes the siren sounded during school hours. Since the primary school near the
church had no cellar, we had to run home immediately. One day I did not follow orders
but stood under the overhang of a nearby house in our street and wanted to see the bomb-
ers. My mother came out of the house, frantically looking for me and shouting for me to
come back in immediately. She saved my life, because minutes later a bomb hit our house
and killed a young boy and his mother in the attached neighboring home. After some time,
my grandfather succeeded in digging us out of the rubble of bricks and foul-smelling
mortar. We climbed over the debris into the street, and our entire bedroom on the upper
floor was exposed with the white bedcovers hanging out, which I found quite funny. We
were "evacuated" to a much larger house on the main street with a barn of cows and pigs

in the back. Our great game was jumping from the ceiling rafters into the hay and straw with an umbrella as a parachute over our heads.

It was here that one day in April 1945 two men in green uniforms with guns came through the window on the street into our cellar hideout. I recall that my grandfather gave them some bottles of wine as a gift, and they left without hurting us. As I later noticed, they had parked their big tank right against the house, and another man on top of the tank smiled and threw some sweets toward me. I screamed as loud as I could and ran away down a lane. I thought I had seen the devil in person. It was my first encounter with a black person. We had been taught never to pick up sweets or toys from an enemy. Suddenly everywhere white bedsheets hung out of street windows as signs of surrender. My grandfather, enlisted in the Volkssturm (a kind of senior's squad for last resistance), had long ago thrown his gun and uniform into the septic holding tank near the outside toilet. The war was over, the sirens were silent, and I was relieved that I no longer had to wake up at night.

There were other war events I remember vividly. Our village lay nestled between a major railway line and the river Main. One evening my mother had gone on her bicycle to our destroyed home near the railway, and my brother and I were left alone at home. Suddenly, low-flying planes attacked the aircraft guns stationed on rail carriers. The fighter planes repeatedly swooped down, while powerful searchlights tried to locate them amid loud gunfire. It was a spectacular sight, but to this day I hate fireworks and love strong searchlights. My mother did not return home for several hours, and my fear that she had certainly been killed is indescribable.

The Americans had set up a mortar and observation post right in our kitchen upstairs, because it had a clear view onto the river, about half a kilometer away. I was no longer allowed to enter the kitchen. On the other riverbank a big German gunboat was anchored for weeks, probably to protect an adjoining lock system. Then shots were exchanged, and a U.S. soldier was killed on our street. The gunboat burned for days. I wondered why the soldiers on the boat had stayed in this trap and did not run away. I was told that they had orders not to desert.

I still mull over why such orders were followed, because disobedience could have saved my father. My father, drafted into the army, was somewhere in Russia. I remember him fondly, coming home for two weeks of summer vacation in 1944 and putting me on his bike for a ride into our vegetable garden on the outskirts of the village. When I refused to eat my food, he mushed it all into "a cake" and insisted that I eat it, and I did. He taught me how to swim in the river by simply letting me fall from his arms. When the news came that he was unlikely to return from a Russian prisoner camp, I refused to believe the message, as did my mother, living with eternal hope. Most "war widows" refused to remarry and proclaimed faithfulness. They made a virtue out of necessity, because there were no men left. Why did my father not desert in 1944 when he was flown back into a beleaguered Crimean peninsula and it was clear that the Germans had already lost the war anyway?

The first years after the war were years of hunger and chaos. Masses of displaced people walked east and west, pushing heavily loaded baby prams and bicycles. The old currency had become worthless, and our household economy ran on bartering. Shops were empty. Wine, paintings, stamps, carpets, and cigarettes were exchanged for essential food on the "black market." U.S. troops had set up camp in parts of our school, and we begged or stole their leftovers. Our gang of wild boys even raided goods trains when they had to stop before a red signal that we had manipulated. Our garden became a crucial resource for fruit and vegetables. My grandfather kept a large flock of chickens and pigeons. Every day I had to collect grass for a dozen caged rabbits. On weekends a chicken or rabbit had its throat slit in front of our dog, which eagerly slurped the warm blood. I still wonder why SA township dwellers do not keep pigeons or fast-breeding rabbits as an essential source of protein. With hindsight I think it may not have been so bad for later health and life expectancy that our childhood was starved of fat and sugar and I tasted my first piece of chocolate at the age of 12, sent in a U.S. "Care packet" for malnourished German children. However, I also remember the frequent colds and infections my brother and I suffered. When the fever rose above 38°C, one of three village nuns who worked as auxiliary doctors came to the house and bundled me up with blankets and towels like an Egyptian mummy to sweat for a day in a dark room. The hated brutal cure normally worked. In another sickness episode, a huge tapeworm was finally extracted from my stomach and demonstratively hacked into pieces by my grandfather, to my great relief.

We did not learn much in four years of frequently interrupted primary school, which was run by teachers who rapped our heads with their knuckles or punished us with rulers on our palms. The decisive moment for German pupils is the entrance examination for high school at age 10. I would not even have been registered for this selection had it not been decided that I was destined for the Catholic priesthood. Should I fail the daylong tests, I was told, I would end up in the nearby quarry, where all the "village idiots," as they were called, shaped paving stones. Every good Catholic family at the time was supposed to donate one of their children to the church, as either a priest or a nun. My younger brother was labeled "good with his hands" but not with his head, because he had once fallen from an apple tree and suffered a slight concussion. Ours was a typical working-class home without books at home. Learning to play a musical instrument, as my daughters and grandchildren have done with diligence, was never in our horizon. My mother could not help me with school homework or confer with teachers, which I would have considered embarrassing. I was on my own in the world of learning. However, as a volunteer assistant librarian in the Catholic village library, I found my access to the "adult section" intriguing. Like every German boy, I not only had absorbed most of the sixty-five volumes by Karl May about the adventures of the noble native "Winnetou" and his friend "Old Shatterhand" but also had access to restricted books by Joseph Flavius about orgies in the Roman empire and ladies caressing small boys at the court of Caesar. This indirect stimulation of sexual curiosity in an era without TV did not seem to have harmed my development, but I am not certain that can also be concluded regarding the ubiquitous exposure of teenagers to soft porn nowadays. What definitely harms adolescents is the repressive guilt about sexual fantasies, instilled by Catholic teaching.

The driving force of my early destiny was a powerful uncle, himself an academic theologian and later rector of the University of Mainz, with the unfortunate first name "Adolf." He had become my father surrogate, the spiritual head of our extended family, and provider of cash. He organized the early rebuilding of the bombed family home. When he visited with his dog and somewhat obese housemaid, our toilet paper miraculously changed from newsprint to rare proper white rolls. Despite his name, he was not a Nazi. He was in fact imprisoned for three months for an anti-Nazi sermon he had delivered as a young chaplain. Since then he confined himself to the noncontroversial study of liturgy, on which he published dozens of books in his long church career. He was also a keen hunter with lots of stuffed birds and deer horns on one wall of his dark, book-lined study in Mainz. When I once interviewed the retired president P. W. Botha in his "Wilderness" home in Knysna, I was reminded of the similarities of stuffy taste and proclivity for hunting by two archconservatives. In his demeanor and attitude, Uncle Adolf was as cold and dogmatic as his Nazi nemesis. He took me for long walks through our nearby forest, to view deer and wild boars, but also forbade me to ever enter the small Protestant church in our village. When he heard that as a student I had brought home a Lutheran girlfriend, he pronounced, "If you marry this person, the tablecloth between you and me is cut!"

With this background, it was no wonder that I ended up as a regular altar boy in the village church until the age of 18. At the age of 15 I had become head of the Catholic youth group with weekly meetings, frequent excursions, summer camps, and command over dozens of younger boy scouts. My self-confidence and identity during these formative adolescent years resulted from this role. My one-year-older counterpart of the girl's scout, the daughter of the church's organ player, gave me the first serious kiss, which left me first dumbfounded and then excited. I was also sent to Jesuit "exercises" in a Frankfurt monastery, week-long indoctrination sessions where we were not allowed to speak even during meals. In the Offenbach gymnasium I attended for nine years, we learned Latin, in addition to English and French, as our main foreign language. The male teachers were mostly injured war veterans. As a rural boy with an accented dialect, I was not popular with most of them. "Adam, speak German!" our head teacher shouted at me. Our history, geography, and social studies teachers were inspiring exceptions, and I ardently began to read the *Frankfurter Allgemeine*, the high-quality conservative German daily. With great interests in politics and as a strong supporter of Adenauer's CDU party at the time, I wanted to become a journalist. With his connections, Uncle Adolf even had arranged an entry job at a Catholic Frankfurt daily *(Neue Presse)*, after it was clear that the celibate priesthood was not for me.

Yet most of my friends went to a university, and I also explored this option. In a chance meeting with my later professor Helge Pross, a returned Jewish exile from the United States, she asked, "How can you expect to write editorials when you have not studied social science?" It was persuasive, and I started to enroll in sociology, philosophy, political science, and psychology courses in 1956. It was a delightful liberated time in Frankfurt when I finally shed my last links to Catholicism. My family ostracized me, and I had to move out of the village, but my mind had opened.

Although German university attendance is free without the exorbitant fees U.S. institutions charge, the four years toward a diploma were hard for me financially. I had to pay my own rent, and some cash went toward the inexpensive student cafeteria, since I was cut off from any family support. There were no scholarships, but only a small state stipend for all students. I relied on odd jobs during the lecture-free five months and evening casual work, organized by the student council. Every evening at 6:00 p.m., the job offers and vacancies were auctioned by lottery to a large crowd of student work-seekers. For four years I worked on building sites, mixing cement and transporting debris, in private homes removing garbage, unloading goods in warehouses, in offices filing papers, and for the longest time as a deputy warden in a converted bomb shelter for "at-risk" youth refugees from the east. As long as my thirty custodians in the semiprison adhered to the midnight curfew, did not get into noisy fights, and did not come home drunk or with prostitutes in tow, I could study and sleep while earning a salary. In the end I even had some money left to exchange my bike for a used Isetta, the smallest two-seater car, which had a front-opening door. Now I felt like a king, who could unashamedly ask for a date and zip around town with friends, dangerously packed on top of each other in the tiny vehicle.

Absorbing the dynamics of a new antiauthoritarian student movement was exhilarating. When Franz Josef Strauss, then the West German defense minister with a new army, occupied the offices of the news magazine *Der Spiegel*, which was accused of betraying state secrets, we organized the first student protest in Frankfurt. As we sat on the tracks of the streetcars in the city center, we were verbally insulted as "lazy student bums" by most passers-by before the police forcibly removed us.

REMINISCING THE FRANKFURT SCHOOL

This recollection of the renowned Institut für Sozialforschung during the 1960's is written with the benefit of hindsight half a century later. The atmosphere sketched and the vignettes of the Frankfurt luminaries painted have to be understood in the culture of the time, as perceived by a graduate student at the start of his academic trajectory. The account highlights the rigid institutional hierarchy that stifled questioning. It focuses on the neglect of gender, race and colonialism by Eurocentric scholars of critical theory. I tried to fill this gap through an analysis of apartheid South Africa from a Frankfurt School perspective.

On September 15, 2014, *The New Yorker* published an intriguing essay entitled "What the Frankfurt School Can Still Teach Us." It evoked nostalgia. The author, Alex Ross, the journal's music critic, focused mainly on the founding members, particularly Theodor Adorno and Walter Benjamin. Ross laments that even discount used bookstores now hesitate to stock the once-cherished classics, from Max Horkheimer and Adorno's *Dialectic of Enlightenment* to Herbert Marcuse's pessimistic *One-Dimensional Man* to Leo Loewenthal's perceptive *Prophets of Deceit*. I share this regret and proudly display the *Frankfurter Beiträge zur Soziologie* (with my own first book no. 17 with a preface by Adorno) among the bulging shelves in our Vancouver living room. The associated Marxist, Hegelian, and Freudian treatises will be the last ones to be donated to charity sales.

After four years (September 1956 through February 1961) of undergraduate study at the Institut für Sozialforschung, I landed my first regular, full-time academic job as *Wissenschaftlicher Mitarbeiter* (research associate) between 1961 and 1965, working on my Ph.D. at the renowned institution. The appointment resulted from my mentor, von Friedeburg, praising my diploma-thesis on the obstacles of working-class children gaining access to German high schools. Naturally, I was thrilled and felt honored by this recognition. A strict hierarchy operated at the institute, with the three directors, Horkheimer, Adorno and the administrator Friedrich Pollock, at the top, followed by senior lecturers Ludwig von Friedeburg, Helge Pross, Egon Becker, Manfred Teschner, and later Jürgen Habermas, with us four junior assistants at the bottom. We underlings had to be at our offices each day at 9:00 a.m. until 5:00 p.m., regularly monitored by Frau Dr. Gretel Adorno at the office next door, who engaged us with gossipy chats, inquired about the perceptions of her husband among students and our own opinions and ambitions. After her husband passed away from a sudden heart attack in 1969, Gretel Adorno, an accomplished chemist by training, committed a failed suicide attempt that tragically left her brain damaged to the consternation of everyone. Rolf Tiedeman, a lifelong scholar of Benjamin at the Institute, assumed the sad task of caring for her.

Adorno, the brilliant philosopher, sociologist, musicologist and aesthetic expert was at the same time highly narcissistic and longed for recognition. In the biggest university lecture hall across the road, a constantly head-nodding group of admirers, mostly women, sat in the front row to the obvious delight of the articulate performer who cherished compliments. This sycophantic atmosphere hardly encouraged critical questioning. Could we dare to make fools of ourselves by raising objections in light of the debilitating respect for a person with such a high reputation?

The worldly director of the institute, Max Horkheimer, was even more aloof and distant to students and associates alike. When we made inquiries about forming a union to bargain for better pay, he warned us that we would all be fired if we did that. Needless to say, we abandoned the thought in order to keep our cherished jobs. Horkheimer also rejected Habermas's habilitation thesis, for which Habermas had earned a distinction from Wolfgang Abendroth at the University of Marburg. Habermas left Frankfurt after this episode, which remained unexplained and puzzled us. The habilitation theses, later published as *Strukturwandel der Öffentlichkeit*, we all considered a seminal work. Still traumatized by their long exile and potential reemergence of fascism, the heads of the institute eschewed the "praxis" of public activism. When I was asked by fellow students to solicit Adorno's signature for a resolution against the U.S. war in Vietnam, he responded, "Do you really expect me to sign a statement that is formulated in such poor German?!" This all happened at an institute that prided itself on being and was generally recognized to be the intellectual center of the German progressive left at the time.

While generally admiring the insights of the critical theory tradition, *The New Yorker* (September 15, 2014) also remarks, "The Frankfurt School's indifference to race and gender is a conspicuous flaw." Indeed, gender played no role in critical theorizing. Adorno's gender awareness was merely confined to flirting with attractive female students. He seemed particularly in awe of nobility and addressed such persons as Gräfin (Countess). In my life I had only heard of princesses and countesses from fairy tales. His later successor at the helm of the institute, the affable Ludwig von Friedeburg, had even married one of his students in our cohort, which would be frowned upon nowadays in North America and considered exploiting unequal power relationships. At the time, we undergraduates were all envious of Helen's sudden access to the higher echelons. As a wedding present, we selected a typical German garden gnome as a joke symbol of our deferent admiration.

However, even more significant than ignorance of feminist concerns by our academic mentors was their total indifference to the developing world. Horkheimer and Adorno showed no curiosity about any third world country and never visited Asia, Africa, or Latin America. They traveled to the same Swiss luxury hotel each summer holiday. When I introduced my newly arrived South African fiancée to Adorno, he engaged in a long chat with Kogila but did not ask one question about apartheid. Instead, he held forth with stories about the Indian colleagues he had met at Oxford before joining Horkheimer in New York and California after the rise of the Nazis.

Among the Frankfurt School luminaries, Habermas is the outstanding cosmopolitan exception, both in his wide swath of global issues explored and in his personal travel to different continents. He was celebrated at Chinese and Indian universities and in many other remote locations. In the mid-1980s he presented a noon lecture at the University of British Columbia (UBC) to a lecture hall, which was filled to capacity with standing room only. His topic, "On Rationality," pitched at a high theoretical and abstract level, made it difficult to grasp. After half an hour a large portion of the audience had walked out, unaccustomed to the dense complexity of his reasoning. I felt embarrassed by the uncivil behavior of my Canadian colleagues, who probably had come to view a celebrity rather than to be enlightened. For the first time I doubted whether our emigration to a wild theoretical no man's land fifteen years earlier was the right decision. The UBC sponsors had not even made arrangements to look after the visitor. Hence, we offered to take over. We invited Habermas and his wife to our Burnaby home, Kogila improvised a quick dinner with a fresh salmon, and the visitors expressed genuine surprise at how smoothly a diverse society and multicultural household seemed to work. To this day, Habermas is still the moral conscience of Germany, a public intellectual par excellence, of whom friend and foe take notice, not unlike Sartre in postwar France.

Unlike Marcuse and Habermas, most of the first-generation Frankfurt theorists were bourgeois elitists. I can remember that during my five years at the institute as an assistant we were once invited to Adorno's stylish apartment in the Kettenhofweg. We initially sat there shy, intimidated, and uncomfortable, listening to Adorno playing the piano rather than engaging socially until Adorno started to sing in the authentic local (Hessian) dialect, which was applauded enthusiastically. A relaxed Adorno could be warm and caring. When I was hospitalized with hepatitis for three months shortly before my scheduled Ph.D. defense in the summer of 1964, he wrote me a long letter not to worry about work, which contributed greatly to my recovery. Similar to the Oxford tradition, in the German university system one did not receive much specific feedback from one's supervisor during the writing of the dissertation. For years students were left to their own resources to plod away with minimal guidance. Yet Adorno, much to his credit, after the draft dissertation was complete, annotated it extensively with wide ranging comments, which I still keep fifty years later as an original treasure. Similarly, I have collected all the *Raubdrucke* (illicit prints) and some neatly typed lectures by Adorno, which Fräulein Olbricht, his devoted secretary, surreptitiously handed over.

In the stiff hierarchical atmosphere of the institute, none of us junior assistants would have dared to address Adorno ("Teddy") or Horkheimer by their first names, let alone expected to be invited to do so, as is customary among academic colleagues in North America. The exceptions were Leo Loewenthal and Helge Pross, who offered Kogila and me *das Du* in a formal ceremony, accompanied by a glass of champagne, when she visited us once in South Africa and later in Vancouver. Before that "Frau Pross," as I used to address her for a decade, guided my Habilitation (a super Ph.D. and requirement for a professorship) at the University of Giessen. Helge Pross was one of the most productive members of the group, starting with an account of German academic exiles in the United States. Her strength lay in the empirical analysis of everyday questions, on which she published interesting work about the education of young women in Germany, a survey about housewives, top managers in big corporations, and about men's perception of women. She also wrote a regular column for a popular women's magazine, *"Brigitte,"* which was criticized by more radical feminists.

Helge Pross was the most charming and down-to-earth mentor and had been close to Franz Neuman. The author of *Behemoth* and a close friend of Marcuse, was another Frankfurt School analyst who unfortunately had passed away, like Helge Pross, at a relatively early stage of life. They all were part of a wealthy sophisticated bourgeoisie but also tried to come to terms with a rougher, not always civil student crowd of the 1960s.

The theoretical Marxism in place of street activism, had alienated a new generation of politicized students who aimed at "changing the world, rather than merely interpreting it." At a time when a "Red Army Faction" bombed American bases and Bader-Meinhof terrorists assassinated bankers and politicians, even the Institute was attacked by these dogmatists. The slogan "if we leave Adorno in peace, capitalism will never cease" made the rounds. A group of bare-breasted women invaded the stage during an Adorno lecture and mocked him. When the Institute's library was threatened to be wrecked the directors called the police to prevent the occupation. The self-styled revolutionaries were denounced with the controversial label "left fascism." The conservative media reveled in *Schadenfreude* that all this happened to a "left" Institute that was held responsible for fomenting such anti-establishment sentiments in the first place.

In rebellious Berkeley, even "Leo," the longest-surviving member of the school and a most amenable and sociable individual, could not fully shed the habits of his privileged German upbringing. In San Francisco, he once invited Kogila and me to a sumptuous dinner in a fancy restaurant and ordered an exquisite bottle of red wine. After an extended tasting ritual, he sent the bottle back, berating the poor waiter about serving such an inferior product. Löwenthal and Marcuse were the only two Frankfurt exiles who stayed in the United States at the University of California, but they occasionally visited their original homeland. When that happened during the early 1960s, we assistants felt honored to play respectful hosts by showing them around in Frankfurt. I had the distinct feeling that their resident colleagues were not too enamored by these visits, and Adorno kept somewhat of a polite distance. He may even have been envious of the fame Marcuse had achieved around the world as a champion of radical students. A rather disappointing experience remains etched in my memory: when I tried to enlist Marcuse as an ideological missionary. In 1966, I had arranged to visit him at his home in La Jolla with a German friend, Fritz Sack, who had been an assistant of a rival sociologist, Rene König, in Cologne. Fritz, now probably the most distinguished critical criminologist in Germany, also had a fellowship in Berkeley. We frequently argued about the merits of the more hermeneutic Frankfurt School vis-à-vis the more empiricist and, in Adorno's view, "abominable positivist" approach in Cologne. Our pilgrimage to the guru Marcuse was to set my friend finally right. We arrived at Marcuse's abode near San Diego in an old Volkswagen after an exhausting drive along the California coast. The new domineering companion of Marcuse offered us a bowl of strawberries. After a superficial chat of barely an hour with the prophet, she accompanied us to the door, indicating in no uncertain terms that the visit was over.

What do the blind spots about three-quarters of humanity outside Western Europe and the United States indicate? What does it mean for the grand critical theory if the ghetto next door in Los Angeles or the subordination of women is simply ignored by the leading thinkers of the epoch? In all of Adorno's lectures and seminars, I do not recall one reference to color discrimination in South Africa or the United States, from which Marcuse expected a new revolutionary class to emerge. The best-known book by Adorno and colleagues, *The Authoritarian Personality*, with its famous F (Fascism), E (Ethnocentrism), A-S (Anti-Semitism), and PEC (Politico-Economic-Conservatism) scales, surprisingly lacks an R (Racism) and an H (Homophobic) scale. While the attitudes of the syndrome are similar, they are not identical. During the immediate postwar decades in Frankfurt, the prism on racism had been narrowed solely to anti-Semitism, partly under the overwhelming trauma of the Holocaust and partly because there were few black people living among the German population. The vast secondary literature on the luminaries of the Frankfurt School has yet to explore such questions of Eurocentric blindness.

One of the lasting lessons learned in Frankfurt concerned the critical reading of Marx together with the insights of Freud. Long before Euro-communism in Italy distanced itself from the official Marxist-Leninism taught in the Soviet Union and its satellites in Eastern Europe, the early Frankfurt theorists recognized that Lenin had perverted Marxist ideals in theory and praxis. Without abandoning a political economy analysis, Horkheimer and Adorno eschewed dogmatism of any kind, particularly the Leninist notion of a vanguard prescribing what is good for ignorant masses. Valued ideals should never justify undemocratic means to attain them. Our mentors instilled a firm moral compass in their students. Moral relativism was assailed and no allowances were made for prominent anti-Semites, like Richard Wagner or Heidegger, who had flirted with the Nazi regime. They were red flags for Adorno in particular.

When I became involved in South African politics in 1966, I tried to apply such critical theorizing. I aimed at filling the gap of race, colonialism, and underdevelopment that the Frankfurt School left unaddressed. South Africa was full of self-declared Marxist analysts at the time—but of the orthodox kind. The liberation movements had defined the institutionalized racism of apartheid as a variant of fascism and expected racial capitalism to collapse as soon as the backward peasants and oppressed working class would have awakened and been mobilized for militant action. Ethnicity was considered false consciousness and identity concerns a distraction from class struggle, which the overlap of race and class would override in one of the most unequal societies. Indeed, the "Nazis of Africa" initially confirmed for me, too, the validity of Marxist class struggle.

However, the Frankfurt School had also taught us to distrust and interrogate dogma. A more nuanced analysis would look at the evidence rather than apply a preconceived formula. That meant in contrast to the *extermination* policy of Nazism, apartheid relied on *exploitation*. Without the black working class supplying cheap labor, there would be no white profits. That necessitated labor policies that enhanced productivity and predictability. No Hitler- or Stalin-type personality cult existed in South Africa. A group dictatorship corrected and limited arbitrariness. Instead, an ethnic oligarchy adjusted its racism according to shifting economic needs rather than being ruled by an inflexible ideology. Even some opposition was tolerated in an authoritarian rather than European totalitarian system. In that 'democratic police state' anti-apartheid resistance could utilize many strategies, from courts to industrial action to media mobilization. Above all, the German Nazis could only be defeated militarily. In contrast, regime change in South Africa could also be achieved through negotiations. By adhering to the fascist definition of apartheid, the liberation movements missed the opportunity to prepare for a 'negotiated revolution.'

And so my lifelong obsession with issues of race, ethnic conflict, colonialism, and liberation started in the shadow of my Frankfurt School–acquired sensibility, self-confidence, and even arrogance toward alternative perspectives. When my *Südafrika: Soziologie einer Rassengesellschaft* was published 1969 in the famous alphabetically listed Suhrkamp series, I was childishly proud that I ranked directly above Adorno's many titles on the same page.

Although I greatly value the inspiration and insights I gained at the celebrated institute, I felt liberated when I left for Berkeley on a U.S. scholarship from the Thyssen Foundation after receiving my Ph.D. in 1965. Upon returning from the United States and South Africa two years later, I turned down an offer to rejoin the institute, choosing instead to seek teaching opportunities abroad and finally deciding on Simon Fraser University in Vancouver. As a newly married happy couple, Kogila and I resisted being stuck in familiar routines. We voluntarily and without necessity wanted to explore new worlds, even if it meant bidding farewell with a heavy heart to the comforts of a cherished culture, language, *Heimat*, and friends, facing the uncertainties of all new emigrants to a foreign land.

PEACEMAKING IN DIVIDED SOCIETIES

The following passages are portions of a mandatory public lecture I gave at Simon Fraser University after I received the 2008 Sterling Prize in support of controversy, in which, as honoree, I was asked to focus on controversies in my career.

I feel honored and also humbled when I look at the list of distinguished colleagues who preceded me receiving this recognition. Courting controversy easily brands one as a troublemaker, particularly in a consensus-oriented society such as Canada. I never wanted to be seen as a troublemaker courting controversy. However, frequently controversy courted me during my academic life. One cannot always practice moral fence sitting and avoid offending people who do not share one's reasoning. At the risk of sounding like a self-absorbed narcissist, let me suggest that we walk together through some of the controversies that I experienced after joining SFU in 1968.

After studying theories of fascism and anti-Semitism with the author of *The Authoritarian Personality* in Frankfurt during the early 1960s, two German geographers with close connections to the apartheid government needed a sociologist for a six-month study tour of South Africa in 1966. The ultraconservative leader of the group, a friend of SA Prime Minister J. B. Vorster, was also the father of my then-serious girlfriend. Since I had no direct experience of German Nazis as a little boy and constantly argued about race and South Africa with my prospective father-in-law, I jumped at the opportunity to explore the "Nazis of Africa," colonial fascists, *Herrenvolk* types of a master race, as Pierre van den Berghe had labeled them, because some of them had ideologically borrowed heavily from the German predecessors. Indeed, the racial subjugation legalized as apartheid and ideological rationalizations of racial inferiority seemed to confirm the appalling similarities. I was also persuaded by the Left literature that such a violent system could only be overthrown through stronger counterviolence by the then-fledgling liberation movements. Apartheid South Africa was a Marxist's dream: a visibly oppressed and exploited majority without political rights and with a clearly visible minority of oppressors, a society ripe for revolution.

Fate intervened and I met my future wife when I was invited to lecture to her class at the segregated Indian university in Durban. I abandoned my two distressed German colleagues and began to explore SA on my own. It was illegal for any person of the master race to have normal social relations, let alone intimate cross-racial contact with a nonwhite individual under the infamous "Immorality Act." Prominent academics like John Blacking were prosecuted and imprisoned for such libidinous transgressions. Nevertheless, in 1967 I returned to a one-year visiting appointment at the University of Natal to win over Kogila's skeptical family. Protected by liberal colleagues and friends, we socialized more or less underground and learned a lot from our association with academic dissidents, like Fatima Meer, Tony Mathews, Jairam Reddy, Rick Turner, and Hamish Dickie-Clark. That did not escape the attention of the authorities in a police state. For example, we used to play tennis with Jairam Reddy and the U.S. consul, John Savage, on Sunday mornings at the empty university courts until I received a written instruction from then-university principal Owen Horwood to desist from such interracial activity prohibited under the Group Areas Act. To cut a long story short, Kogila was fired from her job on the urging of the security police, and I was banned from the country with an official letter that any future visa applications would be refused.

The unintended consequences of this widely reported controversy brought Kogila to Berlin on a DAAD fellowship and me back home to Frankfurt, where we were subsequently formally married. Shortly afterward we emigrated to Vancouver, where Kogila could pursue her Ph.D. in the English language. Since we both were trained in the same discipline (Kogila had an MA from Michigan at the time and later received her Ph.D. from UBC), we have collaborated closely ever since. She deserves as much credit as I for our five coauthored books. Kogila is my reality principle, more radical, but also with much more polished social and diplomatic skills. Combating institutionalized racism in apartheid South Africa has remained our obsession long after we moved to SFU at the invitation of Tom Bottomore, who aspired to establish the equivalent of the LSE in Vancouver.

From the real conflicts in South Africa, I landed in the heated but comparatively trivial disputes of a boycotted twenty-five-member Political Science, Sociology and Anthropology (PSA) Department, which I chaired between 1970 and 1972 (our history colleague, Hugh Johnson, has described this period in his comprehensive book *Radical Campus*). Having just experienced real repression, I found the claims of the pampered students and some faculty to be "the niggers of Canada oppressed by a fascist university administration in cahoots with a right-wing provincial government" a bit far-fetched. In as much as the outlook of the government was a crude frontier-type vision of fast development at the time, neither it nor the university administration interfered in what and how we should teach or who should teach. As long as this essential academic freedom was respected, there was no need to pose as antiauthoritarian warriors. Instead of occupying university buildings and disrupting classes, I argued, we faculty should utilize the freedom to educate our restless students in critical reasoning. Echoes from Frankfurt and Berkeley about "theory and praxis" and the Bader-Meinhoff gang's "direct actions" against "capitalist pigs" a few years earlier had followed me to Vancouver. The Adorno-Habermas argument that "critical theory is praxis" found little support. Initially, I had never heard of "Robert's Rules of Order," but for two years I had to chair constant departmental emergency meetings of our twenty-five teaching and suspended Political Science, Sociology, Anthropology and Archeology (PSA) faculty. Previously we had all agreed on a departmental constitution. Yet in one meeting, my intervention that a proposed action was unconstitutional was rebuffed by an enraged colleague, who rose dramatically, tore the constitution apart, and shouted, "In times of crisis a constitution does not matter." All the fuss was not about an ideological left or right issue but the reinstatement of some suspended faculty who had gone on a teaching strike. Our "rump" department was at the brink of disintegration, neither appreciated by the conservative administration and faculty for bringing the whole institution into disrepute nor supported by the liberal profession, but ultimately saved when I persuaded the Pulitzer Prize winner and social theorist Ernest Becker together with Karl Peter to join, followed later by the internationally known constitutional expert Ted McWhinney.

To my own surprise and reluctance, I had to revise my assumptions about the Nazis of Africa after my empirical research into Afrikaner attitudes in 1966–1967. Simplistic analogies are good for mobilizing indignation, but inadequate for analysis, because the differences outweigh the similarities, as I argue later.

As far as apartheid is concerned, my empirical research of attitudes of MPs, senior civil servants, and business executives revealed the need to distinguish between different kinds of racism and explore the possibility of peaceful, reformist liberalization from within. My first two books in English, *Modernizing Racial Domination* (University of California Press, 1971) and the edited volume *South Africa: Sociological Perspectives* (Oxford University Press, 1971), elaborated on the concept of a "democratic police state" and a "pragmatic oligarchy" that constantly adjusted its strategy and ideology of minority rule, unlike the dogmatic Nazi mindset geared to *one* supreme leader. Those activists who insisted on the equivalence of Nazism and apartheid denounced this reconceptualization as counterrevolutionary revisionism by a typical wishy-washy liberal. Yet *Modernizing Racial Domination* experienced three reprints and was widely adopted in courses, perhaps because it held up a different peaceful vision of a negotiated solution.

The idea of "instrumental racism" in the functional sense of exploitation and securing power and privilege by a minority, as opposed to the irrational Nazi genocide, was further explored in a co-authored book with the historian Hermann Giliomee, *Ethnic Power Mobilized* (1979, New Haven: Yale University Press), while we both were fellows in the South African Research Program at Yale University. We argued against popular psychological theories of racism that focused on prejudice, or considered South African racism derived from the Calvinist mindset of a "chosen people." Instead we favored a political economy explanation while recognizing the independent dynamic of ideology and cultural traditions in leader-follower mobilization. A fierce controversy about rationality and racism was later triggered by my articles in the journal *Telos* (nos. 108 and 118).

Another controversy focused on the relationship between capitalism and racism. Was industrialization compatible with a racial caste system? The dominant academic opinion at the time analyzed the SA system as *"racial* capitalism." Outlawing African unions and securing cheap labor with various apartheid laws was viewed as inextricably linked to maximal profit. The downfall of the one would inevitably lead to the collapse of the other. In contrast, my position, shared also by a Canadian sociologist, Rick Johnstone, asserted that "multi-racial capitalism" was not only conceivable with rising costs of minority rule but also more legitimate and functional than the existing colonial and paternalistic labor relations. Our first jointly authored book, *South Africa without Apartheid,* (Berkely: University of California Press, 1986), projected such a "normal" society without the political exclusion of the majority. It focused on the conditions and political alliances that would bring about the downfall of white minority rule. This was of course considered treasonous in the eyes of the ruling group. Yet Mandela in Pollsmoor prison had read the book approvingly and in a personal, hand-written letter asked to have it autographed.

Due to the intervention of a liberal Afrikaner journalist and a reformist government spell in the late 1970s, we were again granted a visa when I was invited to become, together with Arendt Lijphard, one of the two foreign members of the "Buthelezi Commission," chaired by the liberal Dennys Schreiner, vice chancellor of the University of Natal in Maritzburg. The commission had little to do with Chief Buthelezi, who must have lent his name to the exercise but who never participated in any commission session. Unlike the other Bantustan heads, Buthelezi refused to apply for independence, because he claimed legitimacy from precolonial times. Yet Buthelezi (under Mandela's reign later Home Affairs minister) was *the* red flag for the exiled ANC, because he was opposed to the armed struggle and sanctions. With considerable support among rural Zulus at the time, Buthelezi was suspected by the exiled ANC to emerge as a potential internal substitute to the banned ANC. Yet Pretoria too viewed him suspiciously as a stubborn, unpredictable opponent. The commission aimed at working out a nonracial constitution for Natal, the only province in which the National Party did not hold a majority among the white voters. Among much public acrimony the liberal dream failed in the end. The commission was an exercise in futility since neither the Afrikaner nor the African nationalists supported it.

Around that time (1979) I was also invited to deliver the IX Cecil Rhodes Memorial Lecture at the Convocation of Rhodes University in Grahamstown. My lecture speculated on what Rhodes—the most ruthless and greedy, but politically savvy imperialist— would have done 100 years later in apartheid SA. Among other measures I naively suggested Rhodes would have at least invited some representatives of the neighboring impoverished Fingo township to share the sumptuous meal and participate in the festivities. This seemingly uncontroversial suggestion of social integration and fasting in solidarity with the hungry black poor caused consternation among the all-white luminaries, some of whom had arrived in their private jets. The vice-chancellor declined to reconstitute the reception and instead offered to set up a scholarship for a black student to which the distinguished guests could contribute. The colonial establishment bought out its guilt. I abstained from the food together with a few supportive faculty, but contributed the value of the gold medal awarded me to the scholarship fund. The "scandal" was widely reported in the SA press with numerous letters to the editors commenting in rage about "abuse of hospitality" but also in agreement. Even a Vancouver journalist, the right-wing North Shore columnist Doug Collins, got into the act, castigating that idiot up at SFU (me) for wanting to destroy the last bastion of white civilization on a dark continent by "making blacks and whites jump into bed with each other."

During the height of apartheid repression and emergency rule (1986–1987), I served for a year as acting director of the Centre for Intergroup Relations at the University of Cape Town (UCT) and subsequently taught for fifteen years a compulsory social science course, "Business, Society and Government," in the MBA program at UCT's Graduate School of Business. The Centre for Intergroup Relations was headed by that unrecognized pioneer of early ANC contacts, the unassuming Quaker H. W. van der Merwe. One day the notorious riot squad invaded the campus—"Moscow on the hill," in their jargon—after attacking a student demonstration along the highway below. I can still smell the stinging tear gas, which literally blinded everyone for half an hour.

Two longtime close friends, the sociologist and parliamentary leader of the opposition Van Zyl Slabbert and Alex Boraine, had just resigned from a dysfunctional all-white Parliament. They wanted to establish an "extra-parliamentary opposition." With the financial help of George Soros and diplomatic support of Madame Mitterand, they, together with Paris-based Breyten Breytenbach, organized an important meeting with the exiled ANC and about forty Afrikaner dissidents and some English businessmen in Dakar, Senegal, in July 1987. I was invited to join and, as an outsider with access to the banned literature, was asked to write the preparatory paper on the ANC.

The mission to explore negotiations had to be kept secret. The very idea of a negotiated compromise was controversial among both the left and the right extremists. The left ANC "insurrectionist" argued that "you can never win at the negotiating table what you have not won on the battlefield." The Afrikaner right-wing asserted that you simply do not sit around the same table with "terrorists." The SA president, P. W. Botha, called us "Lenin's useful idiots."

The story of the negotiated transition from authoritarianism to democracy was captured in our book *The Opening of the Apartheid Mind,* (University of California Press 1993). It was published in South Africa as *The Negotiated Revolution*, the very possibility denied by all the apocalyptic predictions of an inevitable racial civil war and the victory of the "armed struggle." We argued that class had now replaced race as the basis of inequality. In the book we also warned about the impending AIDS crisis, long before it became a public issue. Such an alarm was not popular, because it was seen as an attack on African sexual mores.

During the 1980s I was also occasionally consulted by then–Canadian external affairs minister Joe Clark, whose department differed with the Prime Minister's Office on sanctions about South Africa. Paradoxically, Brian Mulroney wanted to break Canadian diplomatic relations with Pretoria, while Joe Clark argued for "constructive engagement." I mainly supplied Clark with suggestions on how Canada could better support the internal anti-apartheid opposition and work with SA civil society. Our contracted book, *Democratising South Africa: Challenges for Canadian Policy* (1982), based on extensive interviews with senior Canadian civil servants, suggests that Mulroney's stance was mainly motivated by his desire to replace pro–South Africa Margaret Thatcher as the moral leader of the Commonwealth.

My position on sanctions toward Israel derived from the lesson I learned from the debate about actions against apartheid. The grand gesture of boycott or breaking diplomatic relations, as Mulroney advocated, affirmed the moral purity of the actor, but did not assist the internal opposition. I preferred to support the late Palestinian intellectual Edward Said, who advocated, "I believe it is our duty as Palestinian and yes, even Arab intellectuals to engage Israeli academic and intellectual audiences by lecturing at Israeli centers, openly, courageously, uncompromisingly. What have years of refusing to deal with Israel done for us? Nothing at all, except to weaken us and weaken our perception of our opponent."

Three years after the first SA democratic election in 1994, Kogila and I published the controversial *Comrades in Business* (1997), co-authored with Van Zyl Slabbert. It analyzed the ANC in power, its shift toward neoliberal economic policies, the role of the new black bourgeoisie, and the depoliticization of a liberation movement in favor of autocratic decision-making in the president's office. When Van Zyl and I handed a copy to then-President Mbeki at a reunion of the Dakar group at the Stier estate in Stellenbosch, we could see the cool displeasure in his face.

During the first years of the pending liberation, a serious debate about the future of the South African economy took place. Should it be a command economy à la the Soviet Union with the nationalization of the mines, or a free-market economy in accordance with the Washington consensus? I argued for neither, but advocated a social democracy. What lessons should South Africa draw from the collapse of the Soviet Union? The chief theorist of the ANC at the time was the head of the SA Communist Party, the late Joe Slovo. After Mandela and Chris Hani, Slovo was the most popular and influential politician. A jovial man, but previously a stern Stalinist, he nevertheless explained the Soviet disintegration as the mistake of the leader, a pilot error, so to speak, rather than a systemic failure of Leninist Marxism. Although South Africa headed toward a mixed economy, Slovo renounced a social-democratic label for the "democratic socialism" he now advocated. At a roundtable discussion on the national TV show *Slabbert on Sunday* with George Soros and Slovo on Easter 1993, I challenged Slovo on why he insisted on the Marxism-Leninism label, but Slovo did not budge. Incidentally, on that occasion I also learned that the archcommunist Slovo had not known who the archcapitalist Soros was (and probably vice versa), but both paid each other compliments as "enlightened representatives of their class."

A two-year teaching stint at the American University in Cairo (1972–1974) led to an abiding interest in the politics of the Middle East. At that time, Egypt under Sadat was still in the Soviet camp and was officially at war with Israel. We sat out the short 1973 "October War," or what the Israelis call "Yom Kippur War," with packed suitcases in Cairo, ready to be evacuated at short notice. We nonetheless visited Israel several times via Cyprus and roamed other countries from Lebanon to Syria and Jordan. During the past six years we worked on the most sensitive project: what can be learned from successful peacemaking in South Africa for the elusive and seemingly intractable Israeli-Palestinian conflict. When we announced this project to one of our SA friends, Michael Savage, he replied, "Are you suicidal?" Yet several research visits to Israel and the West Bank convinced us otherwise.

On the Israeli-Palestinian issue, one can adopt essentially three approaches: The Nobel Laureate Elie Wiesel maintains, "As a Jew I see my role as a . . . defender of Israel. I defend even her mistakes." The British philosopher Ted Honderich argues the same blind loyalty for the Palestinian cause, advocating "liberation-terrorism to get freedom and power for a people when it is clear that nothing else will get it for them." Neither of the two will ever mention the atrocities committed by his adopted side. Wiesel explicitly says, "Either speak up in praise, or keep silent." A preferred third approach avoids the pitfalls of such blind patriotism that elevates fallible policies into the realm of the sacred.

Our book *Seeking Mandela: Peacemaking between Israelis and Palestinians* (Temple UP and Wits UP, 2005) tries to draw lessons from South Africa for the seemingly intractable conflict in the Middle East, without falling into the trap of simplistic analogies of two distinct situations. We question the exhortations that the Israeli occupation of Palestinian land can and/or should be combated with the same methods as used in the anti-apartheid struggle. We highlight similarities and differences of the two situations and argue that any search for solutions must take into account the specifics of the Middle East situations rather than rely on emotional apartheid comparisons. Six crucial realms stand out for comparison in both contexts: economic interdependence, religious divisions, third-party intervention, leadership, political culture, and violence.

In summary, on most counts, the differences between apartheid South Africa and Israel outweigh the similarities that could facilitate transferable conditions for a negotiated compromise. Above all, opponents in South Africa finally realized that neither side could comprehensively defeat the other, short of the destruction of the country. This perception of stalemate, as a precondition for negotiating in good faith, is missing in the Middle East. Peacemaking resulted in an inclusive democracy in South Africa, while territorial separation of the adversaries in two states is widely hailed as the solution in Israel/Palestine. For 95 percent of Jewish Israelis a SA scenario of a binational or one-state solution is a nightmare, because Israel would no longer be a Jewish state, but ironically with its current policy of territorial expansion on Palestinian land, Israel is heading in the direction of a one-state solution.

Many lessons for an Israeli-Palestinian solution can be drawn from the South African negotiated transformation. Preparing an indoctrinated public on both sides for a painful transition through a Truth Commission remains perhaps the most important lesson. While the SA Truth and Reconciliation Commission (TRC) showed many flaws in its design and execution of its task, at least it held out a less divided "truth" about the past. Victims were affirmed and some perpetrators exposed, although beneficiaries were left unchallenged. Denial of past crimes became impossible, although interpretations of causes, guilt, and blame continue to differ. Peace between Israelis and Palestinians requires a modified TRC, an introspective investigation into each side's own abuses. Andrew Rigby has stressed, "It is vital that people learn to acknowledge the validity of other people's truths." A parallel Israeli and Palestinian Truth Commission (IPTC) could attempt this shared narrative by undermining the sectarian stranglehold on history. The effort would have to originate from a civil society initiative, since neither official authority is likely to support a critical scrutiny of its record.

In order to get an Israeli-Palestinian Truth Commission off the ground at all, its task would have to be different and more modest, not aiming at ascertaining guilt, punishment, redress, forgiveness, or healing, but merely establishing a common historical record. The opposing metanarratives currently poison relations. What Mahmood Mamdani has argued for postgenocide Rwanda applies equally to Israel/Palestine: "It is not possible to think of reconciliation between Hutu and Tutsi in Rwanda without prior conciliation with history." While all other TRCs have focused on postconflict reconstruction after the violence has ceased or a regime has changed, the unique role of an IPTC would lay the essential groundwork for bringing about this end in the future. It could bridge the mental disconnect through political education for a mutually acceptable compromise. Only when the "cognitive maps" of both publics resemble each other by similar acknowledgments of past traumatic events will the peace accords of elites resonate among their constituencies.

While on a Humboldt fellowship in Berlin in 1999 and several times thereafter, I was again confronted with how Germany had dealt with its unsavory past, how and why xenophobia and anti-Semitism waxed and waned simultaneously. In several public lectures in Germany, I extolled the virtues of Canada as a model for selecting economic migrants and refugees with a more rational and humane immigration policy. Of course, the German audience was not persuaded that the country needed an immigration policy at all, since it considered itself officially not an immigration society. It brought home to me that unlike Europe and South Africa, Canada is not a xenophobic society.

Postscript 2015: Since that lecture in 2008, my privileged academic life has continued in the same vein, oscillating annually between Vancouver, Berlin, and Cape Town. Another book, *Hushed Voices: Unacknowledged Atrocities of the Twentieth Century* (Berkshire Academic Press), was published in 2011. It is a collection of the 15 best essays in a collective effort by my class in the SFU Graduate Liberal Studies Program. The precise impact of such laborious academic publishing and lecturing cannot be assessed. Whether this new effort of reflections on xenophobia and comparative immigration policies in this book makes any difference beyond narcissistic pleasure for the authors remains to be seen.

References

Abraham, David. 2010. "Doing Justice on Two Fronts: The Liberal Dilemma in Immigration." *Ethnic and Racial Studies* 33 (6): 968–985.

Adam, Heribert. 1971. *Modernizing Racial Domination: The Dynamics of South African Politics*. Berkeley: University of California Press.

———, ed. 1971. *South Africa: Sociological Perspectives*. London: Oxford University Press.

———, ed. 1983. *South Africa: The Limits of Reform Politics*. Leiden: E. J. Brill.

Adam, Heribert. 2002. *Peacemaking in Divided Societies: The Israel-South Africa Analogy*. Pretoria: HSRC.

———, ed. 2011. *Hushed Voices: Unacknowledged Atrocities of the 20th Century*. Highclere, U.K.: Berkshire Academic Press.

Adam, Heribert, and Hermann Giliomee. 1979. *Ethnic Power Mobilized*. New Haven, CT: Yale University Press.

Adam, Heribert, and Kogila Moodley. 1982. *Democratising Southern Africa: Challenges for Canadian Policy*. Ottawa: Canadian Institute for International Peace and Security.

———. 1986. *South Africa without Apartheid: Dismantling Racial Domination*. Berkeley: University of California Press.

———. 1993. *The Opening of the Apartheid Mind: Options for the New South Africa*. Berkeley: University of California Press.

———. 2005. *Seeking Mandela: Peacemaking between Israelis and Palestinians*. Philadelphia: Temple University Press.

Adam, Heribert, Frederik Van Zyl Slabbert, and Kogila Moodley. 1997. *Comrades in Business: Post-Liberation Politics in South Africa*. Cape Town: Tafelberg.

Adam, Kanya. 2000. *The Colour of Business: Managing Diversity in South Africa*. Basel: Schlettwein.

Adams, Michael. 2007. *Unlikely Utopia: The Surprising Triumph of Canadian Pluralism*. Toronto: Viking.

Adorno, Theodor, et al. 1950. "The Authoritarian Personality." New York: Harper.

Alba, R., and M. Johnson. 2000. "Zur Messung aktueller Einstellungensmuster gegenüber Ausländern in Deutschland." In *Deutsche und Ausländer: Freunde, Fremde oder Feinde?*, edited by R. Alba, P. Schmidt, and M. Wasmer, 229–253.

Alexander, Jeffrey. 2013. Struggling over the mode of incorporation: Backlash against multiculturalism in Europe. Ethnic and Racial Studies, 36 (4): 531–556.

Amisi, Baruti, et al. 2011. "Xenophobia and Civil Society: Durban's Structured Social Divisions." *Politikon* 38 (1): 59–83.

Banks, James A. 1997. *Educating Citizens in a Multicultural Society.* New York: Teachers College Press.

Banting, Keith G., Thomas J. Courchene, and F. Leslie Seidle, eds. 2007. *Belonging? Diversity, Recognition and Shared Citizenship in Canada.* Montreal: Institute for Research on Public Policy.

Bekker, Simon. 2010. "Explaining Violence against Foreigners and Strangers in Urban South Africa: Outbursts during May and June 2008." *African Yearbook of International Law 2010*, 125–149.

Benatar, Solomon R. 2001. "South Africa's Transition in a Globalizing World: HIV/AIDS as a Window and Mirror." *International Affairs* 77 (2): 347–375.

Ben-Rafael, Eliezer. 2004. "Where Stands Israel?" *Ethnic and Racial Studies* 27 (2): 310–316.

Bhana, C. Connolly, S. Jooste, and V. Pillay. 2005. *South African National HIV Prevalence, HIV Incidence, Behaviour and Communication Survey 2005.* Pretoria: HSRC Press.

Bischoff, Christine, et al., eds. 2010. *Images of Illegalized Immigration.* Bielefeld: Transcript Verlag.

Bochel, H. 2009. "Political Literacy." In *Active Learning and Active Citizenship: Theoretical Contexts (C-SAP Higher Education Academy Network)*, edited by M. McManus and G. Taylor, 150–168. Retrieved February 19, 2012, from http://www.lulu.com/items/volume_71/6983000/6983481/5/print/Text_all.pdf.

Bonacich, E. 1972. A Theory of Ethnic Antagonism: The Split Labor Market. *American Sociological Review*, 37 (5): 547–549.

Brodkin, Karen. 2005. "Xenophobia, the State and Capitalism." *American Ethnologist* 32 (4): 519–520.

Brubaker, R. 1992. *Citizenship and Nationhood in France and Germany.* Cambridge, MA: Harvard University Press.

Bystydzienski, JM. 2011. *Intercultural couples: crossing boundaries, negotiating difference.* New York: New York University Press.

Campbell, Eugene. 2003. "Attitudes of Botswana Citizens toward Immigrants: Signs of Xenophobia?" *International Migration* 41 (4): 71–109.

Carrim, Nazir. 1998. "Anti-racism and the 'New' South African Educational Order." *Cambridge Journal of Education* 28 (3): 301–320.

Charman, Andrew and Laurence Piper. 2012. "From Local Survivalism to Foreign Entrepreneurship: The Transformation of the Spaza Sector in Delft, Cape Town." Transformation 78: 47–73.

———. 2012a. "Xenophobia, Criminality, and Violent Entrepreneurship: Violence Against Somali Shopkeepers in Delft South, Cape Town, South Africa." *South African Review of Sociology*, Vol. 43, No.3: 81–105.

Chipkin, I. 2007. *Do South Africans Exist? Nationalism, Democracy and the Identity of "the People."* Johannesburg: Wits University Press.

Chisholm, Linda. 2003. *Streamlining C2005: Implementation Plan.* Pretoria: Ministry of Education.

———. 2008. "Migration, Citizenship and South African History Textbooks." *South African Historical Journal* 60 (3): 353–374.

Citizenship Foundation. 2012. *Political Literacy Explained.* Retrieved January 9, 2012, from http://www.citizenshipfoundation.org.uk/ main/ page.php?12.

Clarke, Peter. 2007. *The Last Thousand Days of the British Empire.* London: Allan Lane.

Cohen, Stanley. 1972. *Folk Devils and Moral Panics.* London: McGibbon Kee.

Cole, Mike. 2009. "A Plethora of 'Suitable Enemies': British Racism at the Dawn of the Twenty-First Century." *Ethnic and Racial Studies* 32 (9): 1671–1685.

Coplan, David B. 2009. "Innocent Violence: Social Exclusion, Identity, and the Press in an African Democracy." *Critical Arts* 23 (1): 64–83.

Crick, Bernard. 2000. *Essays on Citizenship.* London: Continuum.

Crick, Bernard., and Ian Lister. 1978. "Political Literacy." In *Political Education and Political Literacy*, edited by B. Crick and A. Porter, 59–74. London: Longman.

Croucher, S. 1998. "South Africa's Illegal Aliens: Constructing National Boundaries in a Post-Apartheid State." *Ethnic and Racial Studies* 21 (4): 639–660.

Crush, Jonathan. 2000. "The Dark Side of Democracy: Migration, Xenophobia and Human Rights in South Africa." *International Migration* 38 (6): 103–133.

———. 2001. "Making Up the Numbers: Measuring 'Illegal Immigration' to South Africa." SAMP Migration Policy Brief no. 3, Cape Town.

———, ed. 2008. *The Perfect Storm: The Realities of Xenophobia in Contemporary South Africa.* Johannesburg: Southern African Migration Project, no. 50.

Crush, Jonathan, and S. Ramachandran. 2009. *Xenophobia, International Migration and Human Development.* New York: UND Human Development Report, no. 47.

Dambrun, M., D. Taylor, D. A. McDonald, J. Crush, and A. Meot. 2006. "The Relative Deprivation-Gratification Continuum and the Attitudes of South Africans towards Immigrants." *Journal of Personality and Social Psychology* 91 (6): 1032–1044.

Danso, R., and D. A. McDonald. 2000. *Writing Xenophobia: Immigration and the Press in Post-Apartheid South Africa.* SAMP Migration Policy Series no. 17, Cape Town.

Decker, O., and E. Braehler. 2012. *Die Mitte in der Krise: Rechtsextreme Einstellungen.* Bonn: Friedrich Ebert Stiftung.

Degenaar, Johan. 1994. "Beware of Nation-Building." In *Democratic Nation-Building in South Africa*, edited by Nic Rhoodie and Ian Liebenberg, 23–30. Pretoria: HSRC.

Desai, Ashwin. 2008. "Xenophobia and the Place of the Refugee in the Rainbow Nation of Human Rights." *African Sociological Review* 12 (2): 49–68.

Di Giusto, Gerald M., and Seth K. Jolly. 2008. "French Xenophobia and Immigrant Contact: Public Attitudes toward Immigration." Conference paper for American Political Science Association, Boston, MA, 28–31 August 2008.

Diehl, Claudia, and Ingrid Tucci. 2011. "Who Can Become German? Xenophobia and Attitudes towards Naturalization." *DIW Economic Bulletin* 1 (3): 3–8.

Dlamini, Jacob. 2009. *Native Nostalgia.* Johannesburg: Jacana Media.

Dodson, Belinda. 2010. "Locating Xenophobia: Debate, Discourse and Everyday Experience in Cape Town, South Africa." *Africa Today* 56 (3): 4–22.

Douglas, A. 2002. *Educating for Real and Hoped for Political Worlds: Ways Forward in Developing Political Literacy.* [Retrieved July 15, 2013] http://www.citized.info/pdf /commarticles/Anna_Douglas.pdf.

Downie, Michelle. 2012. *Immigrants as Innovators: Boosting Canada's Global Competitiveness.* Ottawa, ON: Conference Board of Canada.

Dryden, Sarah. 1999. Mirror of a Nation in Transition. MA diss. in Education, University of Cape Town.

Du Toit, Pierre, and Hennie Kotze. 2011. *Liberal Democracy and Peace in South Africa.* Johannesburg: Palgrave Macmillan.

Elhanan-Peled, Nuri. 2007. Speech at a Demonstration in Tel Aviv Commemorating 40 Years of Occupation. M. Marshall, transl. *Middle East Policy*, 14 (3): 41–44.

Ellis, Stephen. 2012. *External Mission.* Johannesburg: Jonathan Ball.

Everatt, David. 2011. "Xenophobia, State and Society in South Africa, 2008–2010." *Politikon* 38 (1): 7–36.

Falk, Richard. 1995. *On Humane Governance: Toward a New Global Politics.* Cambridge: Polity Press.

Fine, J., and W. Bird. 2006. *Shades of Prejudice: An Investigation into the South African Media's Coverage of Racial Violence and Xenophobia.* CSVR Race and Citizenship in Transition Series.

Fireside, Harvey. 2002. "The Demographic Roots of European Xenophobia." *Journal of Human Rights* 1 (4): 469–479.

Freud, Sigmund. (1930) 1961. *Civilization and Its Discontents.* New York: Norton.

Galston, William A. 2004. Review of *Civic Literacy: How Informed Citizens Make Democracy Work. Journal of Politics* 66 (4): 1341–1343.

Geschiere, Peter. 2009. *The Perils of Belonging: Autochthony, Citizenship and Exclusion in Africa and Europe.* Chicago: University of Chicago Press.

Gevisser, Mark. 2007. *Thabo Mbeki: The Dream Deferred.* Johannesburg: Jonathan Ball.

Gibson, N. 2011. *Fanonian Practices in South Africa: From Steve Biko to Abalahli base Mjondolo.* Durban: University of KwaZulu-Natal Press.

Giliomee, Hermann. 2012. *The Last Afrikaner Leaders.* Cape Town: Tafelberg.

Giliomee, Hermann, and Charles Simkins, eds. 1999. *The Awkward Embrace: One Party-Domination and Democracy.* Cape Town: Tafelberg.

Gilroy, P. 2005. *Postcolonial Melancholia.* New York: Columbia University Press.

Giroux, Henry. 1983. *Theory and Resistance in Education: A Pedagogy for the Opposition.* Westport: Bergin and Garvey.

Godwin, Peter. 2006. *When a Crocodile Eats the Sun.* New York: Little, Brown.

Goupil, S. 2004. Labour market integration of immigrants to Canada. Discussion paper, 9th International Metropolis Conference, Geneva, 28 September.

Gouws, Amanda and Daiva Stasiulis, eds. 2013. "Gender and Multiculturalism," Special Issue of *Politikon*, 10 (1) April: 1–14.

Hall, Stuart. 1999. "From Scarman to Stephen Lawrence." *History Workshop Journal* 48: 187–197.

Harber, Clive. 1998. "Desegregation, Racial Conflict and Education for Democracy in the New South Africa: A Case Study of Institutional Change." *International Review of Education* 44 (6): 569–582.

Harding, Jeremy. 2012. "Europe at Bay." *London Review of Books*, February 9.

Harris, Bronwyn. 2001. "A Foreign Experience: Violence, Crime and Xenophobia during South Africa's Transition." *Violence and Transition Series*, vol. 5. Braamfontein: Centre for the Study of Violence and Reconciliation (CSVR).

———. 2002. "Xenophobia: A New Pathology for a New South Africa?" In *Psychopathology and Social Prejudice*, edited by D. Hook and G. Eagle, 169–184. Cape Town: University of Cape Town Press.

Hassim, Shireen, Twana Kupe, and Eric Worby, eds. 2008. *South Africa: Go Home or Die Here: Violence, Xenophobia and the Reinvention of Difference in SA.* Johannesburg: Wits University Press.

Heitmeyer, Wilhelm, ed. 2009. *Deutsche Zustände.* Frankfurt: Suhrkamp.

Helen Suzman Foundation. 2010. Roundtable Discussion on Strangers and Outsiders: Overcoming Xenophobbia. Johannesburg, 18 August.

Hjerm, Mikael. 2001. "Education, Xenophobia and Nationalism: A Comparative Analysis." *Journal of Ethnic and Migration Studies* 27 (1): 37–60.

———. 1998. "National Identities, National Pride and Xenophobia: A Comparison of Four Western Countries." *Acta Sociologica* 41 (4): 335–347.

Hlatshwayo, Mondli. 2011. "Is There Room for International Solidarity within South African Borders? COSATU's Responses to the Xenophobic Attacks of May 2008." *Politikon* 38 (1): 169–189.

Holborn, Lucy. 2010. *The Long Shadow of Apartheid: Race in South Africa since 1994*. Johannesburg: South African Institute of Race Relations.

Holden, Paul, and Hennie van Vuuren. 2011. *The Devil in the Detail: How the Arms Deal Changed Everything*. Johannesburg: Jonathan Ball.

Hook, Derek. 2012. *A Critical Psychology of the Postcolonial: The Mind of Apartheid*. New York: Routledge.

Horowitz, Donald L. 2001. *The Deadly Ethnic Riot*. Berkeley: University of California Press.

Human Rights Watch. 1998. *Prohibited Persons: Abuse of Undocumented Migrants, Asylum Seekers and Refugees in South Africa*. New York.

Human Sciences Research Council (HSRC) of South Africa. 2008. "Citizenship, Violence and Xenophobia in South Africa: Perceptions from South African Communities." Pretoria: HSRC.

Igglesden, Vicki. 2002. "Public Education to Combat Xenophobia." Working Paper No. 117, Department of Planning Unit. University College, London.

Ignatieff, Michael. 1993. *Blood and Belonging*. New York: Farrar, Straus and Giroux.

Johnson, R. W. 2009. *South Africa's Brave New World*. London: Allen Lane.

Johnson, R. W., and Lawrence Schlemmer. 1996. *Launching Democracy in South Africa: The First Open Election, 1994*. New Haven, CT: Yale University Press.

Joppke, Christian. 2010. *Citizenship and Immigration*. Cambridge: Polity Press.

Joshee, Reva. 2009. "Multicultural Education Policy in Canada." In *The Routledge International Companion to Multicultural Education*, edited by James A. Banks, 96–108. New York: Routledge.

Kakar, Sudhir. 1996. *The Colors of Violence*. Chicago: University of Chicago Press.

Kihato, Caroline Wanjiku. 2007. "Invisible Lives, Inaudible Voices? The Social Conditions of Migrant Women in Johannesburg." In *Women in South African History*, edited by Nomboniso Gaza, 397–410. Pretoria: HSRC Press.

Klaaren, J., and J. Ramji. 2001. "Inside Illegality: Migration Policing in South Africa after Apartheid." *Africa Today* 48: 35–48.

Klandermans, Bert, et al., eds. 2001. *The State of the People: Citizens, Civil Society and Governance in South Africa, 1994–2000*. Pretoria: Human Sciences Research Council.

Klotz, Audie. 2012. "South Africa as an Immigration State." *Politikon* 39 (2): 189–208.

Kovel, Joel. 2007. Overcoming Zionism: Creating a Single Democratic State in Israel/Palestine. London: Pluto.

Kunda, John, E. L. 2009. "Xenophobia in South Africa: Revisiting Tutu's Handwriting on the Wall?" *Critical Arts* 23 (1): 122–123.

Kymlicka, Will. 2010. *The Current State of Multiculturalism in Canada and Research Themes on Canadian Multiculturalism 2008–2010*. Ottawa: Citizenship and Immigration Canada.

Landau, Loren B., ed. 2011. *Exorcising the Demons Within: Xenophobia, Violence, and Statecraft in Contemporary South Africa*. Johannesburg: Wits University Press.

Landau, Loren B., and Fremantle, Iriann. 2010. "Tactical Cosmopolitanism and Idioms of Belonging: Insertion and Self—Exclusion in Johannesburg." *Journal of Ethnic and Migration Studies* 36 (3): 375–390.

Landau, Loren, and Jean Pierre Misago. 2009. "Who to Blame and What's to Gain," *Africa Spectrum* 1: 99–110.

Lenten, Alana, and Gavan Titley. 2011. "The Crisis of Multiculturalism." *Open Democracy* 18 July 2011. [Retrieved 15 July 2013] http://www.opendemocracy.net/ourkingdom /alana-lentin-gavan-titley/crises-of-multiculturalism.

Lewin-Epstein, N., and Levanon, A. 2005. "National Identity and Xenophobia in an Ethnically Divided Society." *International Journal on Multicultural Societies* 7 (2): 90–118.

Licata, Laurent, and Klein, Olivier. 2002. "Does European Citizenship Breed Xenophobia? European Identification as a Predictor of Intolerance Towards Immigrants." *Journal of Community and Applied Social Psychology* 12: 323–337.

Lund, Christian. 2011. "Property and Citizenship." *Africa Spectrum* 3: 71–75.

Madsen, M. 2004. "Living for Home: Policing Immorality amongst Undocumented Migrants in Johannesburg." *African Studies* 63: 173–192.

Mamdani, Mahmoud. 1996. *Citizen and Subject: Contemporary Africa and the Legacy of Late Colonialism*. Princeton, NJ: Princeton University Press.

———. 2001a. When Does a Settler Become a Native? Citizenship and Identity in a Settler Society. *Pretext: Literacy and Cultural Studies* 10 (1): 48–68.

———. 2001b. *When Victims Become Killers: Colonialism, Nativism and Genocide in Rwanda*. Princeton, NJ: Princeton University Press.

Mangcu, Xolela. 2008. *To the Brink: The State of Democracy in South Africa*. Scottsville: University of KwaZulu-Natal Press.

Marais, Hein. 1998. *South Africa: Limits to Change*. Cape Town: Oxford University Press.

Matshiqi, Aubrey. 2010. In Helen Suzman Foundation, Roundtable.

Matsinhe, David Mario. 2011. "Africa's Fear of Itself: The Ideology of Makwerekwere in South Africa." *Third World Quarterly* 32 (2): 295–313.

Mattes, Robert. 2002. "Democracy without the People?" *Journal of Democracy* 13 (1): 22–36.

Mattes, Robert, Yul Derek Davids, and Cherrel Africa. 2000. "Citizen's Commitment to Democracy." In *Pulse: Passages in Democracy-Building: Assessing South Africa's Transition*, edited by Wilmot James and Moira Levy. Cape Town: Idasa.

Mattes, R., D. Taylor, D. McDonald, A. Poore, and W. Richmond. 1999. Still Waiting for the Barbarians: SA Attitudes to Immigrants and Immigration. SAMP Migration Policy Series No. 14, Cape Town.

Menasse, Robert. 2012. *Der Europäische Landbote: Die Wut der Bürger und der Friede Europas.*Vienna: Zsolnay.

McDonald, D. A. 2005. Understanding Press Coverage of Cross-Border Migration in Southern Africa since 2000. SAMP Migration Policy Series No. 37, Cape Town.

McDonald, D. A., and Jacobs, Sean. 2005. "(Re)writing Xenophobia: Understanding Press Coverage of Cross Border Migration in Southern Africa." *Journal of Contemporary African Studies* 23 (3).

Melzer, Ralf and Sebastian Serafin, eds. 2013. *Rechts-Extremismus in Europa* (Berlin: Friedrich Ebert Stiftung).

Milner, Henry. 2002. *Civic Literacy: How Informed Citizens Make Democracy*. Hanover, NH: University Press of New England.

Minnaar, A., and M. Hough. 1996. *Who Goes There? Perspectives on Clandestine Migration and Illegal Aliens in South Africa*. Pretoria: HSRC.

Mngxitama, Andile. 2008. "We Are Not All Like That: Race, Class and Nation after Apartheid." In *Go Home or Die Here: Violence, Xenophobia and the Reinvention of Difference in South Africa*, edited by Hassim, Shireen et al., 189–208. Johannesburg: Wits University Press.

Moodley, Kogila. 1971. "Dialectic of Higher Education for the Colonized." In *South Africa: Sociological Perspectives*, edited by Heribert Adam, 197–213. London: Oxford University Press.

Moodley. 1995. *Multicultural Education in Canada: Historical Development and Current Status*. In: J. A. Banks & C. McGee Banks, eds. Handbook of Research on Multicultural Education. New York: Macmillan. 801–820.

———. 2000. "African Renaissance and Language Policies in Comparative Perspective." *Politikon* 27 (1): 103–115.

———. 2010. "South African Post Apartheid Realities and Citizenship Education." In *Globalisation, the Nation-State and the Citizen: Dilemmas and Directions for Civics and Citizenship Education*, edited by Alan Reid, Judith Gill, and Alan Sears, 50–63. New York: Routledge.

———. 2012. "Political Literacy and Education." In *Encyclopedia of Diversity in Education*, edited by James A. Banks, 1671–1674. Thousand Oaks, CA: Sage.

Moran, Anthony. 2011. "Multiculturalism as Nation Building in Australia." *Ethnic and Racial Studies* 34 (12): 2153–2157.

Morris, Alan. 1998. "Our Fellow Africans Make Our Lives Hell: The Lives of Congolese and Nigerians Living in Johannesburg." *Ethnic and Racial Studies* 21 (6): 1116–1136.

Nattrass, Nicoli. 2012. *The AIDS Conspiracy: Science Fights Back*. Johannesburg: Wits University Press.

Ndlovu-Gasheni, Sabelo J. 2010. "Do Africans Exist? Genealogies and Paradoxes of African Identities and the Discourses of Nativism and Xenophobia." *African Identities* 8 (3): 281–295.

Neocosmos, Michael. 2006. "From 'Foreign Natives' to 'Native Foreigners': Explaining Xenophobia in Post-Apartheid South Africa." Dakar, Senegal: CODESTRIA.

Nyamnjoh, Francis. 2006. *Insiders and Outsiders: Citizenship and Xenophobia in Contemporary Southern Africa*. London: Zed Books, 2006.

Okri, Ben. 13th Annual Steve Biko Lecture, UCT, September 12, 2012.

Olssen, M. 2004. "From the Crick Report to the Parekh Report: Multiculturalism, Cultural Difference and Democracy-The Re-visioning of Citizenship Education." *British Journal of Sociology of Education* 25 (2): 179–192.

Ong, A. 1999. *Flexible Citizenship: The Cultural Logics of Transnationality*. Durham, NC: Duke University Press.

Oucho, J., and J. Crush. 2001. "Contra Free Movement: South Africa and SADC Movement Protocols." *Africa Today* 48: 139–158.

Owen, Ken. 2012. The Sound We Hear. In: Under the Baobab (no ed): Essays in Honour of Stuart Saunders on his Eightieth Birthday. *Africa Yearbook of Rhetoric*, 2 (2): 47–60. Cape Town: Africa Rhetoric Publishing.

Peberdy, S. 2001. "Imagining Immigration: Inclusive Identities and Exclusive Immigration Policies in the 'New' South Africa." *Africa Today* 48: 15–34.

———. 2009. *Selecting Immigrants: National Identity and South Africa's Immigration Policies, 1910–2008.* Johannesburg: Wits University Press.

Pillay, Suren. 2011. "The Scandal." *Chimurenga*. February 10: 12.

Polzer, Tara, Segatti, A. 2011. From defending migrant rights to new political subjectivities: Gauteng migrants; organizations after May 2008. In: LB Landau ed. *Exorcising the Demons Within*. Johannesburg: Wits University Press. 200–225.

Proctor, Elspeth. 2001. Talking Democracy in Grade 7. Master of Education Dissertation, University of Cape Town.

Pugh, Sarah A. 2014. "Advocacy in the Time of Xenophobia: Civil Society, the State, and the Politics of Migration in South Africa." *Politikon*, 41, 2 August 2014. 227–248.

Putnam, Robert. 1993. *Making Democracy Work: Civic Traditions in Modern Italy*. Princeton, NJ: Princeton University Press.

Ramphele, Mamphela. 2001. "Citizenship Challenges for South Africa's Young Democracy." *Daedalus* 130 (1): 1–17.

Reitz, Jeffrey. 2011. "Taxi Driver Syndrome." *Literary Review of Canada*, March.

Rippl, S. 2008. "Zu Gast bei Freunden? Fremdenfeindliche Einstellungen und Interethnische Freundschaften im Zeitverlauf." In *Migration und Integration: Köner Zeitschrift für Soziologie und Sozialpsychologie*, edited by F. Kalter. Sonderheft 48: 488–512.

Samara, Tony Roshan. 2011. *Cape Town after Apartheid: Crime and Governance in the Divided City*. Minneapolis: University of Minnesota Press.

Sarrazin, Thilo. 2010. *Deutschland Schafft Sich Ab*. Berlin: Deutsche Verlags-Anstalt.

Saunders, Doug. 2012. *The Myth of the Muslim Tide: Do Immigrants Threaten the West?* Toronto. Alfred A. Knopf.

Sayed, Yusuf, and Jonathan Jansen, eds. 2001. *Implementing Education Policies*. Cape Town: University of Cape Town Press.

Schlemmer, Lawrence. 2001. *Race Relations and Racism in Everyday Life*. Johannesburg: Institute for Race Relations.

Sears, A. 2010. Citizenship Education in a Multinational State: The Case of Canada. In: A. Reid, J. Gill and A. Sears, eds. *Globalization, the Nation-state and the Citizen: Dilemmas and Directions for Civics and Citizenship Education*. New York: Routledge. 191–205.

Sharp, John. 2008. "'Fortress South Africa': Xenophobic Violence in South Africa." *Anthropology Today* 24 (4): 1–3.

Smith, Anthony D. 1986. *The Ethnic Origin of Nations*. Oxford: Blackwell.

Soudien, Crain. 2012. *Realising the Dream: Unlearning the Logic of Race in the South African School*. Pretoria: SSHRC.

South African Human Rights Council. 1999. *Illegal? Report on the Arrest and Detention of Persons in Terms of the Aliens Control Act*. Johannesburg.

Soysal, Yasmin. 1994. *Limits of Citizenship: Migrants and Postnational Membership in Europe*. Chicago, IL: University of Chicago Press.

Steenkamp, Christina. 2009. "Xenophobia in South Africa: What Does It Say about Trust?" *The Round Table* 9: 403, 439–447.

Steinberg, Jonny. 2014. *A Man of Good Hope*. Johannesburg: Jonathan Ball.

Steyn, Melissa. 2001. *"Whiteness Just Isn't What It Used To Be: White Identity in a Changing South Africa."* New York: State University of New York Press.

Talijaard, Raenette. 2012. *Up in Arms: Pursuing Accountability for the Arms Deal in Parliament*. Auckland Park: Jacana Media.

Thompson, Bruce. 1997. "On Ernest Gellner's Conditions of Liberty: Civil Society and Its Rivals." *Stanford Humanities Review* 5 (2).

Trimikliniotis, Nico, et al. 2008. "Globalisation and Migrant Labout in a 'Rainbow Nation': A Fortress South Africa?" *Third World Quarterly* 29 (7): 1323–1339.

Vaknin, Sam. 2011. *Malignant Self Love: Narcissism Revisited*. Prague: Narcissism.

Vale, Peter. 2002. "Migration, Xenophobia and Security-Making in Post-Apartheid South Africa." *Politikon* 29 (1): 7–29.

Van den Berghe, P.L. 1981. *The Ethnic Phenomenon*. New York: Elsevier.

Van der Vliet, Virginia. 2001. "AIDS: Losing 'The New Struggle'?" *Daedalus* (Winter): 151–184.

Vertovec, S. 2007. Super-diversity and its implications. *Ethnic and Racial Studies*, 30 (6): 1024–1054.

Volkan, Vamic. 2006. *Killing in the Name of Identity*. New York: Ingram.

White, Caroline. 1998. "Democratic Societies? Voluntary Association and Democratic Culture in a South African Township." *Transformation*. 36: 1–36.

Whitehorn, Alan. 2007. *Ancestral Voices: Ethnic Roots, Identity and Genocide Remembered*. Winnipeg: Hybrid.

Williams, Michelle Hale. 2010. "Can Leopards Change Their Spots? Between Xenophobia and Trans-ethnic Populism among West European Far Right Parties." *Nationalism and Ethnic Politics* 16: 111–134.

Wimmer, Andreas. 1997. "Explaining Xenophobia and Racism: A Critical Review of Current Research Approaches." *Ethnic and Racial Studies* 20 (1): 17–40.

Yuval-Davis, Nira. 2011. *The Politics of Belonging: Intersectional Contestations*. London: Sage.

Zafar, Samiera. 1998. *School-Based Initiatives to Address Racial and Cultural Diversity in Newly Integrating Public Schools*. Durban: Educational Policy Unit, University of Natal.

Index of Names

Heribert Adam is Professor Emeritus of Sociology at Simon Fraser University in Vancouver. He is the co-author of *Seeking Mandela: Peacemaking Between Israelis and Palestinians* (Temple).

Kogila Moodley is Professor Emerita, Educational Studies at the University of British Columbia, where she was the first holder of the David Lam Chair. She is the co-author of *Seeking Mandela*.

Also in the series *Politics, History, and Social Change,*

Brian A. Weiner, *Sins of the Parents: The Politics of National Apologies in the United States*

Heribert Adam and Kogila Moodley, *Seeking Mandela: Peacemaking between Israelis and Palestinians*

Marc Garcelon, *Revolutionary Passage: From Soviet to Post-Soviet Russia, 1985–2000*

Gőtz Aly and Karl Heinz Roth, translated by Assenka Oksiloff, *The Nazi Census: Identification and Control in the Third Reich*

Immanuel Wallerstein, *The Uncertainties of Knowledge*

Michael R. Marrus, *The Unwanted: European Refugees from the First World War through the Cold War*

www.ingramcontent.com/pod-product-compliance
Lightning Source LLC
Chambersburg PA
CBHW030647270326
41929CB00007B/241